THE UPPER ROOM

Disciplines

2015

UPPER
ROOM BOOKS®
NASHVILLE

An Outline for Small-Group Use of Disciplines

Here is a simple plan for a one-hour, weekly group meeting based on reading *Disciplines*. One person may act as convener every week, or the role can rotate among group members. You may want to light a white Christ candle each week to signal the beginning of your time together.

Opening

Convener: Let us come into the presence of God.

Others: Lord Jesus Christ, thank you for being with us. Let us hear your word to us as we speak to one another.

Scripture

Convener reads the scripture suggested for that day in *Disciplines*. After a one- or two-minute silence, convener asks: What did you hear God saying to you in this passage? What response does this call for? (Group members respond in turn or as led.)

Reflection

- What scripture passage(s) and meditation(s) from this week was (were) particularly meaningful for you? Why? (Group members respond in turn or as led.)
- What actions were you nudged to take in response to the week's meditations? (Group members respond in turn or as led.)
- Where were you challenged in your discipleship this week? How did you respond to the challenge? (Group members respond in turn or as led.)

Praying Together

Convener says: Based on today's discussion, what people and situations do you want us to pray for now and in the coming week? Convener or other volunteer then prays about the concerns named.

Departing

Convener says: Let us go in peace to serve God and our neighbors in all that we do.

Adapted from *The Upper Room* daily devotional guide, January–February 2001. © 2000 The Upper Room. Used by permission.

The Upper Room Books website: books.upperroom.org

Cover design: Left Coast Design, Portland, Oregon

Cover photo: Steve Terrill / steveterrillphoto.com

Writers of various books of the Bible may be disputed in certain circles; this volume uses the names of the biblically attributed authors.

ISBN: 978-0-8358-1237-5
Printed in the United States of America

CONTENTS

FOREWORD

The steadfast love of the LORD never ceases,
   his mercies never come to an end;
they are new every morning;
   great is your faithfulness.
"The LORD is my portion," says my soul,
   "therefore I will hope in him" (Lam. 3:22-24).

I find these words from Lamentations liberating. No matter where I find myself or what circumstance I face, God's love and mercy never end. They are new every morning, and I can depend on them.

I first encountered this scripture and considered its meaning through the use of *The Upper Room Disciplines*. My life and ministry have been shaped through participation in this guide of biblical study and prayer. The daily practice of searching the scriptures has not only helped me connect to God and God's love but has also led me to take action that has helped heal the pain, injustice, and inequality of our world. I have found it impossible to stay in love with God and not desire to see God's goodness and grace shared with the entire world.

I entered the ministry believing that I was responding to God's call to make a difference in my family, my church, my community, and the world. I wanted to participate in loving the world as God had loved me. Over my forty years in ministry, I have grown in God's love and pursued a lifestyle that makes a difference by following what has come to be called The United Methodist Method. John Wesley articulated this approach in the General Rules of the Methodist movement. He wrote that we continue on the way of salvation, which is living in harmony with God, "by attending upon all the ordinances of God."*

"The ordinances of God" refers to the practices that keep our relationship between God and one another vital, alive, and growing. Wesley named public worship of God, the Lord's Supper, private and family prayer, searching the scriptures, and fasting as essential to a faithful life. He saw these disciplines as central to growing in faithfulness to God. The consistent practice of these spiritual disciplines kept Jesus-followers in touch with Christ's presence and power so they could fulfill their desire to live as faithful disciples. The Methodist movement began in the eighteenth century as a spiritual awakening that resulted in tremendous economic, social, and political change. Wesley's approach held personal piety and social holiness in tension. This tension spurred persons' faith development and led to their deeper engagement in day-to-day relationships and ministry.

I believe John Wesley was on to something when he supported the pattern of searching the scriptures, of reflection, and of prayer. *The Upper Room Disciplines* is a tool that assists us in hearing and responding to God's direction. Through our encounters with scripture we learn to trust God, stay in love with God, and mature in our love for the people around us.

I pray that you will join me and countless others in becoming a new generation of Christians who embrace these practices as we acknowledge and affirm that no matter our situation or circumstance, God's love and mercy never end. They are new every morning, and we can depend on them.

—Dr. Timothy L. Bias
General Secretary
The General Board of Discipleship
The United Methodist Church

---

*The General Rules can be found in ¶104, pages 75–78, *The Book of Discipline of The United Methodist Church*—2012.

What God Imagines

JANUARY 1–4, 2015 • CAROLYN WHITNEY-BROWN

THURSDAY, JANUARY 1 ~ *Read Psalm 8 and Ecclesiastes 3:1-13*

NEW YEAR'S DAY

I want to propose a challenge for the New Year: Memorize Psalm 8 and Ecclesiastes 3:1-13. Psalm 8 offers a perspective both calming and energizing, especially in these pre-Epiphany days. As Christmas lights disappear from homes and businesses, the psalm speaks of a different kind of epiphany. Consider the creation around you, the amazing perfection of each exquisite, interconnected piece. Deeper than our wisdom is the mystery of God the Creator. In this new year, take a moment to let your heart breathe.

And we humans—where do we fit into this abundance and beauty? The psalmist suggests that we notice all that God has put under our feet. We read Psalm 8 not as an invitation to trample or dominate but to locate ourselves in God's creation, marveling at all that sustains, nourishes, and delights us.

But how do we live rightly in God's creation? As we walk gently and attentively on this earth, we can pray using the words of Ecclesiastes 3:1-13. There is a time for everything. What are we called to *now* in 2015? These words help us understand: The common experiences of our human lives have not changed. We still must ask God's help to discern our own times, the challenges of our lives, and our historical moment.

God, throughout this year of 2015, open our hearts to walk on this earth as you desire, to see our lives from your perspective, and to know how to live in these times. Amen.

Fellow at the Centre for the Study of Religion and Society at University of Victoria, British Columbia; faculty member of St. Jerome's University at University of Waterloo Ontario: coordinator of the L'Arche International Founders Project

I received a great blessing this year from my new friend Peter. Some might see Peter's intellectual disability or blindness, but he doesn't define himself that way. He offered me counsel as though he were my guardian angel, exhorting me to stand tall, to hold my head up, to refute the voices inside me that might try to tell me I'm not good enough. "Don't be afraid; don't be afraid," said Peter, in his rich voice that sings the blues so wonderfully, "You'll never walk alone. You are beloved."

In Matthew 25, Jesus tells a story of reciprocity: We must receive. This can be hard when we're vulnerable and want to protect ourselves. I haven't been in prison, but I have felt poor and I have been a stranger. I have experienced hunger and fear, and I have been sick.

In those terrible times, I have received abundant kindness and generosity, often from unlikely sources. Our dignity and self-respect take a beating when we find ourselves as broken people in humiliating circumstances. I didn't feel like Jesus, but perhaps I was.

It's hard to be needy, to receive, to feel exposed. But those are the times when we discover one another, times when it's not about poor and rich or us and them. We are all poor; we are all rich. When we are poorest and most broken, we have a gift to offer—though we might not see it. We can care for one another. And this applies to communities and nations as well as individuals. The story of Jesus asks not only how can I help people in need but also what can I receive? How am I needy?

God, open our hearts to offer our vulnerabilities and suffering as well as our gifts to build community. Amen.

Praise! This exuberant psalm addresses the issue of finding our place among all God's beloved creatures and landscapes. It is most definitely not about owning, possessing, or controlling anything.

This is a curious time of year. Christmas has come and gone. The twelve days of Christmas stretch on even as we take decorations down; nearly everyone has lost the taste for Christmas cookies; and sales brochures urge everyone to find comfort and joy in buying something more.

Praise! It's a hard concept: It doesn't fit into New Year's resolutions to be better people or do more good deeds or lose weight or budget better or visit that lonely person who tugs at our hearts. Perhaps praise can put all those resolutions in perspective, but the psalmist doesn't suggest any salutary result of praise. It has no goal.

Praise goes deeper than gratitude. Gratitude is still about ourselves, while the praise of this psalm dwarfs all our concerns.

Praise! It's a gesture, a stance, an orientation toward the world. We are not alone in praising God; we're part of an enormous chorus of praise.

Do something countercultural today. Join the angels, the shining stars, the sun and moon, things above the highest heavens. Praise God!

God, we praise you with open hearts and deep delight. Amen.

EPIPHANY SUNDAY

A rise, shine. . . . " I love this passage. I memorized it so long ago that I can't even remember why. My imagination comes alive envisioning everyone responding to this call: "Arise, shine; for your light has come, and the glory of the LORD has risen upon you." All who wonder how they can make a difference: old people who fear their lives have lost value, powerful people with wealth and generosity, artists and writers and musicians, aboriginal people integrating their old and new traditions, people labeled handicapped, children, new immigrants, people who endure negative voices both inside their heads and from people in their fearful and judgmental society, big-hearted refugees, every frightened person with crushed dreams—what would happen if we *all* rose and shone—in every part of the world. Imagine the joy and excitement if we all discovered that this is *our* moment, the moment that our light has come and the glory of God has risen upon each of us!

Darkness covers the earth and thick darkness the peoples. We can't deny it. Sometimes I despair that our society wastes so many gifts because it cannot receive the unique gift of an autistic child or persons so sensitive and wounded that they have self-medicated with alcohol or drugs or the weary refugee who has traveled so far already. But—over *you* the Lord will rise!

Consider the world that God imagines, where people suddenly leap up in the fullness of their beauty to take their role in a society that values their unique contribution, shaped by their own suffering and wisdom. There is an unrepeatable grace in the life of each person. I love that Isaiah calls us to imagine how our world would look if each person arose and shone because the Light has come.

God, encourage all your people everywhere to arise and shine your light into the dark places of their part of the world. Amen.

Baptism of the Lord

JANUARY 5–11, 2015 • MYRON WINGFIELD

MONDAY, JANUARY 5 ~ *Read Genesis 1:1-5*

Steve Padilla draws sunspots. Daily, for nearly forty years, he has climbed to the solar telescope perched atop Mount Wilson near Los Angeles, California, to sketch images of the sun and its ever-changing surface. Padilla has added to the over 28,000 images that date back to 1917. Once a week, he goes down the mountain for groceries, dinner with friends, and church. Otherwise, he sits on the mountain and draws sunspots. Using colored pencils and ten-by-twenty-inch sheets of paper, he sketches a new image every day. Meteorologists use the sketches to predict solar flares. "The value," Padilla says, "is not so much in the individual achievement but in maintaining the daily record." (*Los Angeles Times*, October 28, 2013)

Reading "the daily record" of creation in Genesis, I also recall a writer who advised would-be writers to watch the sun set every day for a year. He could not say exactly how that practice helped him, but he knew it made him a better writer.

There is constancy in the expression of God's creating and recreating Spirit. Creation's story unfolds one day at a time, and each day ends with the comforting refrain, "And there was evening and there was morning." In the Bible, the verb "create" indicates an exclusively divine activity. Only God creates, and God continues to create and to recreate in and among and around us every day. There is a reason this daily guide to scripture and prayer is called *Disciplines*, for there is wisdom and grace to be gained when we align our daily rhythms with the constancy of the Holy Spirit.

God, make us constant in devotion. Amen.

Assistant General Secretary, General Board of Higher Education and Ministry, The United Methodist Church

Our firstborn was baptized when he was four months old. Jesse was a mellow infant inclined toward contentment, often passed around like a basketball, showing ease of adaptability even among strangers. The moment I handed him to the bishop, however, he started to fret, arched his back and squirmed, then squalled in baby-speak, "I do not like this—make it stop!" Quickly and at some risk of dropping him, the bishop applied the water, invoked the triune God, and handed Jesse back to me. Everyone exhaled and said, "Amen." After the service, I tickled Jesse under his chin and, for the first time, he laughed—just like that, a four-month-old in full chuckle.

Genesis 1 tells of God's bringing order and light to chaos and dark; but in the process, I can't imagine that everything simply fell into place without some resistance and fretting. I imagine the darkness put up a fight before retreating; chaos arched its back, squirmed and squalled before submitting to order. Yet, at day's end, God said it was all good—just like that, a one-day-old creation laughing, in full order and light.

By relating the two watery, Spirited accounts, I'm not suggesting that Jesse suddenly grasped the meaning of creation and recreation through baptism. I simply and gratefully marvel at how he, in his own squirming, squalling, and laughing, pointed to the journey that we all take in baptism. Through it, we are led by the graceful, ordering Spirit of God on a course that leads through high anxiety and deep peace, through unfathomable loss and ineffable joy, through ordinary consternation and ordinary acceptance, through the breathless solitude of being forsaken and the awe of taking flight on the wings of grace. Remember your baptism, and be thankful.

Reflect on how grace has worked to form you through suffering, joy, and all in-between.

A friend of mine recently visited a church and noticed that none of the men and few of the women sang when the praise band led the music. Lyrics projected on the screen and the band leader's enthusiastic encouragement led to only a few of the hundreds gathered joining in. The majority simply stood, swayed, and kept their mouths shut.

A few weeks earlier, I had worshiped with a traditional Church of Christ congregation that employs no instrumentation—no organ, no piano, no guitar, not a single drum or tambourine. I once heard a Church of Christ member joke that he resists the urge to clap in church because his hands would be considered a percussion instrument. Instead, all of the music is rendered by singing in four-part harmony. It was beautiful. At the peak of the congregation's harmonization, the members did sound like "heavenly beings."

The psalms advocate for both vocalization and instrumentation for celebrating God's presence, not to mention stillness and silence—so I am not inclined to pick one way over another. I do believe there is good reason to revisit John Wesley's Directions for Singing (*The United Methodist Hymnal*, vii). Research indicates that group singing has both physical and mental health benefits, but the early Methodists did not need neuroscience to confirm what the psalmist knows: We are strengthened in body, mind, and soul when we lift our voices with other members of the body to "ascribe to the LORD glory and strength."

When we gather to raise our communal voice of praise, we can also hear the Voice that makes us strong and gives us peace.

Today, sing your own song using these words: "May the LORD give strength to his people! May the LORD bless his people with peace!"

Read more: http://ideas.time.com/2013/08/16/singing-changes-your-brain/

As I noted in the second entry for this week, my infant son Jesse was too young to apprehend the import of baptism. But several years later, when our younger son, Luke, was about four, he had some working awareness of God's creative ways. He was raking leaves with me one day when he stopped to look at a bush of miniature roses in full bloom. His eyes widened as he smiled and said, "I bet God sure is proud of those!"

This same child had no fear of climbing trees, loved to go out in the rain and tramp around in the puddles—never mind the thunder that roared and shook the air or the wind that swirled through the trees and made them dance or the lightning that clapped and lit up the darkened sky. He soaked it all up as his clothes soaked up the rain, and in it he saw the splendor of God's creating ways.

Today we join the psalmist and all creation in a state of awe before the power of God made known through the mystery and majesty of the created world. The power of God's voice breaks cedars, flashes flames of fire, and shakes the wilderness. We join in calling attention to "the glory" and "holy splendor" of God's creating power. There is no end to it. Just as Genesis records a rhythmic constancy to God's creating days, so the psalmist leads us in a rhythmic declaration of inspired worship and praise. The psalmist wants us to know that this is the same God who first moved "over the waters" to bring order and peace from chaos and distress. God's brooding, loving Spirit still does. We pause in wonder and cry, "Glory!"

Awe-inspiring God, may we witness your power emerging from chaos and darkness to bring beauty and joy. Bring strength to all, and bless us with your peace. Amen.

The book of Acts records several instances when an individual has an isolated, solitary encounter with the divine—Saul's experience on the Damascus road (Acts 9:1-6), Peter's hunger-fueled vision of unlimited inclusivity (Acts 10:9-16). But we also read of divine activity in groups of folks who gather. The Holy Spirit seems to prefer a community setting as the context for stirring things up. That is what happens in today's reading when Paul happens upon a group of new believers.

In Wendell Berry's novel *Jayber Crow*, Jayber is the barber in the fictional town of Port William, Kentucky. In addition to barbering, Jayber cleans and cares for the little community church. He starts attending Sunday services when he becomes janitor because he does not want to appear "indifferent," and he doesn't mind receiving the women's compliments for his good work either. While lacking in appreciation of most of the sermons, he loves the singing, the ringing of the church bell, and the "naturally occurring silences." What he loves most is simply sitting among the people.

I understand that. Like others, I can bear witness to deeply personal experiences of God's grace, but I've never been able to separate them from the communion of saints into which I was born and reborn and by which I've been borne along in baptism. With Martin Marty, I would say, "I am much more a communal believer than an individual believer" (from *NewsHour Online*, National Public Radio, June 4, 1998).

With a nod and a wink, Luke records, "There were about twelve of them in all" that day who, with Paul, gave witness to the presence of the Holy Spirit (Acts 19:7, RSV). It is his way of saying that baptism is a community experience; through baptism, the Holy Spirit creates community. There are no individual believers; we're all communal believers held together by One who transcends all time and place through eternity and grace.

Dear God, we pray, "Come, Holy Spirit." Amen.

Baptism of the Lord

Reading Luke's Gospel and his book of Acts together is sort of like being in an echo chamber. "Didn't I just hear that?" the reader asks? In this passage, John's disciples become Jesus' disciples when they are baptized in Jesus' name. The Holy Spirit comes to them and, lo and behold, they speak in tongues and prophesy. With a wry smile, Luke gives us a wink—it's Pentecost all over again. (See Acts 2.)

If speaking in tongues is not enough of a hint about what is happening, Luke gives us another: He writes that there are "about twelve" of them. You can see why he thinks we need a hint. After all, it was Peter (one of Jesus' twelve) who explained the first Pentecost to "about one hundred and twenty persons" in Jerusalem (Acts 1:15; 2:1, 14), and this is Paul explaining matters to "about twelve" all the way out in Ephesus. With a wry smile, Luke gives us another wink—it's Pentecost all over again.

Acts is full of these "Pentecost repeats": the baptism of the Ethiopian eunuch (8:26-39), the baptism of Saul (9:17-19), the baptism of Cornelius and his household (10:44-48), the baptism of Lydia and her household (16:11-15), and on and on it goes.

The book *By Water and the Spirit* reminds us that through baptism, "God bestows upon baptized persons the presence of the Holy Spirit, marks them with a seal, and implants in their hearts the first installment of their inheritance as sons and daughters of God" (p. 46). When these twelve are baptized by Paul, their joyful utterances are the first signs of that enduring inheritance. From that moment on, they will be in Jesus, with Jesus, always growing to be more like Jesus through the power of the Spirit. Remember your "Pentecost repeat," and be both thankful and joyful.

God, through baptism, give us the joy of being your sons and daughters. Amen.

BAPTISM OF THE LORD SUNDAY

This is one of the great mysteries of our Christian faith: Jesus being baptized by John who, by his own account, is unworthy to stoop and untie the laces on Jesus' walking shoes. Yet Jesus walks right into the Jordan with John (did John really take Jesus' shoes off first?) and takes the treatment. What do we make of that? That's a tough one but not much tougher than the question of what we make of our own baptism.

A friend of mine reflecting on his baptism, said he was nine months old when it happened. Neither of his parents had been baptized at the time. In fact, my friend was ordained for ten years before his parents were baptized. What do we make of that? I don't know. He says he doesn't know either.

My friend makes this observation: "Just because we don't understand doesn't get us off the hook for promising more than we realize. We tend to think that we shouldn't be held responsible for anything we didn't understand at the time." If that's the case, he says, then much of life—getting married, having children—would result in failed promises because who truly understands what they're getting into at such moments? As he noted, "We're in over our heads in these things. We always have been."

But my friend knows this: throughout the New Testament the word *faith* is best translated "trust," and the Latin word for faith—*credo*—has the same root word as "cardio." What happens in baptism is not something we "know" with our minds. Baptism is about trusting God with all our heart.

Baptism is an act of trust, of faith in God, that puts us "in over our heads." The good news is that Jesus is not only there but is with us in all the life that follows. You can trust that.

Remember your baptism, and be thankful.

Faces of Revelation

JANUARY 12–18, 2015 • J. DANA TRENT

MONDAY, JANUARY 12 ~ *Read 1 Samuel 3:1-9*

Thousands of messages inundate us daily. It's no wonder we sometimes feel we don't know God. The constant noise that surrounds us can muffle even God's powerful voice. It often takes repeated attempts and the wisdom of others to help us discern our Creator's call.

First Samuel is set in the early life of Israel, a precarious time when the "word of the LORD was rare." Though the Israelites had known strong leaders like Moses, tribal wars threatened to destroy the nation because "all the people did what was right in their own eyes" (Judg. 21:25).

Samuel is now a young boy. His mother, Hannah, had dedicated him to the Lord as soon as she weaned him (1 Sam. 1:27-28). As Christians we dedicate ourselves to God's service through baptism, which can occur at different ages based on the tradition.

The Lord calls to young Samuel several times before Eli realizes what is happening and tells Samuel how to respond. As baptized Christians, how many times do we miss God's call? How many times do we mistake God's voice for a human voice? Like Samuel's call, our spiritual purpose is not necessarily loud or disruptive; it may be a quiet murmur in the night. We often find it difficult not only to hear our call but to understand its meaning. Our loved ones and colleagues can help us discern God's purpose, just as Eli instructed Samuel to return to his place and tell God he was listening. Though we may miss God's call at first, God continues to stand before us until we answer.

God, help us learn to respond, "Speak, LORD, for your servant is listening." Amen.

Ordained Baptist minister; author of *Saffron Cross: The Unlikely Story of How a Christian Minister Married a Hindu Monk*

Samuel's first oracle from God brings troubling news and uncertainty about what to do next. We can picture ourselves in Samuel's shoes, holding a difficult piece of information with hesitation.

Eli's sons, Hophni and Phinehas, have descended from a priestly line and are destined to serve the temple—but they have acted improperly, using their position of power for ill instead of good. Because of his sons' blasphemy and an earlier prophecy, Eli anticipates the harsh contents of the Lord's first message for Samuel, as it was foretold in 1 Samuel 2:27-36. Though the aging prophet's eyesight has "grown dim," he can clearly see the outcome of his failures. Eli listens to Samuel's words and responds, "It is the LORD; let him do what seems good to him."

How often do we approach God with such humility, even in the midst of such terrible news? Do we sometimes find it difficult to allow control to slip from our hands and submit to the One who is all-knowing?

Both Samuel and Eli teach us how to be servants of God. They remind us to listen, respond, and accept that God's thoughts are not our thoughts, nor are God's plans our plans. Sometimes our busyness with church, work, family, errands, and meetings makes our lives too full for us to sit, wait, and listen with such acceptance. Perhaps we fear that God will call us out of our comfort zones for the sake of the gospel. Or, like Samuel, we might be afraid to share what we've heard. What will my church, family, colleagues think of my calling?

No matter the message, we seek to live into the fullness of our baptisms as beings created for a purpose.

God, help us to listen like Samuel and be humble like Eli. When the message is tough, give us strength both to bear and convey the news. Amen.

The early Christian desert fathers and mothers of the fourth century memorized and prayed the Psalms aloud; it helped them keep their minds and bodies focused on God. Today, we still turn to the Psalms for assurance of our deep connection with God. The psalmist poetically describes his intimacy with God. Using the pronouns "I" and "you," the psalmist suggests the familiarity we share with our closest family and friends.

After reading these verses, how does it feel to live into what the psalmist describes as God knowing our every movement, our thoughts, and our personal tendencies? The knowledge described here is unique to God; no human can emulate it. But this kind of communion can be frightening. After all, if God knows all that we think and do, why would God still love us?

God loves us because this kind of affection is unique to the Creator and the created. God's knowing us this deeply does not pose a threat to our independence as individuals with free will but comes as a gift of good news.

Have you considered the feelings that accompany being loved in this fashion—loved inside and out for all that you are, all that you do, think, and feel? When you feel absent from God's presence, deep in stress and suffering, reread these verses to remind you of the unbreakable connection with your omniscient God, the one who "knows" you—inside and out.

Like the fourth-century desert monastics, we rejoice in such knowledge, remembering our indestructible link to our Creator.

God, you know our ways, our hearts, and our missteps. Lord, have mercy on us as we humbly accept and embrace our truest calling as your people. Amen.

What does it mean to be "fearfully and wonderfully made"? Our culture associates the word *fear* with unpleasantness. In verse 14, the word *fearfully* is derived from the Hebrew verbal root *yara'*, which means to evoke awe and reverence.

Consider the miracle of creation and relationship: infants in their mothers' wombs; forever families knitted together with love, not DNA. God's connection with us existed before we were flesh and bone. God laid hands on each of us, forming our days "when none of them as yet existed." The psalmist celebrates a Creator who knows us from beginning to end.

How do we live as if we were "fearfully and wonderfully made" and "intricately woven in the depths of the earth," a phrase that hearkens back to the Creation story of Genesis? If we truly lived as the sacred beings described in verses 13 through 18, our postures might be more apt to turn toward God rather than toward the stress, anxiety, and hustle and bustle that often consume us.

"I know where you live" are words we often say in jest, an indication of our relationship to another individual in an effort to enforce or emphasize a point. But have we considered that God says this to us each day? In times when we wrestle with uncertainty, obstacles, and trials, we can slow down and look into the divine face of revelation in Psalm 139. Then we can walk in the world living into what it means to be "fearfully and wonderfully made," assured of God's care and all-seeing nature.

God, how incredible it is to be made by you! Help us to remember who and whose we are. May we respond to the calling of being "fearfully and wonderfully made" in a way that glorifies you. Amen.

The Corinthian community to whom Paul writes attempted to affirm that their Christian status meant that all things were lawful for them. They embraced a separation of body and spirit that allowed them to engage in unhealthy behaviors. Paul calls them to a full-bodied spirituality by reminding them that their bodies are for the Lord, that they are temples of the Holy Spirit. Perhaps the most telling comment comes when Paul closes with these words: "You are not your own. . . . you were bought with a price."

What would it mean to live into our calling as "fearfully and wonderfully made" and use our bodies to the glory of God? As members of the body of Christ, we are more likely to view and treat our bodies as instruments when we embrace our spiritual connection to Jesus. In this way, we consider living a more integrated life of both physical and spiritual nourishment. We might practice radical self-care, even as we continue to care for others.

Our bodies are "holy temples" in which all our parts: our feet, legs, arms, hands, mouths, hearts, and minds are used to the glory of God. Imagine a day when we employ our aching joints for service to visit a lonely friend. Imagine a day when we use our mouths to the glory of God by speaking kind words. Imagine a day when our chronic illness inspires someone to take courage to face their own declining health. How might we orient our day and body to mirror Christ's servant heart?

Affirming and caring for our bodies as part of our spiritual self-care helps us experience the one who created us. Christ has set us free not so we can do whatever we want with our bodies, but so we can serve God with love.

God, our bodies can feel like a burden sometimes. Instead, help us to remember that they are holy temples, created by you and filled with your love. May we use them to glorify you each day. Amen.

In the opening chapter of John's Gospel, John the Baptist has proclaimed Jesus' identity as the "Lamb of God" and the "Son of God" (v. 34). Shortly thereafter, Jesus begins calling his disciples, including Philip. Philip then tries to recruit the less-than-enthusiastic Nathanael. Philip confesses Jesus' divine nature to Nathanael, linking Jesus to the prophets and the law. But Philip also reveals Jesus' human nature as the "son of Joseph from Nazareth." Jesus has not only fulfilled the scriptures as the Messiah, but he has an earthly father. Nathanael, who comes from a Galilean village that despises Nazareth, responds, "Can anything good come out of Nazareth?" How could an almighty savior possibly be born to a family in Nazareth? But Philip's reply echoes Jesus' words in verse 39: "Come and see."

Perhaps at times we too doubt that the savior of the world could be born in a humble village to unwed teenage parents. Like Nathanael, many bring their skepticism and prejudices to the church. Even as baptized Christians, we often fail to see the power of a narrative in which a wandering evangelist with no earthly possessions changes the world for nearly two thousand years and counting.

"Come and see" invites us into the upside-down reality of God's reign. Jesus himself—his ministry, healing, death, and resurrection—reveals the radical nature of the Messiah.

John's Gospel encourages openness to God's many faces of revelation. Are we listening like Samuel? Are we following like Philip? Or are we skeptical like Nathanael? How is God inviting us to "come and see"?

God, help us to "come and see," that we may affirm Jesus as your son, your very face among us. Amen.

Nathanael has dismissed Philip's "Messiah sighting," but then he meets Jesus himself, who proclaims that Nathanael is "an Israelite in whom there is no deceit." Similar to our reading from Psalm 139, Jesus knows Nathanael as only God would. Jesus reveals his divine nature when he explains that he saw Nathanael under a tree—the place where students often went to learn from their teachers. Like Nathanael and the psalmist, we can take comfort in the fact that even though we sometimes doubt, we are known by God. Nathanael's actual experience of Jesus changes his mind. How often do we enter a situation with skepticism, only to change our minds once we've had the experience? Like Nathanael and many others in the Gospel narratives, we too must decide whether we are for or against Jesus.

Nathanael confesses Jesus as Son of God and King of Israel, and Jesus offers promises of greater things yet to come and of seeing heaven opened. Nathanael will witness the miracle at Cana and come to understand and believe in Jesus as the ultimate link between here and eternity. Later in John's Gospel, Nathanael will be among the disciples who meet the resurrected Jesus on the seashore (chapter 21).

God has many faces of revelation: a prophecy given to young Samuel, a "knowing" Creator revealed to an appreciative psalmist, and the doubting pilgrim Nathanael. How has God been revealed to us? When God calls, do we listen? Do we mistake God's voice for someone else? Do we reject the call because of our prejudices? Or do we take the time to be still and discern, to remember our unbreakable link to the One who knows us?

God, help us to have faith in you even when we don't witness a miracle. Help us to remember your voice in the story of Samuel and Eli and your love from the psalmist. May we accept our bodies as holy instruments. May we embrace the invitation to follow you—even when at first we doubt. Amen.

Proceed toward Promise

MONDAY, JANUARY 19 ～ *Read Jonah 3:1-5*

Second chances often begin with someone covered in vomit. (See Jonah 2:10.) Perhaps our own second chances began with the nauseous feeling produced when truth and denial converged inside of us. In this way, Jonah's story is similar to our own. The first time God spoke to Jonah and called him to the onerous task of offering grace and forgiveness to his nation's archenemy, Jonah ran from the promise of a second chance for Nineveh. Today's passage begins with a second chance for Jonah. God speaks to Jonah a second time and calls him to proclaim God's impending judgment on Nineveh. This time, freshly spewed from his recent denial of God's ability to forgive and embrace all people (regardless of nationality or history), Jonah proceeds toward the promise of a second chance—for himself and for the Ninevites. By moving toward the promise of a second chance, Jonah lives into his vocation; and the Ninevites, acknowledging their own need and desire to live in unity with God, repent of their hateful ways.

Like Jonah, we may have doubted the nudge of God's Spirit when the radical nature of God's grace offended our personal sense of righteousness. Like Jonah, possibly we have rejected outright the clear direction of God's intent to love us, our neighbors, and our enemies unconditionally. However, this passage offers the assurance that God is invested in offering second chances. Today, we hear again what God can do in us and others when we proceed toward the second chance God offers.

Help me, God, to recognize the difference between your truth and my denial and to take a step toward the promise of a second chance. Amen.

Minister, Maple Grove United Church of Canada, Toronto area

The people of Nineveh hear divine accountability and justice in Jonah's voice, and they respond to God's clarion call for a change in their way of life. The Ninevites wear their repentance and remorse as sackcloth and ashes, and they come face-to-face with the reality of their own mortality and with the power of God to overthrow even the fiercest human warriors. In an unexpected turn of events, the Ninevites prostrate themselves before God; and God changes God's mind. Instead of bringing the intended calamity, God proceeds toward the promise of a people who receive and respond to God's message.

Occasionally, we face the teaching that God has certain plans for us that cannot be amended, especially if we fail to meet God's expectations. We can become paralyzed by an understanding that God simply won't be affected by our life situations, by our failure to live with courage or even by success in overcoming adversity with unanticipated strength. Living with a belief in an inflexible God who seems unresponsive to both our pitiful mistakes and our unexpected accomplishments promotes a perception of life as a crossword puzzle: one wrong letter nullifies the rest of our good work.

Today's passage reminds us that God holds us accountable for stewardship of the life we have been given. However, God is not stuck in a predetermined rut of accountability, even if our past choices have been less than faithful. God is responsive to us as we (made in God's image) can be responsive to God. The Lord can and will proceed toward the promise of a people who receive and respond to the divine message even if it means God has to make a change in the plan.

Mysterious God, who is unchanging yet able to change, in the freedom you give may I receive and respond to your word today. Amen.

In the early verses of Mark 1, John readily admits that he is a messenger of a different sort than Jesus; John proclaims his ministry as subservient to the ministry and work of Jesus. Even so, John baptizes Jesus in the Jordan; Jesus rises from the waters as God's Beloved, beginning his ministry with forty days in the wilderness. In the wake of John's arrest, Jesus returns to Galilee and exhorts the people to believe the good news, to recognize that the kingdom of God is at hand, and to repent. John was arrested because of this message (and speaking truth to power); yet, Jesus goes throughout the land proclaiming the news.

Jesus proceeds toward the promise of the good news despite hearing of John's arrest. Jesus moves forward in the face of certain opposition from religious and civil authorities who will be threatened by his power and unnerved by his disregard of "the old ways." Jesus proceeds toward the promise of the good news with authority recognized in the synagogue and in the streets by the unclean, the sick, and the sinful.

In our lives we struggle to be faithful to God's call when adversity draws near. Often we wonder what we might do to avoid adversity and still remain faithful to the work of God's kingdom. In the church, we sometimes find ourselves considering accommodation to bullying attitudes and mean-spirited gossip in order to be "nice" and to avoid confronting those who work against the good news of God. John faced it; Jesus met it; and, as disciples, we can also expect resistance when we proceed toward the promise of the good news.

Friends, receive the power of Christ to proceed toward the promise of the good news—even when adversity draws near.

Jesus, help me to release my fears and have the courage to live your good news. Amen.

Simon, Andrew, James, and John proceed toward the promise of a new identity as followers of Jesus, to become fishers of people; they leave their nets behind. The disciples let go of what has been extraordinarily useful in their prior lives. In this new vocation, they won't need the same tools or the same environment. So, with empty hands, knowing nothing except the desire for the new identity offered by Jesus, they walk away from what they have known.

How often have we yearned for God to bring about a change in our identity, a shift in our desires and wills? How often have we resisted the change for which we have yearned when the Spirit of God reveals the need for us to retool our thinking, our habits, our prayers, and our ways of being? How often have we recoiled from meaningful opportunities because we fear letting go of the familiar?

As Jesus' disciples, we live by faith, trust, and hope. We listen for the call of Christ in our lives to the best of our ability. We follow the leading of God's Spirit, aware of the fears that would entangle us; yet, we walk into a new identity and new reality despite our unknowing. Perhaps our prior knowledge proved useful to that old identity; but if we want to proceed toward the promise of a new identity, we must be willing to let go. We can let go of formerly useful thinking, habits, prayers, and ways of being that have no place in a changed identity. We can let go of prior environments that will not nurture a changed desire and will. We can let go and proceed toward the promise of a new identity, following Jesus Christ in whom we place our faith, trust, and hope.

Enliven within me, O Christ, the wisdom to know what I need to leave behind in order to truly follow you. Amen.

In today's passage, Paul references the expectation that Christ will come again soon. Upon Christ's return, the greater reality of God's final judgment and the fulfillment of God's salvation will overshadow the concerns of the present circumstances. When Christ returns in final victory, marriage, grief, joy, possessions—anything of the Corinthians' present existence will no longer hold the same degree of sway in their lives. Thus, Paul urges the church in Corinth to proceed toward the promise of an eternal reality that supersedes present circumstances.

Whether Christ's return happens tomorrow or in two thousand more years, Paul's teaching remains valuable for us today. We inventory our lives and ask, "What of all this will last? What will come of my daily investment of time, energy, and resources in particular relationships, emotions, and experiences? Do my current circumstances point me toward an eternal reality or to an ephemeral one?"

Viewing our lives in this way does not mean we deny the gifts of our relationships or focus so much on the hope of Christ's final victory that we ignore the work of the Holy Spirit in this very moment. Rather, Paul encourages the early church and us to participate in our present circumstances while knowing a definitive reality is yet to be spoken in our lives. In so doing, we will find that all our relationships, emotions, experiences, and resources are placed within the larger context of a God who will make all things right forever. We too can proceed toward the promise of an eternal reality that will not belittle our life; instead, this eternal reality will supply our life with its fullest meaning.

No matter what I am dealing with right now, help me, O God, to see my life within the context of your eternal work in me and in the rest of creation. Amen.

The psalmist knows well that God, God alone, is everything we need. Assailed and battered; bearing the brunt of lies, curses, and deception, the writer of Psalm 62 has given up all illusions that the heart can be soothed and saved by any other than God. In silence and in an awareness that all else will fail to meet our deepest needs, the psalmist voices the refrain for us, "God alone."

"Will what we need most come from people, even those we love and respect?"

" No. God alone."

"Can anything else satisfy the depth of our longing for belonging and for wholeness?"

"No. God alone."

Do you remember the shape sorter, the one we find in many infants' rooms? The shape sorter is the cube or ball with shaped holes in its sides. One shape is a triangle; another is a circle. Other common shapes are diamonds, hearts, squares, and ovals. The shape sorter provides the opportunity for a young child to learn the contours of a shape and match the shaped objects with shaped holes. Hearts will fit in the heart-shaped hole and nowhere else. Diamonds will fit only in the diamond-shaped hole. And, no, the triangle will not fit in the circle-shaped hole.

We are often no more than spiritual toddlers attempting to match the shape of our need with the misshapen holes of this broken world. But we know, in the quiet recesses of our prayers, that the shape of our need and the contours of our hope can only be nestled safely in God alone.

Proceed, dear ones, beloved of God, toward the promise of God alone.

Help sort me out, O God. With your gentle and tender Spirit, help me identify where in my life I might be expecting more from the world than the world can give. Amen.

The psalmist speaks and sings these words to a trustworthy God who is characterized by steadfast love, to a God upon whom salvation rests. The psalmist knows God as a refuge from the persecution of others and as a righteous judge who knows and will repay the true work of all people. Where else than to that God would the psalmist go with the deepest concerns of his heart? And so, the psalmist urges us to proceed toward the promise that we also can pour out our hearts to God.

Many of us did not grow up in homes and churches that taught us of a God like the psalmist describes. Instead, we may have learned about a jealous and vengeful God who would never speak to us with compassion and understanding. We may have learned of a God who stands ready to strike us down when we make a wrong move or a bad decision. Perhaps we learned of a God whose "love" is characterized by conditions of our perfection (a perfection we never achieve and thus routinely cause God to be disappointed in us).

Who we believe God to be and how we understand God to act and respond will determine the distance between our hearts and God. If we assume the psalmist's understanding of God, our hearts—full of secrets and longings and disappointment and pain—reside safely in God's hands. If we know only an angry, vengeful, demanding God, we will be unable to disclose our failures, weakness, and vulnerability.

Regardless of what we have been taught, maybe this is the day for us to proceed toward the promise of a God with whom we can share our hearts.

Before I share my heart with you, God, I need to know your love. Amen.

Hear and Heed

MONDAY, JANUARY 26 ~ *Read Deuteronomy 18:15-20*

Transitions are challenging, whether it's a new job, a new house, a new community, or a new church. We react in a variety of ways during transitions. Sometimes we are cranky, sometimes we quietly turn inward, and sometimes we just keep ourselves busy. In the uncertainty, we want certainty. While we cannot gaze into a crystal ball and know the future, this passage assures us that God will guide us and continue to speak to us.

Moses addresses the people of Israel as they prepare to enter the land of promise. He tells them that God will provide leadership through a prophet like himself. The prophet may bring words that cause discomfort because Israel is to be distinctive among the nations. The people are to heed the prophet's words to avoid the seducements of the land in which they will settle.

Today prophets rise up among us. They challenge us and call us to repent. As Christians we too are to be a distinctive people. We are not to fall prey to the idols of the land in which we settle.

Transitions require leadership and discernment to understand what God has to say to us in this time and in this place. It will be a word that challenges us and makes us uncomfortable. It will call us to make sacrifices. We must heed the words that the prophets speak in God's name.

O God, you promise to speak to us. Help us to recognize and heed the prophet. We trust in you today and in all the days to come. With all gratitude and praise. Amen.

Associate for denominational women's organization relations, Bread for the World, Washington, DC

While the promise that we can trust God to continue speaking to us is comforting, we might not like what God has to say. The prophecy business was a tough one—and continues to be a tough one. The job of the prophet is always to challenge the status quo—to push God's people beyond their comfort level, to stretch them and help them grow.

The prophet's authority comes directly from God—unmediated by scripture or tradition. The prophet bears accountability to God for speaking God's word to the people. The people are to listen and heed the prophet's words. Unlike other nations, Israel is led by God's purpose through the human agent of prophet. During the periods of the monarchy, God established the prophets who rose above the political realm of the kings, to hold both the kings and the people accountable to the God of the Exodus.

The prophets' message calls for a reorientation of lives toward God: to follow the law, to make decisions, to live with God in the forefront. By remembering God's justice and love in all that we do, vulnerable members of the community are cared for, workers are not exploited, and sojourners are welcomed into the community.

In our own time, we hear prophets speaking through the words of those who challenge the powerful institutions that exploit vulnerable people in our world. We hear the voices of the prophets calling us to repent, to turn back toward God, to be guided by God's love for us. May we respond to that call, let go of our personal desires, and align ourselves with God's desires for the world.

God of love, may I hear and heed the prophetic voices of my time. Align my desires with your desires for my life and the world. In Jesus' name. Amen.

The psalmist praises God's nature and God's activity in the world. God's activity and work leads to some understanding of who God is and what God's nature reveals. The psalmist praises God for the provision of food, for a place among the nations, and for God's mindfulness of the established covenant. Through God's good works, the world is made good.

What would it look like to see God through divine activity in the world? What would we understand about our powerful God? Whom would we love? What activities would engage our time? What does it mean to honor a Creator who provides and calls everything good and who repeatedly forgives our turning away? As Christians we affirm a God who displays God's nature and being through activity in the world. We worship a God who has shown the divine face in the face of Jesus Christ.

This God chooses the lost child to lead people to freedom or a small tribe to be God's chosen people or lifts up the sinners and the outcast, the vulnerable and the poor. This God provides and cares for those the world neglects.

Where do we see God at work in the world and glimpse a bit of God's nature? Perhaps we see God in the movement to cut hunger around the world in half by the end of 2015. We might glimpse God through the lens of people who work in food banks or who volunteer at food pantries. And that glimpse can empower us to act on God's behalf and reflect God's nature. We can take a small step to share love with others by offering a smile to a stranger, sponsoring a child in a low-income country, or working to improve the situation of minimum-wage employees. "The LORD is gracious and merciful," and so must we be.

O God of great works, open our eyes to you and your movement in the world. All glory, honor, and praise belong to you. Amen.

Paul is writing to a blended community. Some members come from the Jewish tradition, while others come from pagan traditions. The quarrel involves purity laws around food sacrificed to idols. Paul explains that food is food and that rituals around food preparation do not defile us. But he cautions those who understand this idea not to judge those who need to refrain from the food in order to "remain clean." He also cautions those who follow the law by avoiding food sacrificed to idols to refrain from judging those who do not eat it.

Conflicts in community arise when any group digs in its heels and insists that its knowledge or understanding is right. Some people get puffed up with ego and feel more righteous than others. Paul cautions them and us to allow love to guide our attitudes. We are to support one another in our journeys of faithfulness. And we, like the Corinthian factions, should be mindful of the influence our behavior might have on others.

At times our desire to be right overrides our love and compassion. We get caught up in blaming, which drives wedges among us instead of building relationships in love. Members of our local congregations often struggle between those who like the "way we have always done it" and those who want to try new ideas. There is wisdom in both options; but when we dig in our heels, we can't hear the other's wisdom.

By letting love guide us, we gain an openness to others. We can find ways to support the spiritual growth of others in the community. We in the body of Christ are to be about the work of building relationships of love that strengthen us in our commitment to others' well-being.

O God, you have all knowledge of me. You know when I am filled with love and when I am puffed up by knowledge. Open my heart and fill it with your love so that I may support the weak and not be a cause of their falling. Amen.

When modern people talk about idols, we often talk about where we put our energies or how we get distracted from God. Sometimes we talk about getting caught up in work. Idols are those things we put our trust in. They help us feel in control in a constantly changing world.

The believers in Corinth were a diverse group. Some continued to sacrifice to pagan gods in return for good fortune or well-being or success. Others in the community believed that eating the food from sacrifices to other gods made them unclean. Paul argues that because there is no other God, these foods cannot defile them.

It helps to remember that our idols are not gods. We can sacrifice for them, but ultimately they will not be our strength in times of change and suffering. If we trust in Jesus, if we make Jesus the center of our world, then everything else will fall into place. It doesn't mean that we won't suffer or that things won't change. But Jesus is our rock.

The other aspect that Paul mentions is the importance of our impact on those around us. The value always resides in the community rather than individual freedom, and we are to respect and value all in the community, despite our individual view or our theological strength. We are not to become stumbling blocks to the weak. So we take care as we consider potential idols in our lives so that we don't lead others astray.

O God, may we experience the joy of trusting in you. Guide us to be good neighbors as we value others' differing views and opinions. Amen.

Mark, in his storytelling, tries to set Jesus apart from the scribes. He attempts to convey to his readers and hearers that their trust is better placed in Jesus' teachings than those of the establishment religion, for Jesus' authority comes directly from God. While Jesus comes from the tradition of the scribes, he brings a new message that critiques the ways that the powerful exploit the weak. Jesus offers a critique of the leaders who continue to exclude those who are vulnerable and marginalized.

We are Christians because something about Jesus captures our imagination—we believe that Jesus is our Lord and Savior. The authority of his teaching and the way he teaches speak to us. But now, *we* are the establishment religion. Jesus' critique of religion focused on the fact that religion exploited the most vulnerable.

What would the critique be for our church, the church that is established in denominational structure and independent sects? What would Jesus say about the ways we honor God by serving those who are marginalized and vulnerable? How do we as the church speak with the authority that moves people to spread the word around the world?

O God, we are grateful that you sent your son to speak on your behalf and that he spoke with such authority as to wake us up. Give us the courage to speak without fear and to share with the world your words and your will. Amen.

We like to think that unclean spirits don't exist in our time or that our greater sophistication moves us past such juvenile thoughts. But we probably all believe that evil exists in the world, that there exist forces at work that are driven by something evil. They manifest themselves through greed and selfishness and lead to the dehumanization of people. Emotions can consume us from inside, taking over our lives through our thoughts and feelings. Maybe they are not unclean spirits, but these "unclean" thoughts and feelings divert our attention from God. What do we do with these forces?

Jesus enters the synagogue and teaches. The focus is on his authority; the people gathered are astounded at his teaching. They may ask, Who is this man? Whose power does he draw on? And then as if to answer the questions, the unclean spirit in the man cries out to Jesus. The unclean spirit knows the answer to the questions and knows where the authority lies. We learn nothing about the man; the demon is cast out, and those in the gathered community now stand amazed. Those in hearing distance of the miracle ask, "What is this?"

Jesus' "fame" spreads, and we have heard these reports as well. We encounter evil forces, experience "unclean" thoughts and feelings. As we consider what to do with these forces, we move beyond the bystanders' question of "What is this?" We have the answers to the questions: Who is this man? Whose power does he draw on? With Jesus as our acknowledged Lord and Savior, we also acknowledge our uncleanness; we cry out for healing. "What have you to do with us, Jesus of Nazareth?" And the answer comes back: I have everything to do with you. We bow before that authority and are healed.

O Great Healer, cast out the unclean spirits in our bodies and minds. We bow before your authority; make us well. In Jesus' name we pray. Amen.

God's Freely Given Love

FEBRUARY 2–8, 2015 • V. BRUCE RIGDON

MONDAY, FEBRUARY 2 ~ *Read Isaiah 40:21-31*

Have you ever felt as if there were no hope for anything good in your life to happen, as if every possibility for your dreams to come true had been destroyed? That was the plight of those to whom this passage is directed. Babylon had invaded Judah, destroyed the Temple, threatened all of the institutions from which the people expected God's faithfulness to be manifested and had carried many of its inhabitants into a long and bitter captivity. How could things have been worse?

The prophet's words remind his readers and all of us that God is not like any other god. God is the source, the creator of everything that exists. God actively cares about everything that exists. Past, present and future, all things are in God's hands.

We cannot hide from God or presume that God does not know or care about our affairs. God is the source of all the energy in the cosmos. Nothing exhausts God, and God gives life, energy, and renewal as God sees fit. Therein lies our hope!

God cares about us so much that God strengthens the weak, the faint, and the powerless. Doesn't that describe us? And if we get tired and grow weary or grow old and sick, God renews our strength so that we can walk, run, and, yes, even fly. It's enough to cause a rebirth of hope! So, what do we have to do to experience this renewal of courage and hope? "Wait," the prophet says. Wait for God to act. And in the meantime live as if the promised reign of God is already here!

Loving God, teach me to see your presence in the world around me and to respond to the needs of my neighbors, especially the weak, the powerless, the poor, and the discouraged. Amen.

President Emeritus, Ecumenical Theological Seminary, Detroit, Michigan; former Professor of Church History, McCormick Theological Seminary in Chicago

This story of the exiles in Babylon holds two dramatic elements in tension with each other. On the one hand, disaster has already befallen them. They are victims living in captivity in a foreign land. It must appear to them that Yahweh has allowed this to happen to them or, worse yet, that Yahweh was unable to prevent it.

On the other hand, Isaiah is reminding the Israelites that this is no local deity but the powerful Source of all that is. This God will deliver them, bring them home, and heal their broken hearts. How can these seemingly contradictory things be true, especially when institutions like the Temple and its priesthood through which Yahweh has blessed Israel have been destroyed?

We too agonize about why God allows tragedy to befall good people. And we often despair because the usual ways and the ancient institutions through which we expect God's action appear too weak to be viable.

The prophet reminds us that we are not God, that our ways are not God's ways, and that God works in ways beyond our conceiving or imagining. What matters is that God cares about each of us, calls us by name and will keep God's promises to us. Faith takes the risk that God is trustworthy.

Faith, therefore, involves a holy and expectant waiting—not a passive waiting but an active and responsive life that anticipates what God is doing in the world. D-Day, for example, was not the end of the Second World War in Europe; but for those who belonged to the resistance movements against Nazism and fascism, it signaled a certain end to the struggle. It encouraged those engaged in the struggle to take greater risks than ever, despite the fact that some of the worst days still lay ahead.

Gracious God, teach me to trust you daily and to see your hand at work around me. Amen.

Psalm 147, from beginning to end, utters a powerful doxology, which clearly locates it in the context of worship. We hear the voices of Jews and Christians, Israel and the church, raised to give God thanks and praise. For what is this thanksgiving offered?

In its historical and literary context the psalm celebrates God's faithfulness. God keeps promises and justifies the trust by which God's people live. God is building up Jerusalem once again and gathering together the outcasts and the exiles. God is healing those with broken hearts and tending graciously to the wounded. God lifts up the downtrodden; that is, all those who have gotten the short end of the stick: the poor, the sick, the disadvantaged, and the disabled. To all those who need God's presence, mercy, and love, God responds with generosity.

If this were not enough, God determines the number of stars and gives to each its name. It would appear that God loves not only us, humankind, but God deeply loves the entire creation and everything in it. God cares so much that, when necessary, God even brings down the wicked! Yet God continues to be bigger and greater than anything we can possibly comprehend. The only way to "know" God is to love God.

Taken together, Isaiah 40 and Psalm 147 make a special pair. They emphasize the fact that life is full of dangers, tragedies, pain, suffering, and death. No one is immune from such possibilities and realities. But the cosmos is God's beloved creation. God's people have promises from God that darkness will never overcome the light and that death will never destroy life.

Faith is the risk we take to trust God with everything in life and in death. Doxology and praise are essential and joyful human responses to a God who cares.

Creator God, give me grace to see your image in everyone I meet. Amen.

All of us have known relationships that seemed to have dried up. Often one of the signs and causes of such a breakup is the failure to express heartfelt thanks and appreciation to the other. That failure indicates the death of love. Love thrives and grows by finding joy in the other and expressing it in praise and thanks. "Sing to the LORD with thanksgiving; make melody to our God on the lyre," commands the psalmist.

The heart of the psalmist is full of joy and thanks. He praises God for clouds and rainfall, for grass on the hillsides, for the feeding of animals and birds, and for delighting in those who love God and who hope in God's steadfast love. God seems to take delight in human beings who trust divine promises, obey divine laws, and hope in God's steadfast love.

Human beings need love in order to remain human, in order to thrive. Think of infants and how they thrive on parents' praise as they express the depth of their love and identify the baby as the source of their delight and joy. Imagine what would happen to the infant if all love were denied. The baby's development would be impaired, the infant's humanity threatened. I presume that the child's capacity both to give and to receive love would be badly damaged.

So the psalmist knows that in order to grow into full human beings, full children of God who can give and receive love, we need to learn the art of praising God with all our hearts, with all our souls, with all our strength, and with all our minds. Only then can we love our neighbors as ourselves. And this offering of praise needs to occur regularly since it changes our lives. It is our way of knowing God.

Oh, yes, there is a reason we are able to love God. It is, very simply, because God first loved us.

Redeemer God, give me the grace to love and serve you with all my heart and strength. Amen.

Paul is working in Corinth as he carries out his apostolic mission. In the midst of his work, the issue arises as to how the Corinthians will pay Paul for his labors. Teachers and philosophers received support in several ways. Paul chose what must have been the least popular: earning his own way by manual labor. Paul became a tent maker in the most literal sense.

But interestingly enough, this decision comes only after Paul himself has established his right to be paid for his labors. If Paul were a volunteer he would have the same right as anyone else to earn his living as a minister or servant of the church. He would then be someone who had decided voluntarily to give his time and his work in return for a salary. But Paul insists that it is not by his own free will that he offers this service but rather that God has commissioned him to be an apostle. The fire of his apostleship burns in his bones, much like the prophets of old. Hence Paul connects the issue of how he will earn his keep with the fact that he is called by God to be an apostle for the sake of the gospel. One authenticates the other.

On this basis Paul claims that he offers the gospel "free of charge," that is, without cost to anyone. To do so requires that he renounce his rights to be paid a just wage for his apostolic work. In Paul's mind, he offers the gospel in a way consistent with the gospel itself. Jesus had renounced any and all rights in order to give himself and the gospel freely to all who would receive it. Paul's mission is to reach as many people as possible with the good news. His understanding of apostleship now frees him to become all things to all people in order to win them, that is, to bring them within hearing distance of the gospel. Christian freedom for Paul allows him to surrender his self-interest on behalf of others' needs. Is this true for us as well?

Lord, give me the courage to be free to give my life to others. Amen.

We are in the opening scenes of Mark's Gospel. Jesus has been baptized by John the Baptist in the Jordan River. He has undergone temptation in the wilderness and has called his first disciples. His true identity remains a secret, but his public ministry has begun. Its starting point is a synagogue where Jesus teaches and heals a man with an unclean spirit. Those who hear him are amazed not only by what he teaches but by the authority with which he speaks. Everyone is curious with regard to the identity of the new rabbi from Nazareth. The so-called messianic secret is a major feature of Mark's Gospel. Who is this one who teaches and heals in Yahweh's name?

From the synagogue we go to a family home in Capernaum— the home of Simon, one of those whom Jesus has called to be his disciple. If you visit present-day Capernaum you can find the archaeological site of this house and an active church that commemorates its significance to early Christians. The author of this Gospel was obviously very aware of the tension between synagogue and house churches in the church's early history.

Among those Jesus has chosen as disciples are married men. Simon's mother-in-law lies in bed with a fever. Jesus goes to her, takes her hand, and lifts her up. She experiences immediate healing. The text states that she gets up and serves Jesus and his friends. Traditional exegesis has assumed that this meant that she prepared food for them. But the verb used for *serve* in this case eventually led the church to describe those who served as deacons. This is the first appearance of a woman in Mark's Gospel, and she reminds us of the many faithful women who followed Jesus—even to the foot of the cross.

Faithful Lord, teach your church to welcome all your children to the joys of serving you in faithful ministry. Amen.

When the sun has set and the sabbath is over, Mark says that the whole town turns out in front of Simon's house to see Jesus. They bring all their sick, and Jesus heals many of them.

Jesus rises well before dawn and goes to a deserted place to pray. This rhythm of intense involvement in the lives of people and his withdrawal for prayer and reflection marks the whole of Jesus' ministry. He prays, experiences God's presence, renews his spirit, and reflects on God's purposes and will for him. These periods of being in God's presence seem to renew his energy, strengthen his resolve, and clarify the issues in his ministry.

This, of course, suggests the wisdom of establishing in our own lives a pattern and rhythm of action and reflection, of engagement and withdrawal so our own spirits have the possibility of refreshment, rest, and renewal. It is a discipline that is difficult to manage, but being in God's presence is essential for life itself.

Soon enough Simon and his companions confront and surround Jesus and tell him that everyone is looking for him. The passage concludes with Jesus telling his disciples that he must go to all of the villages in Galilee to proclaim his message and heal the people.

In his teaching and healing, Jesus proclaims the liberation that God intends for all God's children: freedom from illness and disease, freedom from political and social oppression, freedom from fear and want. No wonder Jesus and his disciples are headed for trouble—trouble with political and religious authorities and everyone who has a stake in the status quo. But Jesus faithfully proclaims the coming reign of God and embodies the power of love at the heart of that reign in his own death and resurrection.

Risen Lord, sustain me with your love and free me from all fear, that I may live joyfully in the reign of God. Amen.

The Light of the Glory of God

FEBRUARY 9–15, 2015 • SARAH S. HOWELL

MONDAY, FEBRUARY 9 ~ *Read Mark 9:2-9*

The Transfiguration is a narrative in which revelation and mystery meet. Jesus' place among the prophets is confirmed as he appears with Elijah and Moses, and a voice from on high declares his relationship to and authority from God. The disciples are bewildered, afraid, and unsure how to respond.

Christian prayers and hymnody have strongly reinforced the idea of giving glory to God or glorifying God. Some traditions prioritize prayer or morality or social justice. While all these aspects have their place within the worship and work of the triune God, often they nudge out time we might spend simply marveling at God's glory. Peter is so thrown by the power of the divine presence that he scrambles to do something to commemorate or preserve the moment rather than receive it.

Glory is not something God needs us to give; when we glorify God, we participate in the glory that comes from God. When we catch a glimpse of God's glory (or perhaps even receive an incredible vision), we do not need to do anything or say anything. Our only response should be one of awe.

The word *awe* in its original sense implied reverence, admiration, and fear. The Transfiguration as an event is "awe-full"— not bad but full of awe. What role does awe play in your life? Do you tend to want to resolve every mystery or explain every revelation? What would it look like for you to see and receive the glory of God in your life today?

God, help me pause today to see the dazzling light of your glory, whether it bursts upon my heart like a sunrise or filters stubbornly through the cracks. Amen.

Assistant minister, Centenary United Methodist Church, Winston-Salem, North Carolina

We witness the passing of the mantle, so to speak, from Elijah to Elisha. The tension of what is coming builds to the dramatic ending as a chariot of fire separates the two, and a whirlwind carries Elijah away.

Elijah repeatedly tells Elisha to stay behind, and Elisha repeatedly ignores him. God is sending Elijah to Bethel, to Jericho, to the Jordan, and Elisha follows. Elisha knows that his master will be taken from him; he ignores the questions of the prophets who badger him along the way. Elisha knows, but he doesn't want to talk about it; he wants only to be near his master.

The relationship between Elijah and Elisha in some ways resembles that of a master and an apprentice; but in other ways, it is that of two dear friends. At the time that Elijah is taken away, we see that the two men are "walking and talking" together. The journey is a shared one in which the prophets keep each other company.

Elijah asks Elisha what he can do for him not after Elisha has performed a great feat or even as an invitation to earn a blessing; the question comes only after Elisha has followed Elijah to Bethel, to Jericho, and finally to the Jordan. Elisha's presence with and attention to his master allows him to witness Elijah's departure and to receive a double share of Elijah's spirit.

The other prophets in the places they visited kept their distance, knowing Elijah would be taken away. But Elisha remains close to Elijah. Other prophets may have known what was about to happen, but only Elisha knew that the most important aspect of relationship came in staying near his master—not in knowing the future.

God, give me the faithfulness required to receive your Spirit, not because I can earn it but because you want me to remain close to you. Amen.

Psalm 50 bears witness to the dramatic inbreaking of God's presence, much like the Transfiguration itself. As Jesus' face shone, so "God shines forth." This light illuminates and reveals, and it reveals more than God's glory. This light shines on us and reveals our shortcomings. In Psalm 50, God is coming "that he may judge his people." Before this image of devouring fire and mighty tempest, we may feel as terrified as the disciples were on Mount Tabor.

This scene reminds us that we are people of a covenant. We find ourselves in a particular relationship with God that calls us to a particular way of life. God's love, while neither permissive nor punitive, makes demands of us and holds us accountable to the covenant made by sacrifice.

God shines forth not simply to inspire but to remind us of who we are. We are called as God's faithful ones. The implied question being, have we been faithful? Who are we to respond to such a quality of fidelity?

We take courage in the final statement of this passage: "God himself is judge." The light that shines upon us gives us the opportunity to examine ourselves; to seek forgiveness, reconciliation, right relationship with God and one another—but in the end, we judge neither our neighbors nor ourselves.

Only God is judge. We stand in the light of God's judgment, exposed for who we truly are. This exposure may be painful, but it offers the opportunity for confession and forgiveness,which makes us more and more like the "faithful ones" God calls us to be.

God, I hear your summons and will respond to your call. Shine your light into my heart and give me strength to face whatever is revealed, offering it to you in your mercy. Amen.

We often see the adjective "Christian" attached to things with little clarity as to why it is there or what it means. The church can become a social club whose membership rules involve participating in Christian activities, buying Christian products, and eating at Christian restaurants.

But the gospel is not about *being* Christian. The gospel is about Christ. The word *Christian* means "little Christ"—so being Christian involves following the teachings and person of Jesus. Christian is not a label that sanitizes secular goods to make them fit for our consumption; it is the name given to those baptized into Jesus' death and resurrection.

The danger in pigeonholing ourselves as "Christians" who do "Christian" things is that our faith and life become more about being "Christian" than about God. We point to ourselves and our Christianity more than we point to Christ.

The good news is that pointing to Jesus instead of to ourselves takes the pressure off us! We are called to be the body of Christ here on earth, to grow in God's likeness, to be perfected in love—and yet we fall short. But when we profess God and not ourselves, we can own our brokenness and proclaim the One who heals; we can admit our sin and witness to the One who takes our sin away; we can confess our hypocrisy and gesture toward the Source of truth. We can remove the veil of "Christian" labels and see Christ clearly by the light of God's face.

When we proclaim God and not ourselves, we practice humility. Humility is not about thinking of ourselves as less than others but about knowing our true place in creation. Our place in creation is as beloved children of God. When we know that, we can point beyond ourselves with humble, thankful hearts.

God, give me the knowledge of your truth but give me also humility so that I always point to you and never to myself. Amen.

This passage tells us where we may see the light of God's glory: in Jesus' face. God's glory is not communicated by words but by *the* Word. The light is not simply the light of knowledge or understanding; it is the light of recognition and connection to another person.

We can be blinded to the light of God's glory in many ways. Today's passage says that "the god of this world has blinded the minds of the unbelievers." Let us expand the definition of "unbelievers" for a moment—not limiting it to atheists or non-Christians but understanding that even within the life of faith come moments of unbelief. This is not necessarily a bad thing. One of my favorite prayers is Mark 9:24, "I believe; help my unbelief!" God can hold our doubt and faith together.

But let us consider another definition of unbelief: separation from God. Where in your life do you feel separated from God? When have you found it hard to trust God's mercy, God's goodness, God's love? When have you experienced dry places in your spiritual life or prayer life and felt distant from God?

Unbelief as separation from God may occur within our own hearts and minds, but it can also happen between us and other people. When we feel disconnected from our neighbors, we will feel separated from human beings who were made in the image of God. We then find ourselves separated from the possibility of seeing God in them.

May we seek Jesus' face in all people at all times in all places, becoming faithful believers by healing separation from God wherever we encounter it.

God, may I be a light to others, so that even if their sight is veiled in unbelief, they will see your truth and love in my words and actions. Amen.

What comes to your mind when you hear the word *justice*? Our cultural understanding of justice is largely punitive: criminals being held accountable for their crimes and locked up or otherwise punished. Our justice system favors this approach.

In the Hebrew Bible, justice and righteousness go hand in hand, but the justice is seldom punitive. In Psalm 50:6, the word translated as "righteousness" may, in other places, be rendered "justice," but this justice has a deeper meaning than the one we attribute to the word. One Hebrew word for "justice," *mishpat*, has more to do with governance and the establishment of Jewish law; but the word *tzedakah*, which we find in verse 6, does not have a comparable equivalent in English. We may translate *tzedakah* as "justice," "righteousness," or "charity."

In English, the words *charity* and *justice* convey different concepts, coming from the Latin roots *caritas* and *iustitia*. In some circles, "charity" may evoke images of monetary assistance isolated from relationship building. "Justice" (especially "social justice") may conjure up ideas of politics and rhetoric disconnected from people's immediate needs.

However, the word and concept of *tzedakah* inextricably links charity and justice. Only when these concepts come together do we discover true righteousness. This idea speaks not only to our role as God's people in an unjust, uncharitable world but also to our understanding of God's character. God serves as a just judge. God's justice is tied to God's charity—God's mercy and love. God is righteous because in God these two qualities are one. We can trust God's fair and loving judgment, and we hope that we can participate in God's righteousness.

God, judge me in your justice, and remind me that your justice cannot be separated from your mercy and love. Amen.

TRANSFIGURATION SUNDAY

The disciples' reaction of fear in seeing God's glory explode on the scene does not surprise us. Fear often has more to do with the unknown than with actual danger. In this case, what is happening lies beyond anything they have seen or known—so they are "terrified." Being in the presence of the living God is a fearful thing indeed. God—in all majesty, glory, and power—lies beyond our comprehension, and it is only human that such an experience would provoke fear in us.

Peter's proposition of building memorials to Jesus, Moses, and Elijah is ignored. Dazzling presence gives way to cloudy overshadowing, and the voice of God speaks, "This is my Son, the Beloved; listen to him." The words come as a baptismal reaffirmation and a confirmation of commissioning. The Transfiguration is more than an end in itself; the disciples will not remain on the mountaintop. They must follow Jesus down into the valley.

As terrifying as the Transfiguration event seems, perhaps the disciples have even greater—or at least different—fears about returning to where they have been. In the previous chapter, Jesus tells the disciples that those who follow him will deny themselves and "take up their cross" (Mark 8:34). Whatever that meant, it does not sound pleasant. The terror of God's dazzling presence might have been preferable to the prospect of shouldering the heavy beams of a literal or metaphorical cross.

Though the disciples do not find release from their fears, they are given Jesus' own presence. Jesus accompanies them down the mountain. Whatever fears may confront us, whether the wild, joyful fears of the mountaintop or the dark, dangerous fears of the valley, God is always with us.

God, calm my fears; give me the courage to follow you down the mountain of revelation into the world of kingdom building. Amen.

Walking through Lent

FEBRUARY 16–22, 2015 • TIM WHITAKER

MONDAY, FEBRUARY 16 ~ *Read 2 Corinthians 5:20b–6:10*

At one time we experienced the grace of baptism as a bath and a new birth and an infusion of light into our hearts. Then we let ambitions, daily preoccupations, and distractions put the memory of our experience of God's grace behind us.

It is not only those who forsake the church and the Christian life who do not fulfill their baptism. Even those of us who remain in the church acknowledge seasons when our conviction of God's truth and our enthusiasm for Christian living become dull.

Today the apostle Paul calls to us, "We urge you also not to accept the grace of God in vain." Isn't our deepest spiritual yearning not to miss the grace God has to give us and to become the person God created us to be? This is our true desire, but embarrassment about our need, fear of change, or hesitancy about making commitments have kept us from fulfilling our baptism for too long. Before it is too late, we can approach this Lent as our time, the time we need to renew our faith so that we do not walk in vain.

Walking in the Christian life is not easy. Paul speaks eloquently about the sacrifices he and the other apostles made. Yet what shines through his testimony is his conviction: It has been worth it! See how we have been transformed! If we had resisted Christ's call, we would never have grown in "purity, knowledge, patience, kindness, holiness of spirit, genuine love, truthful speech, and the power of God."

Spirit of the living God, enable me to seize this time of renewal so that I do not walk in vain. Amen.

Retired bishop of The United Methodist Church, living in Virginia

Tomorrow, Ash Wednesday, we begin our observance of Lent by praying Psalm 51. This psalm is David's prayer when he confesses to the Lord the sin of abusing his power as king. He had arranged the death of one of his soldiers, Uriah, in order to cover up his adultery with Uriah's wife, Bathsheba. (See 2 Samuel 11–12.) Israel's ideal king is guilty of a merciless act, but Israel's Lord shows him mercy by forgiving his sin. In this masterpiece of a psalm, I am David, and David's Lord is my God.

We may think we have not done anything as evil as David's actions. We may recoil from identifying ourselves as sinners. We may even denounce a religion of introspection and guilt for cultivating in us unhealthy attitudes toward ourselves. If so, then let us think again about what this psalm is about.

This psalm can only be prayed by a person who knows that God is "steadfast love," that this boundless love frees us to face the truth about ourselves, and that confession of our sin to this God offers the way to be made whole. Psalm 51 invites us to walk in truth, for God "desires truth in the inward being."

To confess our sins does not make us spiritual hypochondriacs; it acknowledges us as fully self-aware persons who are not afraid to face the reality of our human limitation and sin.

Our culture either encourages us to pretend we are OK or tries to destroy anyone who is exposed as a phony. Only before God can we learn to walk in truth, for God's love provides an arena of divine scrutiny of our real self where we are not only known but also accepted and forgiven.

God, in your love, free me to walk in the truth. Amen.

ASH WEDNESDAY

On Ash Wednesday, we hear the invitation to the observance of Lenten discipline, which includes the call "to observe a holy Lent: by self-examination and repentance; by prayer, fasting, and self-denial; and by reading and meditating on God's Holy Word." To most of us, what stands out in this invitation is the call to fast.

Protestants generally neglected fasting as a spiritual discipline. Even Methodists forgot that tucked into one of our General Rules was the charge to practice "fasting or abstinence." We in the Wesleyan traditions are reclaiming many traditional spiritual disciplines, including fasting. In the Gospel reading for Ash Wednesday, Jesus does not say, "if you fast" but "whenever you fast" (Matt. 6:16).

Fasting occurs in many forms. Eastern Christians do not consume milk, eggs, or meat during Lent. Many Christians give up desserts. Others choose to abstain from whatever may get in the way of their relationship to God. However we do it, fasting is an offering to God to overcome being and doing what *we* want so that we may be and do what *God* wants. What does God really want from us? The prophet Micah says that the Lord requires that we do justice, love kindness, and walk humbly with our God (6:8). When we fast, think about that!

In today's reading, the prophet exposes the hypocrisy of those who go through the ritual of fasting while oppressing their workers and neglecting the poor. God says, "Is not this the fast that I choose: to loose the bonds of injustice, to undo the thongs of the yoke, to let the oppressed go free, and to break every yoke?" Because God's purpose is to order a just society, God's relationship with us requires that we walk in justice.

Lord, show us how to walk in justice as we pray and fast. Amen.

The Old Testament reading each Sunday during Lent tells about one of God's covenants—with Noah, Abraham, Moses, and Jeremiah. On the First Sunday in Lent, the reading addresses the covenant with Noah.

The saga of Noah and the ark sets the stage for telling the history of Israel beginning with the call of Abraham. This saga shows that the history of God's covenants with Israel, which come to a climax in the new covenant that Jesus announces to his disciples at the Last Supper, happens in the context of God's purposes for the earth—even the entire universe.

God says that the covenant with Noah is "between me and you and every living creature" and "between me and the earth." The sign of this covenant is the rainbow—as if God hangs a weapon of destruction, the bow, in the sky to symbolize God's purpose for creation: not destruction but preservation of life.

God plans to save all creation. Our personal salvation is part of a cosmic salvation. God intends nothing less than the liberation and transformation of the "the whole creation." (See Romans 8:18-25.) The covenant with Noah looks toward Easter when the risen Jesus signals the transformation of our bodies and all things. (See Philippians 3:21.)

We exist within four relationships—with God, others, ourselves, and the natural world. Often we forget the fourth relationship. God desires that we not only worship God, love others, and know ourselves but that we also take care of the earth and "every living creature" on it. Our walk with the Lord takes place with "every living creature" and requires ecological reverence and stewardship.

God our Creator, help us to walk gently on the earth with every living creature. Amen.

On the First Sunday in Lent, we pray Psalm 25:1-10 as a response to the Old Testament reading of Genesis 9:8-17. The psalmist offers a prayer of thanksgiving for the steadfast love of the Lord on behalf of all creation.

One of our roles as human beings is to be the priests of creation. Of all God's creatures on earth, we alone can pray and give thanks to the Creator on behalf of all creation—the heavenly bodies, the earth and its seas, and all living things. We exercise this role whenever we celebrate Holy Communion and lift up our hearts to exclaim on behalf of all creation, "Heaven and earth are full of your glory!" The sacrament shapes us to offer prayers of thanksgiving every day.

In exercising our role as the priests of creation on behalf of all creatures by offering prayers of thanks and praise to our Creator, we are acknowledging that we and all of creation depend upon the power, wisdom, and grace of God.

Prayer is the most radical act we can perform. Through prayer we learn to live in humility as creatures who depend upon our Creator. The Lord "teaches the humble his way." By praying, we learn to walk in humility, not only in God's presence but also with others.

Humility is self-abnegation but not self-defamation. Paradoxically, by accepting ourselves as God's creature and therefore as a companion creature with others, we also claim our dignity as persons created for communion with God and others. Being humble is not being ashamed; it is being fully aware—aware of the difference between God and us and aware of the differences between ourselves and others.

God our Lord, thank you for the mystery of prayer in which we learn to walk in humility. Amen.

First Peter 3:18-22 is the epistle reading for the First Sunday in Lent because of its connection to the Old Testament reading. It tells the story of Noah's ark as a symbol for baptism, for the eight persons on the ark were "saved through water." It also contains the mysterious comment on the preaching of Christ to "spirits in prison," an allusion to the evil "sons of God" or fallen angels in the saga about Noah in Genesis 6:1-4. Christ's preaching represents his cosmic victory over the spiritual powers of paganism. The text exhorts baptized Christians to be faithful witnesses to Christ and be willing to suffer as he suffered. Those who are out of step with their godless and pagan culture are few in number. But they acknowledge the risen and ascended Christ as the true Lord of life—although the world does not know it.

The author says, "Baptism . . . now saves you—not as a removal of dirt from the body, but as an appeal to God for a good conscience." God's grace through baptism washes us clean. Rather than a physical washing, this spiritual cleansing creates within us a good conscience toward God.

Our conscience is that dimension of our consciousness that pronounces judgment on our thoughts and actions. Through the grace given in baptism, our conscience itself is surrendered to God's good will so that it rightly serves to guide our walk through life.

We find ourselves surrounded by a culture that molds the human conscience to its own standards. We need to practice the spiritual disciplines of worship, searching the scriptures, fasting, and prayer to bind our conscience to the will of God so that we may walk in the world with a good conscience.

Gracious God, cleanse our minds that we may walk with a good conscience. Amen.

FIRST SUNDAY IN LENT

The Gospel reading tells the story of Jesus' baptism and his testing in the wilderness for forty days. The lection epitomizes the whole season of Lent, for during this season of forty days before Easter we remember our baptism and submit ourselves to a time of testing.

Sometimes the church's observance of Lent may seem to instill a "do it yourself" (DIY) kind of religion rather than a "live by the Spirit" walk in faith. Since Jesus' baptism and testing in the wilderness serve as the paradigm for our observance of Lent, notice the emphasis on the Holy Spirit in this story.

During Jesus' baptism, the Spirit descends on him so that he may hear that he is God's son. In Jesus' baptism we see our own: The Spirit also descends on us so that we may hear the word that Jesus is God's son and our Lord and thereby become the sons and daughters of God our Father.

Following Jesus' baptism, "the Spirit immediately drove him into the wilderness" to be tested. If the Spirit "drove" Jesus into testing, then we should not look upon Lenten disciplines as inconsistent with a life in the Spirit. To the contrary, we expect the Spirit to use all kinds of testing to enable us to grow as God's own children.

However, we also recognize that spiritual disciplines do not function as a DIY kind of religion but as a means for learning together how to let the Holy Spirit illumine, lead, guide, and empower us to be faithful disciples of Jesus Christ. During Lent the church provides the means. What happens to us when we use them depends upon our willingness to walk by the Spirit.

Triune God, empower us to walk in your Spirit. Amen.

Worthy of Trust

FEBRUARY 23–MARCH 1, 2015 • ELISE ERIKSON BARRETT

MONDAY, FEBRUARY 23 ~ *Read Psalm 22:25-31*

The aspect I found most terrifying about being a mother to infants was the absolute trust they placed in me. I could have been terrible or wonderful, loving or abusive—on that first day, they loved me just because I was there.

But babies learn quickly whether or not they have trustworthy caregivers. They notice if they will be fed when they are hungry, if they will be kept clean, if they will be picked up and cuddled, if their bids for connection will be met by loving attention. With every feeding in the wee hours, every sponge bath, every snuggle and smile, I sent messages to my babies. You are loved. You are safe. You can count on me.

I did this imperfectly. But adequate parents teach their children to have faith in them—to ask for what they need, to cry when they are hurting, to rejoice when they appear.

The psalmist says, "Those who seek him shall praise the LORD." Another way to express this might be, "Those who cry out to their Parent will find that God is praiseworthy." Worthy of praise, worthy of trust. Far more than even the most loving human parent and transcending the brokenness we unconsciously imprint on one another, God can be trusted, even by those who sleep in the earth, who have gone down into the dust. And once we learn in a hundred small ways that our hunger will be satisfied, that we will be tenderly cleansed, and that the Voice speaking to us out of the loneliest nights is full of love, we will feel free to trust and, thereby, to live.

Loving Parent, help me seek you as unself-consciously as a crying infant, and teach me how trustworthy you are. Amen.

United Methodist pastor, pastor's wife, mother to three, musician, and writer, Spartanburg, South Carolina

Perhaps you remember participating in those awkward "trust falls" at college orientation or youth group meetings—you know how it goes: One person stands, arms crossed over her chest and eyes closed, another person stands a few steps behind her, braced and ready. At the leader's command, the person in front squeezes her eyes shut and falls straight backward, hopefully into the arms of the other student. Trust falls gone awry result in bruised backsides and hilarity, usually nothing worse. They are intended to foster a sense of trust among the group members, creating a shared experience of putting personal physical safety in the hands of another and ideally having that safety protected, that trust justified.

In this passage from Genesis, God invites Abram and Sarai to perform the ultimate trust fall with their lives. "Come," God says, in so many words. "I realize that you're ancient, both of you, but I'd like to make a great nation out of you. You are going to be exceedingly fruitful. . . . as in centenarians having babies. All you have to do is trust me. . . . Oh, and change your names. And I'd like you to leave the home you've known for a century and move to a land you've never seen."

This invitation requires more than simply deciding whether it's worth the risk to fall into the arms of the sophomore you outweigh by thirty pounds. God invites Abram and Sarai to a free fall off a cliff, away from security, away from the known, away from a life that seemed to be winding down more or less comfortably. God speaks to Abram and Sarai, and although the specifics seem utterly ridiculous, what they hear apparently convinces them that God is worth trusting. The covenant is only as good as the One who makes it.

Calling God, let us hear you clearly enough that we are willing to trust you, to fall into your safe arms. Amen.

What is faith? Is it a belief? Like flipping a light switch from the off to the on position, flipping our inner ideology from disbelief to belief, from no to yes?

The Genesis passage seems to imply that faith, *saving* faith, is more than a flip of the switch. Faith requires more than intellectual assent to a proposition or set of statements about God. Instead, faith is an active trust, an orientation of our lives toward One we have met and find trustworthy. Faith is less about the details about what we believe, more about the transformation of our very lives.

Paul reminds us of what this looked like for Abram and Sarai. They did not just say to God, "Yes, we believe that you are the Lord" and go back to business as usual. Once Abram and Sarai met God, everything changed. And the change did not come because they found a statement about God intellectually compelling. When God encountered them directly, they chose to trust God with everything.

The promise, Paul says, depends on faith and rests on grace —in the presence of the God in whom Abraham believed, the God who gives life to the dead and calls into being the things that are not. When we are aware of and open to God's presence, when God meets us, we share the saving faith of Abraham: not a mental backflip to try to believe something unbelievable but a life-altering trust in the One we come to know. Knowing God, living in the presence of God—this will lead us into the faith that sets us right with God and with one another. We, like Abram and Sarai, open ourselves to the power of a surprising God and refuse to settle for life as usual.

God, I want to be present with you. Come close enough to me that I can trust you fully—not always understanding but believing that I can trust you with my very life. Amen.

Years ago, my husband and I attended a wedding in northern California. Living in the South, we were accustomed to the folks around us having some exposure to Christianity. We were one of only a handful of religious types at this wedding, however, and as a matched set of United Methodist pastors, we attracted interest. People were warm and genuinely curious: "What does a pastor do?" "Wow, I've never met someone who was a professional religious person!"

After an intelligent and respectful interchange about the whole "religion" thing with one man, he finally shook his head. "I mean, it'd be great to have a framework like that for your life, and I think there's a lot of good in it. I just can't make myself believe some of that stuff—that there's a heaven with angels and harps, that all those miracles happened—can't buy it. But part of me wishes I could."

If faith consists in our making ourselves believe what we find unbelievable, we are sunk. Paul goes to great lengths here to show us just how unlikely God's promises to Abraham to make him a great nation were: His elderly body was already "as good as dead," and Sarah's womb was barren. Still, Abraham hoped against hope. Why? Because the promises made sense? No. Because Abraham had met God. And once he met God, he trusted God—even to make good on a future that seemed, to put it politely, unlikely. This trust, actively pursued and lived, made Abraham righteous—set right with God. Our willingness to trust in God's Christ, Paul says, puts us in right relationship to God. Even when the path is unlikely. Even when the promises seem impossible.

Help me trust you, God, even when your promises seem unlikely to be fulfilled. Amen.

C. S. Lewis's *The Screwtape Letters* is a series of fanciful communiqués written from a senior demon to his nephew, who is young and inexperienced in the ways of tempting humans. In one letter, the nephew has been gloating over some trial his particular human is experiencing. The nephew, it seems, holds a faulty assumption: In this world, faithful people get blessings, and failing people get punishments. We've heard this view expressed quite bluntly: "Your hardship happened because God is punishing you." Or, it can be more subtle: "If you'd prayed harder or prayed more faithfully or changed your life, God would have shown up and saved the day."

The senior devil stops his nephew short by stating that times of trial don't necessarily indicate that evil is winning. In fact, some people who are closest to God end up experiencing longer, more difficult periods of suffering than anyone else. In those times of suffering and pain, these humans grow into the kind of creatures God intends them to be.

The psalmist has been there, has experienced affliction. We don't know what: warfare? hunger? sickness? death of a loved one? Has his community come to believe painful gossip about him? Whatever his affliction, in his time of suffering he called out to God. And God did not despise him, did not abhor him, did not hide from him. Instead, God heard him.

This is no small thing, as you know if you have ever been truly heard by another. God heard the psalmist. And even out of our experiences of suffering can grow deepened trust in God. If we cry out in our affliction, God listens and hears.

Ever-present God, hear my cry. I am afflicted by _____.
Help me know that you hear me. Amen.

Picture your favorite politician or celebrity. He's in the middle of an upsurge in popularity, in demand on television, viral online. And you—you!—are one of his most trusted friends. An insider. You're the one ducking out of the limo right behind the flavor of the moment, and while you know all the cameras are flashing at him, you also know that everyone in the crowd wishes they could be you, to be close to the action, one of the few who really know what this person is like.

So imagine that one day while you're waving and smiling and following in the wake of your famous friend, he suddenly raises his hands for silence and, in front of the reporters and cameras, starts saying things like this: "It's all about to end. I know you all love me right now, but in just a little while, you'll be spitting at the sound of my name. I'm going to be arrested. Not only that, I'm going to receive the death penalty."

You are appalled. Not only is this terrible news (and surely it's an exaggeration?), but it's not the way to nurture this wave of momentum. So you run up, confident in your insider role, and pull him aside. "Hey, friend, we've got to lay off all this death and failure stuff—people don't want to hear about that." He looks at you with grieved eyes. "Back off, tempter," he replies. "You've misunderstood it all. This was never about the biggest numbers or the popularity or about success on someone else's terms. I'm only concerned with God's priorities. And God's priorities are so different from the priorities of this world that they seem painfully foolish if you're out of step with the way of life I'm trying to show you."

God, keep us from measuring your work and call by the success standards of our culture. Amen.

SECOND SUNDAY IN LENT

Two years ago, my husband began a battle against lymphoma, which eventually culminated in a bone marrow transplant. It was the closest I've come to losing my life. I temporarily lost everything I valued most. I didn't see my children for months; my marriage morphed into a caregiver/care receiver relationship; and I was far from my networks of support. Perhaps you've had a similar experience—a military deployment, a serious illness, a traumatic loss. These experiences press us beyond our ability to cope, beyond our ability to pretend that we're just fine.

This is the space—this dark space beyond the edges of the life I'd built for myself—where I fell before God over and over, raging, exhausted, and despairing, and found myself loved—not abandoned but more fully myself than I had ever been. I had lost my life only to find it. This is the space in which Jesus promises us we will find the life God meant for us all along. We catch glimpses of this life when suffering and loss push "life-as-we-know-it" aside. We sense it despite our frantic efforts to control and to protect ourselves and those we love from harm.

But Jesus seems to suggest another way. We don't have to be pushed beyond our endurance to lay our lives down. Our God is worthy of trust, even with our precious, fragile lives. And when we come to know the God who knows and loves us more deeply than we know and love ourselves, we will realize that we can place our very lives in God's hands. Then we discover—beyond the borders of our tight and frightened attempts at control—the life that was meant to be ours all along.

Trustworthy God, I am yours. Relax my frantic clutch on my plans, my worries, my goals. Give me what I need to lay my life down so you can show me what it means to truly live. Amen.

Wisdom without Words

MARCH 2–8, 2015 • BILL DOCKERY

MONDAY, MARCH 2 ~ *Read Psalm 19:1-6*

One evening a few years ago, I took my children to a remote farm, away from the noise and lights of Knoxville. A farmer had created a maze in one of his cornfields and was charging school kids and parents for the fun of getting lost in it. The youngsters quickly disappeared into the raspy rows of cornstalks. I stepped away to a pasture where the cars were parked.

The faint glow of twilight outlined the horizon. A thin husk of moon hung in the sky, punctuated by the brightness of the evening star. Suddenly as I gazed, the blue-black sky gained depth, and I sensed the whirling of planets and moon through space, speeding me on unimaginable paths. Terror gripped me. Like a kid on a runaway merry-go-round, I felt I might be flung into that inky sky. Instinctively, I wanted to flatten myself against the earth to keep from being hurled into the void. I knew immediately that I was in the presence of the Holy. I became aware of my true place in the world.

That overwhelming awe, tinged with terror, is what the psalmist celebrates in the first verses of Psalm 19. "How clearly the sky reveals God's glory!" (TEV) Accustomed to a desert sky unobscured by human activity, the psalmist can readily grasp the universe as the incarnation of the Creator. Yet, the psalmist tells us, "No speech or words are used, no sound is heard" (TEV).

Though words are needed to sing of the experience, the psalmist wisely celebrates the wordlessness of the sacred wisdom that emanates from God's universe.

God of creation, help us see behind our words to your deeper wisdom. Amen.

Retired journalist; Knoxville, Tennessee

The psalmist who wrote Psalm 19 takes care not to leave us with only a wordless appreciation of how God is manifest in the natural world. The song quickly moves into a celebration of the law that God has given: "The law of the LORD is perfect; it gives new strength. The commands of the LORD are trustworthy, giving wisdom to those who lack it" (TEV). Like the mute testimony of the heavens, God's law offers the Israelites the possibility of a right relationship with God and the world. Following the law leads to happiness and wisdom and helps the Israelites avoid their tendencies toward faults and willful sins.

The centerpiece of that law is the Ten Commandments, laws from God to the children of Israel as they struggle for both survival and identity. Given at a moment of high drama in the desert at Mount Sinai, the divine laws weld the Israelites into one people, God's people. In succinct language, the commandments lay out a covenant between the Israelites and Yahweh. The first three govern the ways humans relate to God. The next two suggest how humans must take care of themselves and their families. The final five cover the fundamental rules for living with other people.

The Ten Commandments are among the most famous lists in the history of world civilizations. Unlike more extensive codes from other early Middle Eastern civilizations, the commandments do not list specific punishments for transgressors. Only failing to honor God (who admits to being a "jealous" God) will call down wrath on the Israelites.

As a code of conduct, the Ten Commandments provide a fundamental guide for a just and righteous society. For those who want to be part of God's people, following them is vital to a right relationship with God and others.

Guide my daily actions, O God, that I may grow closer to you. Amen.

The Ten Commandments remain at the forefront of contemporary culture but not in the reverential way they were taken in biblical times. Today the commandments are as much a source of controversy as they are a guide for righteous living. Factions use them iconically to posture in political disputes about freedom of speech and religion. This is not the first time the commandments have been misused for secular purposes.

In 1956, one of the most famous movies of all time began to appear in theaters across the nation and around the world: *The Ten Commandments.* The movie, a Hollywood epic, dramatized how Moses led the children of Israel out of bondage in Egypt and into a covenant with God in the desert.

Cecil B. DeMille, the producer-director of the film, devised an unusual publicity stunt to advertise his picture. Working with a civic group, he had granite monuments engraved with the commandments erected in the yards of hundreds of courthouses across the country, all for the purpose of promoting the movie.

Engraving the commandments on a stone and posting it in a public place seem to be a kind of idolatry forbidden by the third commandment. These principles from God should be posted in the individual heart and furnish a standard by which we measure our own actions toward God and the world.

In any discussion of the commandments, we must keep in mind Jesus' response to the young lawyer who challenged him: "Which is the great commandment in the law?" (KJV). Without hesitation, Jesus stripped away the negative formulations: "Thou shalt love the Lord thy God with all thy heart, and with all thy soul, and with all thy mind. . . . And the second is like unto it, Thou shalt love thy neighbor as thyself. On these two commandments hang all the law and the prophets" (Matt. 22:35-40, KJV).

O God of truth, may I never use your words to deceive others—or myself. Amen.

In his willingness to profit from the faith, C. B. DeMille had nothing on the merchants of first-century Jerusalem. When the Israelites rebuilt the Temple after the exile in Babylon, its outer courtyard quickly became the commercial hub for people who want to profit from the needs of observant Jews following traditional religious rituals. Visiting the Temple before Passover, Jesus finds a scene of unbridled exploitation: merchants tending livestock for sale to people wanting to make a sacrifice, dove vendors selling birds to those who could not afford a larger sacrificial animal, and speculators who would exchange foreign currency for the local specie—all for a price.

All four Gospels record Jesus' anger and his quick response. John tells us, "Making a whip of cords, he drove all of them out of the temple, both the sheep and the cattle," "poured out the coins of the money changers," and ordered the dove sellers to leave.

"Stop making my Father's house a marketplace!" he said. Officials of the Temple immediately question his authority to take such actions, challenging not his legal authority but focusing specifically on his religious credentials: "What miracle can you perform to show that you have the right to do this?" (TEV)

In terms of traditional rational discourse, Jesus' answer is a *non sequitur*—it just doesn't make sense. "Destroy this temple, and in three days I will raise it up." The meaning of his statement is lost on the officials who immediately point out the nonsensical nature of his claim: "This temple has been under construction for forty-six years, and will you raise it up in three days?"

Only after Jesus' death and resurrection will his own disciples understand the trivial nature of traditional Temple sacrifices and the significance of a Temple rebuilt in three days. Sometimes in the silence after an event, what seems to be nonsense turns out to be profound wisdom.

Everlasting God, give us patience to wait for understanding that comes with time. Amen.

What seems to be nonsense turns out to be profound wisdom. The disciples come to understand that fact after the Resurrection drama has played out on Golgotha and in a nearby tomb. That drama explains matters to them that would have seemed incredible had someone told them in advance. Paul got it too, as he shows in his first letter to the church at Corinth: "The message about Christ's death on the cross is nonsense to those who are being lost; but for us who are being saved it is God's power" (TEV).

A sophisticated Jew who was as at home in a contemporary Hellenistic environment as he was in Hebrew culture, Paul writes to encourage a congregation beset on the one hand by Jews who want religious miracles for proof and on the other by Greeks who lean on philosophical wisdom to explain the world. Paul is blunt: Neither miracles nor reasoning will do in the face of Jesus' resurrection and the saving grace it offers to believers.

The apostle reminds the Corinthian congregation of Isaiah, where the prophet writes, "These people claim to worship [God], but their words are meaningless, and their hearts are somewhere else. Their religion is nothing but human rules and traditions, which they have simply memorized. . . . Those who are wise will turn out to be fools, and all their cleverness will be useless" (29:13-14, TEV).

Paul makes a powerful case against letting human wisdom overshadow the fundamental fact that, as implausible as it may sound, faith in the sacrifice and resurrection of Jesus is the only path to salvation. "God in his wisdom made it impossible for people to know him by means of their own wisdom" (TEV).

For Paul and for Christians today, an acknowledgment of the truth of that fundamental "nonsense" is the key to identifying with the Christ.

Humble me today, O God, that I may choose your truth over my own. Amen.

Wisdom without Words   77

It is hard to imagine faith without words or wisdom without reason. "In the beginning was the Word, and the Word was with God, and the Word was God," the Gospel of John states right up front. Many Christians have identified themselves as "people of the book," testifying to the importance of written scriptures for faith. And many Protestant denominations focus on the proclamational (or preaching) aspects of their faith instead of the sacramental elements. Getting the words right has been central to Christian theology for two thousand years.

But what if the words don't matter? What if the heavens can proclaim the glory of God and "no speech or words are used"?

My daughter, Haley, has a problem with speech. Because of developmental disabilities, she has a speech impairment that makes her verbalizing aloud hard to understand. She also has intellectual delays that limit her ability to read scripture or the words to a hymn. The deeper meaning of the religious words she hears is lost on her as well.

When Haley was young, our family shared a table grace at the evening meal. Her brother memorized a simple blessing, but Haley would resort to singing songs that seemed to fit the occasion. Sometimes it would be a garbled "Jesus Loves Me"; other times it might be "Rocky Top," the University of Tennessee anthem. We always accepted her contribution in the spirit of sacred participation.

Recently when I have spoken to congregations, I've sometimes asked Haley to offer a benediction. She always provides what words she can muster. Though it can sound like gibberish, I've come to realize that her participation, like that of the heavens, still proclaims God's glory and shows forth God's handiwork.

Let the words of my mouth and the meditation of my heart —whatever form they may take—be acceptable in thy sight, O Lord, my strength and my redeemer. Amen.

THIRD SUNDAY IN LENT

I recovered from my trip to the maze. The kids found their way out of the cornfield both energized and tired. I too felt energized by the sacredness I had experienced. We loaded ourselves into the car and drove back to an ordinary world where we could lose ourselves in school and work, routine and daily activities.

Yet I find I'm still traveling through a maze. Confusing passageways don't take me where I want to go. I follow dead ends that frustrate me and threaten me with despair. Sometimes it feels I am moving in a circle, revisiting places I thought I had left in the past. But after my "maze" experience, I don't feel so lost.

I've learned how valuable the rules of the road are—those scriptural commandments (Moses' ten and Jesus' two) that help me navigate the rough passages with God and other humans. Like the psalmist, I celebrate both the law and the wordless wisdom of God's creation.

Like the disciples watching Jesus in the Temple, I marvel at the nonsense I witness, but I've learned to wait on the holiness that may be revealed when I don't reject it in advance by expecting a different answer. Like Paul, I have realized that I'm touched by God's wisdom not only through words and discussion but also through the revelation of grace—that amazing, unearned blessing that doesn't make sense to anyone but God.

From time to time I think back to those moments on the farm and remember the wonder that experience sparked in me. I can still see the fingernail moon, that jewel of a planet, and the incredible translucence of the fading light. I gaze toward the heavens every time I can on the off chance that once more the Holy will grab me by the collar and send me spinning into sacred space.

O God, grace me today with a vision of your glory. Amen.

Struggling in Today's Wilderness

MARCH 9–15, 2015 • CHARLENE KAMMERER

MONDAY, MARCH 9 ~ *Read Numbers 21:4-9*

The Israelites go overboard in complaining to God again about their fate. They start living in the past, wanting to go back to Egypt, wishing for leaders other than Moses and Aaron, fearing death in the wilderness, spewing anger at the lack of food and water of their choosing. They start reliving their negative history of not fully trusting God to be their sole Guide and Protector.

And so God allows them to encounter poisonous snakes that overrun them and kill some of their company. The people begin to repent and name their sins. Once again, God's merciful hand intervenes and saves them from the deadly snakes. Moses follows God's instruction to make a serpent. He creates one out of bronze and places it high on a pole so the people can see it. The bronze serpent represents both death and life. When the people look up and remember what God has done for them, trusting and obeying God again, they are saved from the snakes' poison.

How often do we as a people forget that God is in charge? How often do we in the church complain that "if only" we were bigger, had more money, more children and youth, a nicer building, a good preacher, then we would be growing and multiplying our numbers and ministries. How often do we act like we want to go back to the past instead of moving forward to God's Canaan for us? To what do we look to regain our trust in God?

Ever-patient God, stop us in our tracks when we complain incessantly about everything that is wrong in our lives and world. Turn our hearts to you in whom we find strength and joy for the journey of discipleship. Amen.

Retired United Methodist bishop, Lake Junaluska, North Carolina

Let the redeemed of the Lord say so. . . . " Those of us who are United Methodists promise to support our local congregations with our "prayers, presence, gifts, service, and witness." To include the word *witness* in this covenanting phrase has been a good addition. This perfectly reflects our heritage as a body of faith that gives voice to our knowledge and love of God, Jesus, and the Holy Spirit.

As a child growing up in a Methodist congregation, I was encouraged to share my faith witness or to give my testimony of what God was doing in the world and in my life. I learned how to do that by listening to others of all ages give their witness. I felt assured that God would use my authentic witness to encourage other people.

Serving as a pastor, I often gave my witness to different congregations where I served. When I was elected to serve as a bishop, I continued to offer my testimony through the arena of the annual conferences to which I was assigned. I remember so many people being surprised to hear a bishop give a testimony. It was a great way to connect at a deeper spiritual level. Giving witness always makes me feel closer to God.

We should never be timid or discouraged to offer our witness. God will take our words and our actions and use them in ways that will extend God's reign. We can speak about our gratitude for God's love, our fears, our joys, our hopes for a broken world and for healed relationships. When we continue to give witness, we find that it isn't really us speaking—it is God through us.

O listening God, keep me attuned to you so that I am always ready to proclaim your mighty deeds. Amen.

Psalm 107 expresses two uniting themes. One is a call to praise and thanksgiving of God's people as they gather. The second theme involves recalling the story of deliverance of God's people. What prompts God's attention throughout the psalm is a cry for help from any of God's beloved children, anyone bound by covenant and faith to Almighty God.

"Let them thank the LORD for his steadfast love" is a refrain throughout the psalm. The Hebrew people have struggled mightily through the wilderness and wearily arrived in the Promised Land. They have wandered in search of God's promises, hungry and thirsty for salvation and restoration as a people.

The psalmist describes those who are redeemed by God in four categories: those who are dying from hunger and thirst, those who are imprisoned, those who are sick from the result of sin, and those who are threatened by storms at sea.

While traveling with a group following the apostle Paul's journeys, our ship got caught in a storm over the Mediterranean Sea. For thirty-six hours, we were thrown around by the tossing of the ship upon the terrifying waves. We remained in our cabins because we could not walk safely from one area to another. We engaged in constant prayer and tending to those who became seasick. When the waters finally calmed and we reached our destination in Malta, many of us kissed the ground when the ship docked and our feet touched land once more. Let us always thank the Lord for steadfast love.

O powerful God, when we feel overwhelmed by life and fear of death, may we cling to your everlasting strength and salvation. Cradle us in your arms so that we can know your unending love for us. Amen.

The Lord "sent out his word and healed them, and delivered them from destruction." In this psalm, the four stanzas of the hymn format are the same throughout. There is a brief account of the adverse circumstances. Then comes a crying out to the Lord for help. We read the statement of the Lord's deliverance, followed by a plea to thank God and praise God for abundant care and love.

In this instance, the "terminally ill" Israelites do not suffer from physical malady. These people are sinsick, overwhelmed with the consequences of their many transgressions against God's word and law. Yet God steps in to make their souls well, to give them a future that was promised, to help them to be strong and just in their dealings with themselves and others.

For Christians, this passage portends the coming of Jesus, who offers us a second chance to be the redeemed ones who live in concert with God's will. Jesus of Nazareth came and brought divine healing for many physical, mental, social, and spiritual sicknesses.

We can read Psalm 107 as an uplifting hymn of all those who are God's chosen ones, God's beloved. As such, there is great rejoicing in the land and in the hearts of God's people everywhere—for God's steadfast, unending, and eternal love extended to them. God offers this same love freely to us. We are called to be ever thankful for God's gracious gift.

O healing God, wherever there is strife, illness, or destruction, bring your healing power. Open our spirits to receive the gift of your healing mercies. Amen.

I have learned that feeling dead spiritually and feeling totally alienated from the knowledge and love of God are two different realities. In the first instance, all Christians go through periods in life when we are in "desert places," where a veil separates us from full connection to God. Sometimes we can't pray. We might not experience joy in worship or in places of service or our work. Such a time invites us to keep praying anyway, until prayer becomes a source of strength. The community of saints around us can pray on our behalf or stand with us through times of grief, anger, loneliness, illness. In such desert places, we always know that God's love and mercy hover around us, waiting to move within to bring us a renewed spirit—if only we can reach out to receive those gifts of God.

For those who have never known the all-embracing love, mercy, and forgiveness that our Creator God offers to us, there is not just a veil but an absence of connection. We all know people who move through life with no sense of purpose and no knowledge of being children of God. Disciples in the church must share Christ's connection with God and God's abiding love for us—an indescribable gift and discovery, for now and eternity.

On my first spiritual retreat, I learned how to engage in "breath prayers." The participants were asked to name silently our deepest longings, then use only five words to form a prayer. I have used two breath prayers for over thirty years that have sustained me spiritually. One of them is, "Help me embrace my fears." May God in Christ come to you in your desert places.

O searching God, help us to release our deepest longings to you. Give us a spirit of waiting with hope in your presence. Amen.

As a young, newly ordained pastor in my first appointment, I discovered that my home conference was experiencing a painful chapter of discipleship. Glossolalia, the speaking in tongues, was becoming an issue of division within our local churches and the conference connection. A small group of deeply convicted pastors who had experienced this spiritual gift were insisting that every pastor and congregation that didn't exercise this gift was not right with God. There were overt attempts by pastors to bring the use of this gift into play in worship, meetings, and decision making. After several years, churches facing a change of pastors would demand from the bishop a certain kind of pastor. Pastors who were moving who had the gift of tongues would demand only a handful of "pure" churches to which they would go.

A journey of reconciliation began, led by many faithful lay and clergy members. Our shared theology, polity, doctrine, and spiritual practices were named and lifted up in many gatherings with intentionality. Over time, the separation and exclusion lessened. Healing took place in individual relationships and within congregations. In this season every fiber of my spiritual life was alert to God's guidance.

One of the apostle Paul's greatest gifts to the early church and the church of the future was to insist that we cannot be in charge of our own salvation. It is simply and powerfully a gift of God. We cannot work for it, change it, or tweak it. It is ours to accept or reject. "By grace alone and by faith alone" would remain Paul's credo of our salvation experience. Yes, we are created to do good works, but our salvation does not depend on that achievement.

O God of grace, bring us into a place of awe and joy as we continue to receive your salvation as pure grace. May we never boast but show humility in our faith. Amen.

Fourth Sunday in Lent

John's Gospel reading brings us full circle from the Old Testament image of Moses and the bronze serpent (Numbers 21). Moses lifted up the bronze serpent to save his people from the snakebites and their own sinful ways.

John's telling of the good news of Jesus Christ is rich in imagery. John recalls the Moses story and underscores the literal raising up of Jesus of Nazareth in crucifixion and resurrection. John begins his Gospel with the Word that becomes Jesus. He talks about the true light and repeatedly speaks of eternal life. He contrasts living and perishing, being saved and being condemned, and doing what is true versus doing what is evil. John's crescendo of faith is embedded in verse 16: "God so loved the world that he gave his only Son, so that everyone who believes in him may not perish but may have eternal life." God loves the world.

Nicodemus, a leading religious ruler, has come to Jesus at night to ask questions. He and Jesus seem to live in two different realities. They speak past each other. They do not connect. Nicodemus does not understand Jesus. Drawing on a well-known Old Testament account, Jesus implies that he, like the bronze serpent lifted up by Moses, has the power to save his people. We assume that Nicodemus leaves Jesus and goes off unchanged into the night. Jesus is left yearning for him to risk following the true light and way of life.

Once we encounter the living Christ, how will we respond? When we turn our eyes toward Jesus lifted up on the cross, will we be saved—saved from our snakebites of egocentricity, willfulness, and covetousness? What change does the salvific power of Christ make in your life?

O God, open wide our eyes and our hearts so that we see you in every encounter we have with the living Christ. Amen.

New Venues of Obedience

MARCH 16–22, 2015 • M. THOMAS THANGARAJ

MONDAY, MARCH 16 ~ *Read Jeremiah 31:31-34*

Do you realize that this is the only place in the Hebrew Bible where the phrase "new covenant" appears? Ezekiel talks about God's planting a new heart and a new spirit in us (Ezek. 18:31) and mentions how God can "remove the heart of stone" and replace it with "a heart of flesh" (Ezek. 11:19). But Jeremiah offers us a "new covenant" that God promises to make with God's people. The Holy One made an earlier covenant with the people of Israel when delivering them from bondage in Egypt. They broke that covenant and went after a golden calf in the desert and other idols around them. Now Jeremiah announces the days when God will make a "new covenant" with the people.

Why does God offer a new covenant instead of abandoning the people to their disobedience? Here is the clue. God says, "I was their husband." The bond between marriage partners in biblical times was a permanent and unchanging covenant. God's abiding covenant with the people of God cannot be totally broken; it can be made anew.

Even in our disobedience, a new covenant is possible, and God takes the initiative, living into the relationship in "steadfast love." The psalmist rightly proclaims again and again that God's steadfast love endures forever. Lent offers a time of accounting for our disobedience and learning to obey. God is willing to make a new covenant with us even now.

O Holy One, give me the courage to accept your offer of a new covenant and the strength to keep it in total obedience to your will. Amen.

Retired presbyter of the Church of South India; Professor Emeritus of World Christianity, Candler School of Theology, Atlanta, Georgia

As a teacher of theology, I have employed several styles of teaching and learning in the classroom: lectures, small-group discussion, and plenary sessions. Whenever we have group discussions, students enjoy the fun of learning from one another. They report back to the whole class and expect the teacher to add more to their learning. Jeremiah promises a time when the scenario will differ. God says that the days are coming when there will be no lectures, no group discussions, and no plenary sessions to report and refine. All will know; none needs to be taught.

What a sharp discontinuity with the past! You can feel the radical disjunction that is highlighted by the terms "not be like" and "no longer." I no longer need the other to lead me to the knowledge of God because God's law has been put within me.

Does this mean that we no longer need community for our Christian discipleship? No. With the new covenant, God ushers in a new community. We now relate to one another not just as mutual knowers but as known in God and by God. As we interact, we recognize the law of God written on our neighbor's heart. In India people greet each other by placing their palms together in a worshipful posture. The deeper meaning of that gesture is this: The God in me greets and salutes the God in you!

In the new community all members relate through their connection to God. The church is called to be such a community that knows and accepts the fact that God has forgiven our iniquity and does not remember our sin anymore. Today, more than ever, we are called to a new venue of obedience that requires an open and welcoming relation with people "from the least of them to the greatest."

Lord, help me acknowledge your law that is written on my neighbor's heart. Amen.

Psalm 51 is one of the most frequently used among penitential psalms in the life of the church and its liturgy. Its popularity comes in its link to the dramatic story of King David's sin and his repentance, and we can connect it with our experience of failure. It reflects the embarrassing history of humanity's persistent sinfulness and reveals the ubiquitous presence of sin in everything that we do: "All have sinned and fall short of the glory of God" (Rom. 3:23). Therefore we could conclude that Psalm 51 is all about the tragedy of the human predicament. But such a conclusion misses the point.

This psalm concerns God's nature. It affirms the sovereignty of God when the psalmist cries out, "Against you, you alone, have I sinned and done what is evil in your sight." Every human sin is an affront to the sovereignty of God's love. When God condemns sin, God is "justified" and "blameless" in judgment. It seems to imply that God takes no responsibility or accountability for human sin. Yet, it is God who sends Nathan to convict David of his sin and to invite him to repentance. At other times God is like the father who waits for his wayward son to return home and say, "Father, I have sinned" (Luke 15:21). When we come home, God's steadfast love and abundant mercy are ready to "blot out" our transgressions.

For this reason many churches throughout the world insist on confession as an important part of prayer and worship. "Lord, have mercy" is a constant refrain. During the season of Lent we are led both to confess our sin and to affirm the sovereign love of God and God's limitless mercy. Are we willing to confess our sins and the sins of our communities and nations? May our lips speak the words, "Lord, have mercy."

Lord, I hear your invitation to confess and to be reconciled to you in a refreshing way today. I respond with a resounding yes! Amen.

An effective physician is never satisfied with just looking at the symptoms of a disease. He or she wants to know what is going on inside the sick person and discover what triggers these symptoms. Modern medicine has invented several instruments to examine the inner workings of a human body. Thus the medical world uses x-rays, scans of different types, and laparoscopy to understand the inner workings.

God, like a good physician, wants to examine our "inward being." God's only instrument is to nudge and lure a human willingness to open up. That is why the book of Revelation presents Jesus as saying, "I am standing at the door, knocking; if you hear my voice and open the door, I will come in to you" (3:20). King David willingly opens the door. He knows that God desires "truth in the inward being" and therefore pleads with God to teach him wisdom in his secret heart.

Only when we make the request, "Purge me," does God come to clean us up. Only when we say, "Wash me," will God step in to do so. Only when we utter, "Create in me a clean heart," does God come to "put a new and right spirit" within us.

When God calls us to new venues of obedience, God waits for our reply, "Yes, Lord." The Holy Spirit's presence in us perennially calls us to follow God's path. When we say yes to the Spirit, we discover that our joy is restored and "a willing spirit" is sustained in us.

This psalm does not end with pleas to a renewed life alone; it ends with praising God and resolving to sing aloud God's deliverance. When we say yes to God's forgiveness, we sing God's salvation not only through words but with our whole lives.

Create in me a clean heart, O God, and put a new and right spirit within me today. I open my body, mind, and soul to you right now. Amen.

Most images of Jesus seen in paintings and sculptures tend to present him as gentle, meek, mild, totally calm and composed. Even many pictures of the Crucifixion portray Jesus as devoid of pain and suffering because he is in control. This letter presents a Jesus who prays to God "with loud cries and tears." As we read this passage we remember the scene in the garden of Gethsemane where Jesus prayed in anguish and "his sweat became like great drops of blood falling down on the ground" (Luke 22:44). Most artists who paint this scene show us a post-anguish Jesus, not a struggling one. But the Gospels and Hebrews present a Jesus who suffered pain and anxiety.

There are two reasons given for such struggle and pain in Jesus' life. The first is that he chose to express solidarity with humans; such solidarity demanded that he suffer like every other human being. He had to be tested by what he suffered so that he could help those who suffer. Hebrews 5 offers another reason. Jesus, as one chosen to be a high priest "according to the order of Melchizedek," had to perfect himself without glorifying himself and by learning obedience through what he suffered. Every situation of suffering became a learning experience for Jesus.

This is indeed a new venue of obedience for us when we perceive our sufferings as occasions for learning. As James puts it, such trials help us to move toward being "mature and complete, lacking in nothing" (Jas. 1:2-4). We need not get discouraged or sink into despair when we face suffering in our lives; we can turn it into occasions to grow in our Christian discipleship. Jesus stands as our pioneer and model in this approach.

Lord, open my eyes to recognize every event—even times of suffering—as an invitation to grow in my love of you and my neighbor. Amen.

Jyoti Sahi, a Roman Catholic theologian-artist in India, has painted a picture of Christ's resurrection. At the center of that painting is a seed within which Jesus is seated in a yoga position. You would notice on the top portion of the seed the sprouting of a new plant. Under the seed is a serpent (which represents time in the Hindu tradition) folding itself into the shape of infinity, signaling the beginning of eternity. This painting aptly describes what is going on in this Johannine passage.

During a festival at Jerusalem some Greeks wish to see Jesus and approach Philip for help. Philip and Andrew take the Greeks' request to Jesus. In their conversation Jesus mentions how a grain of wheat is of no use when it remains as a single grain. But when it is placed under the soil, it dies and comes up to bear much fruit. This leads Jesus to present the dynamic of Christian discipleship: Only when you lose your life do you gain it. This profound teaching of Jesus says much about how the rule of God operates in the world. He says, "Those who love their life will lose it, and those who hate their life in this world will keep it for eternal life."

Jyoti Sahi's painting highlights the quiet, hidden, and unassuming ways in which God works in the world and invites us to live our lives in such a manner as well. Christians and churches are all too often drawn to the ostentatious, glamorous, and dramatic portrayals of Christian obedience. Our TV programs, revival meetings, and personal testimonies border on such desire for glamor. The church is called back to its savior Jesus Christ, who in dying unnoticed and alone rises to bring transformation and new life. Jesus invites our discipleship: "Whoever serves me must follow me." Are we willing to follow?

Lord, grant me your grace that allows me to live my life like the salt that melts and brings taste and like the grain that dies and sprouts forth, bearing much fruit. Amen.

FIFTH SUNDAY IN LENT

Glory is a recurring theme in John's Gospel from chapter 1. "We have seen [God's] glory" in the Word's becoming flesh in Jesus (1:14). In the next chapter we find Jesus revealing his glory at the wedding at Cana (2:11). Now in chapter 12, we come back to the theme of glory. Jesus prays again, "Father, glorify your name" (12:28). Here a voice from heaven responds, "I have glorified it, and I will glorify it again." In the death and resurrection of Christ we discover the revealed glory of God.

Such glorification occurs by driving out "the ruler of this world" and lifting up the crucified and risen Christ from earth— letting him draw all people to himself. Jesus speaks these words to Andrew and Philip who have come with a request from some Greeks who want to meet Jesus—not Greek-speaking Jews but Gentile Greeks. These same disciples brought Jesus a few Jewish disciples: Peter and Nathanael. Drawing *all* people to the glory of Christ starts right here with the coming together of Jews and Gentiles. The Gospel writer places these words on the lips of the Jewish religious leaders, "Look, the world has gone after him" (12:19).

God's glory is revealed when barriers between people of the world are broken and a new community of peace and justice begins to emerge: "For [Christ] is our peace; in his flesh he has made both groups into one and has broken down the dividing wall, that is, the hostility between us" (Eph. 2:14). Our new venue of obedience in today's world comes when we offer ourselves to Christ to work for peace among peoples, nations, and cultures. Then we become God's instruments of peace.

Lord, make me an instrument of your peace. May I glorify your name by inviting people to the peace that you offer. Amen.

Love Has Us Surrounded

MARCH 23–29, 2015 • PAUL L. ESCAMILLA

MONDAY, MARCH 23 ~ *Read Psalm 118:1-2, 19-29*

Palm/Passion week is one like no other—fraught with triumph and tragedy, festivity and forsakenness, virtue and vice, all woven in a tight weave. In such a context, Psalm 118 is a gift of undergirding, a song of assurance that come what may, nothing will separate us or the world from God's abiding love.

The structure of the psalm reflects the structure of the week in which the psalm presents itself in the lectionary. The first and final verses are identical: "O give thanks to the LORD, for he is good; for his steadfast love endures forever!" We could say they represent Palm Sunday on one end and Easter on the other. Between the two, the psalm, as with the week, presents us with distress, hatred, rejection, even thorns, all bookended by these enduring words of encouragement.

This bookending framework is more than mere poetic license; it is theological affirmation, akin to another we know from Revelation: "I am the Alpha and the Omega," the first and the last (1:8). God is good, all the time and forever; and the steadfast love of the Lord never ceases. This latter phrase evokes the plaintive tones of Lamentations, in which the prophet Jeremiah, deeply distraught with the many burdens of both his work and his world, still affirms, "The steadfast love of the LORD never ceases, his mercies never come to an end; they are new every morning; great is your faithfulness" (Lam. 3:22-23).

The blessing of bookends is their ability to hold us steady during the unsteady time between the times; in other words, to reassure us that come what may, love has us surrounded.

Eternal God, hold us steady with the assurance that your steadfast love never ceases. Amen.

Senior pastor, Saint John's United Methodist Church, Austin, Texas

For many years my morning time of prayer, reading, and reflection has included the recitation of a particular verse from Psalm 118: "This is the day that the LORD has made; let us rejoice and be glad in it." The facet of this verse that intrigues me most is the first-person plural command that begins the second phrase: let *us* rejoice. When I recite this verse during my morning prayers I am seldom in the company of others; in another sense, however, I am always in the company of others when I recite it. With the words "let *us* rejoice," I am practicing the presence of the whole community of faith, remembering that we move through the joys and difficulties, challenges and privileges of each day together rather than alone.

The first half of the verse reminds us that God's love and creative presence surrounds us each and every day; the second part, that we also are surrounded by those who bear steady and sturdy witness to the goodness and faithfulness of that love and presence and who expect us to do the same.

This second assurance may be an especially important reminder as we move toward Holy Week when the shadows lengthen and the powers of darkness seem all the more real. The adage holds true: There is indeed strength in numbers. If we go through these tempestuous days together, then, by the grace of God, we go through them assured, even rejoicing.

O God, this is the day that you have made; we will rejoice and be glad in it. Amen.

Psalm 118 is at one level a running dialogue between an individual and the community of faith. In the midst of this interchange comes an acclamation we may be well acquainted with from eucharistic prayers: "Blessed is the one who comes in the name of the LORD." Who is this "one" who comes in the name of the Lord? Given the dialogue we've identified, it is surely the person who has survived the unnamed distress and lived not only to tell about it but to praise God for deliverance.

In Mark's Gospel, the crowds accompanying Jesus' triumphal entry identify that person as Jesus (11:9). When we share this acclamation in table prayers, it is Christ we have in mind. And certainly as we move through the events of Holy Week, we will identify Christ as one who, like the person in the psalm, has been delivered from death by God's hand and now comes to bring that good news to the world through his resurrection.

Yet the psalm's restraint in identifying this person as a specific historical figure gives us latitude in making that identification ourselves: Anyone who has been delivered or who brings deliverance can find their story or calling sung in this verse.

Psalm 118 celebrates a historical figure who was saved from harm and now comes to give God glory for that salvation or to bring good news to others. But Psalm 118 also issues a summons to any who have a similar story to tell or a calling to fulfill, including you. When you sing, "Blessed is the one who comes in the name of the LORD," the words on your tongue may be singing your own vocation.

Lead me, Lord, to those with whom I can share my witness of deliverance and to whom I can offer compassion and blessing in your name. Amen.

In the midst of a whirlwind of activity surrounding Jesus' last days, a small but significant incident occurs to indicate a deepening of Mark's portrayal of Jesus' nature and identity. A study of Mark's Gospel reveals that Jesus is most often called "Teacher"; once, by Peter, "the Messiah"; also "Son of David" and "Son of Man"; demons call him out as "the Holy One of God." Yet not once so far has the nomenclature of divinity been employed.

However, as Jesus directs the disciples to retrieve a colt on which he will ride into Jerusalem, his instructions contain a new designation: "If anyone asks you why you are doing this, just say, 'The Lord needs it . . .'" "Lord," *kurios* in Greek, is an ascription reserved for royalty and divinity. Jesus, for example, makes reference to God as "the Lord your God" (12:30) and "the Lord" (13:20). Suddenly, this teacher come from God, who casts out demons, feeds the multitudes, and teaches with authority, introduces a new aspect to this portrait: divine presence.

The reference is subtle, as we might expect, for with regard to identifying Jesus' divinity, Mark is the most understated of the four Gospels. But the meaning is clear: The one entering Jerusalem—lionized one moment, vilified the next; celebrated by crowds that would days later clamor for his crucifixion—is no mere teacher; his presence is far too powerful for a mere mortal. The centurion in charge of his execution sums up best the emerging recognition of this figure whose identity is at once so enigmatic and so clear: "Truly this man was God's Son!" (15:39).

Jesus, we call you by many names: Son of David, Teacher, Holy One of God. In these holy days, grant that we may meet you and come to know you more fully and completely by one other title: Lord. Amen.

The Lord has need of it." We've looked already at the subtle suggestion of divinity implied in those words. What is profoundly ironic is that such a divine/royal title, "Lord," emerges in regard to the acquisition of what is essentially a second-rate mode of transportation. The vehicle for ushering "the Lord" into Jerusalem, the city of outrageous hopes and outlandish expectations, is not a handsome steed or warhorse but a colt.

The narrative serves to reinforce what the Gospel of Mark as a whole has conveyed: Jesus does not seek conventional power, status, wealth, or popularity. Rather, his ministry unfolds through service in self-giving ways, eventually to the point of death. A story relegating Jesus to colt status rather than steed status is difficult for us who prefer our leaders to follow escalating trajectories. We are schooled in upward not downward mobility. At this point in his ministry, Jesus should be honored with the very best things that life can offer; he has certainly earned them.

And refused them. If Jesus is to be feted as he approaches the holy city, then it will be in the humblest way; if he is to be triumphantly praised as "Lord," then those expectantly offering the accolade will want to begin now to cope with their disappointment.

Jesus arrives on the scene disinclined to greatness but very much inclined for goodness. Having eschewed the limelight he is ready to proceed unencumbered with the work at hand: facing his accusers in the same spirit of love and self-surrender with which he has carried out his ministry and for which those same accusers will demand his life.

Merciful God, when greatness calls loudly to us from so many quarters, help us to hear the whispered summons to goodness and so follow Jesus on the way that leads to life. Amen.

In a church I served several years ago, three-year old Jett gave an alternate name to Palm Sunday: "Palm Day." Jett's abbreviation became our congregation's amplification. For on that special Sunday of the year and the days that follow, palms become the expression of many emotions, intentions, fears, denials, and ultimately, hopes.

On Palm Sunday, of course, we recall the devotion of crowds who lay palm branches before Jesus as he enters Jerusalem. Later, in an upper room, the disciples of Jesus will hold in their own palms bread and chalice, nourishing signs of Jesus' life given for them and for the world. Soon after we follow them into a garden, where we overhear a prayer that cannot but turn surrendered palms upward: "Thy will be done." As Jesus prays those words, some of the disciples instead make of their palms a pillow, hoping perhaps that on this night of deep foreboding sleep may ease them, if briefly, into some more auspicious realm.

Jesus is abruptly arrested and presented before Pilate. Peter teeters between courage and cowardice, following him at a near distance but then deflecting a bystander's claim that he is one of Jesus' followers. We can imagine his palms lifted upward and away, historically an easily assumed posture for the human creature.

By week's end, Jesus will be nailed to a cross, his palms opened out to the world in unspeakable love and forgiveness. Then finally, when hope seems lost, we will hear again of the great mystery of a tomb standing empty to the sky. On that day our palms lifted high will form their own empty tomb, open and yielding to the joy and mystery of resurrection.

Lord, let my palms quietly open to hold the remarkable gifts given to us this week: love and redemption offered at such cost and without price, your provision for the life of the world. Amen.

PALM/PASSION SUNDAY

One year just after Palm Sunday I was in the foyer of a sanctuary at a nearby church when I noticed a half-emptied box of palm branches sitting in a corner. The shipping instructions printed on the box were these: "Palms for Palm Sunday. Please do not delay."

There was a certain prescience to those instructions, having to do with the awareness on the part of the mail-order supplier that the parade in which a recipient will use those palm branches would not last forever. Too soon that parade would lead its celebrated subject, Jesus, into the patient and determined maw of the holy city of Jerusalem. One moment we would be swept up in a blissful celebration, a storybook tribute to the acclaimed Messiah; the next, we would be moved along to a Passover meal in a borrowed room, then a garden of anguished prayer, followed by an arrest, a legal proceeding in a kangaroo court, and finally the middle cross at a place called "the skull."

"Palms for Palm Sunday. Please do not delay." Because too soon the parade will have passed by, and we'll be needing something other than palms to fit the occasion. We'll be needing minds to seek to make sense of senseless things; eyes to search for love among the ruins; and once found, hearts to ponder the breadth and length, the height and depth of this love that needs so little and offers the world so much.

O God, before the parade passes by, we lift our palms in the air. Then, once the day is done and the cheers subdued to silence, allow us to see how mercy looks beyond the parade grounds where the sign of your love and need for our surrender become real as never before. Amen.

Trusting in God's Presence

MARCH 30–APRIL 5, 2015 • CLAIRE MCKEEVER-BURGETT

MONDAY, MARCH 30 ~ *Read Psalm 36:5-11*

The psalmist speaks truth yet again. For who on this Holy Monday, after Jesus enters Jerusalem, after Mary publicly prepares Jesus' body for burial and for death, who does not need a reminder of the protective, present love of God?

We know where the road to Jerusalem leads. We know that the hosanna shouts and palm-branch waves quickly fade into the background. We know the authorities meet in secret, making deals, sacrificing lives. We know Judas betrays and Peter denies. We know what lies ahead. It was a long week then, and it is a long week now.

Which is why the psalmist's words sing in our hearts, offering us hope, offering us love, offering us light.

Biblical scholars tell us Psalm 36 is a hymn of rejoicing in the Temple. The Israelite people were a people of pain. They knew their share of heartache and betrayal, yet they also knew how to testify to God's love and to celebrate Yahweh's victory.

The ancient songwriters, much like the poets of today, looked to the mountains and the sky, to the sea and to the forest, to the birds of the air and the animals of the land, trusting that in all things God was present with them.

The psalmist trusts in the strength of God's love and the vastness of God's protection and turns to the natural world to tell the love story of God.

Is it any wonder that Jesus quoted the Psalms so often? Is it any wonder that Psalm 36 is part of our reading for this Monday of Holy Week?

Today, help us, O God, to trust in your vast love. May we follow the way of Jesus—the way of salvation, trust, and life. Amen.

Program Interpretation Manager, Upper Room Ministries

A t the end of today's Gospel reading, after Jesus engages in a call-and-response worship experience with the gathered community, he commends the crowd to "believe in the light" so that they might become the light themselves. Then, the scripture says that Jesus departs from them and hides.

Where does Jesus go to hide, we wonder, and what does Jesus' hiding say to us on this Tuesday of Holy Week?

The psalmist offers us another kind of hiding—that of hiding in old age. Known as a "prayer in old age," Psalm 71 takes us through an individual lament: a cry for help; a plea for refuge, safety, and protection; a petition for rescue and salvation. At the very beginning of the psalm, in verse 1, the psalmist says, "In you, O LORD, I take refuge." *In you, O Lord, I hide.*

So perhaps Jesus, after encouraging his followers to go and be light in the world, also hides in the presence of God. Perhaps Jesus' hiding encourages us to do the same. After all, how else will Jesus face a trial, a death, and a resurrection except with time away with God?

Like the psalmist, Jesus needs time—away from the crowds, from the shouts of hosanna, and from the cries for mercy—to petition for his own help, protection, and love. Jesus, the proclaimer of light and goodness, needs time away in hiding in order to share his own light until the end.

Jesus, like the psalmist, knows his enemies pursue him. He knows his death is imminent. He too prays for hope and trust in God alone.

On this Tuesday of Holy Week, where do we hide? Where do we find time to plead our case and pray our cries? Where and how do we trust in God's presence?

Holy God of light and life, help us find places of refuge and renewal so we can return to the world as the light-bearers you call us to be. Amen.

We've all been there, have we not? Sitting at the table to dine with friends and family, basking in the glow of good food and fellowship, when all of a sudden someone says something accusatory and awkward, and the table falls silent.

Today, it's Jesus, the host of the meal, who, after speaking freely about hospitality and love, states quite plainly that someone sitting at the table with him will betray him. The disciples begin to look at one another, bewildered and confused.

We can imagine the feeling of being falsely accused, the wonderment at why a friend would say such a thing. We can even be tempted to think that Jesus had too much to drink, which caused him to speak out of turn.

But Jesus, as he always does, offers us a lesson on this Holy Wednesday. His spirit is troubled, and he senses deep in his bones that something is not right. Instead of avoiding the awkwardness, he speaks honestly with his friends. He confesses that he knows he dines with a betrayer, and we know the betrayer is Judas because Jesus hands him a piece of bread.

Jesus speaks clearly to Judas, saying, "Do quickly what you are going to do." Instead of throwing Judas out of the room or making a dramatic, shameful scene, Jesus releases Judas to his own deceit. Only after Judas leaves does Jesus proclaim, "Now the Son of Man has been glorified."

Perhaps, on this Wednesday of Holy Week, we need to ask ourselves what or whom it is we need to confront and release in order to know God's glory. Are we able to speak honestly with our friends, our family? Are we able to break ties in direct and peaceful ways with those who wish us harm? Are we willing to risk awkwardness for the sake of God's kin-dom?

Help us, O God, to face our fears with peace. Help us, O God, to speak truth in all things. Help us, O God, to trust in you. Amen.

MAUNDY THURSDAY

Maundy Thursday arrives each year, faster than we planned, more surprising than we thought. The night when Jesus, our Savior, kneels to wash feet—an odd twist of plot, not because feet weren't always washed before mealtime but because we, like the disciples, are accustomed to doing it ourselves.

Yet, Jesus shows up saying, "Let me wash you."

Jesus, having had his own body anointed just a few days prior while dining with Mary, Martha, and Lazarus, knows something of the healing touch of another. He kneels on this Maundy Thursday night to return the favor, yes, but also to remind us of the mission of his life—service in love for all—a mission that we also are to adopt and embody if we seek to follow him.

As Jesus kneels to wash the disciples' feet, images of an earlier scene in John's Gospel play before us, when water serves as the image for life. To the Samaritan woman at the well, Jesus says, "Drink from the water I give you, and you will never thirst again" (John 4:14, AP).

And here, in chapter 13, Jesus says, "Unless I wash you, you have no share with me." In other words, the cleansing that Jesus offers makes us a part of him and him a part of us.

So we kneel to wash each other's feet—not because it's easy or fun or normal or perfectly comfortable. No, we kneel to wash each other's feet because Jesus, the one we seek to follow, told us to do so.

On Maundy Thursday, where is the water that cleanses not only our feet but also our souls? What might the water teach us, not only about ourselves but also about one another?

Jesus, the one who gives us water again and again, make us whole not so we may boast of our togetherness but so we may share your love with the world. Amen.

GOOD FRIDAY

We awake on Holy Friday to a different kind of kneeling. Instead of kneeling to wash each other's feet, we kneel to cry. Today is a day of lamentation, the day Jesus dies—handed over to the royal empire out of fear, sacrificed by a government in shame.

Psalm 22 gives perfect expression to our laments. It is a prayer of anguish, a prayer of question, a prayer of anger, a prayer of suffering, a prayer of disillusionment. It is a prayer we hear Jesus pray as he hangs on a cross, struggling to breathe, close to his death.

"My God, my God, why have you forsaken me?"

In hearing Jesus pray this prayer, we receive the freedom to pray it ourselves, to ask where our God might be.

The psalmist uses the first twenty-one verses of the psalm to cry, question, and lament before arriving at the truth undergirding the despondence. In verse 22, the psalmist confesses, "I will tell of your name to my brothers and sisters; in the midst of the congregation, I will praise you." Continuing with the praise, the psalmist offers a litany of God's care for the afflicted and the poor. Indeed, by psalm's close, we are beckoned to live for God and to proclaim God's deliverance for all. So even in this psalm of lament, a psalm that offers us the liberty to scream and cry and wail, even in this psalm we return to the praise of God, the One who creates us, sustains us, and loves us always.

Yes, we awake on Holy Friday to a different kind of kneeling. We awake to a kneeling of pain, suffering, lamentation, and even death. In the presence of our cries, in the frenzy of our questions, in the fury of our fear, are we willing to trust in God?

God, we often wonder where you are in the midst of our pain and suffering. Show us today where you live and who you are. Lead us in pastures of healing. Amen.

Today is the day we fall silent, sinking deeper into our prayers, holding vigil through the night as we usher in the light of God. Today is Holy Saturday, the day when Jesus' friends awoke with swollen eyes and aching heads; the day when Jesus' followers asked in bewilderment, "What happened yesterday?"

Today is the day we wait.

Like our Hebrew ancestors, we search for prayers to pray, songs to sing, poems to recite. We turn to the promise of God's deliverance to guide us safely through the night. In Psalm 114, we receive the hymn song we so desperately need, a poetic offering that recounts God's deliverance of the Israelite people from the enslavement of Egypt.

The poet asks, "Why is it, O sea, that you flee? O Jordan, that you turn back? O mountains, that you skip like rams? O hills, like lambs?" only to answer that the most appropriate response to God's salvation is the trembling of the entire earth. Trembling, then, becomes not only a response of fear but also, and perhaps more appropriately, a response of praise.

So as the women tremble on their way to the tomb at sabbath's end and the Jewish custom of preparing the body for burial begins, God sends a messenger of resurrection. The women's trembling in fear soon shifts to the trembling of praise as they hear, "He has been raised; he is not here. . . . go, tell his disciples and Peter that he is going ahead of you to Galilee; there you will see him."

Today, as we wait for the deliverance of God; today, as we keep watch, hold vigil, pray, and sing, may our trembling find its roots in the promises of God's salvation. May we, as God's people, heed the words of God's messenger—Go and tell!—trusting that we too shall see him there.

Eternal Presence, who is ever with us through both day and night, be with us now as we wait for your salvation. Amen.

Easter Sunday

Today is the resurrection day of Jesus! It is the day when we sing aloud the alleluias that were buried on Ash Wednesday; it is the day we resurrect our jubilant praises to God. What was once dead now lives. May we rejoice and be glad!

But before we sing loudly and proclaim fervently, we must not miss the quiet moment of Mary Magdalene's tears—and our own. Only yesterday we held vigil and kept watch through the night. Only yesterday the disciples hid, fearing for their lives. Only yesterday Jesus' body lay lifeless in a tomb.

The scripture tells us that "Mary stood weeping outside the tomb." She had arrived moments earlier to find the tomb empty. She went to find Peter and the other disciples to tell them of Jesus' missing body. They arrived at the tomb, saw it was empty, and returned home.

But Mary remains at the threshold in tears. The ever-present God who was with Mary and the disciples throughout the trauma of the week prior, who has been with us this entire week of holiness, chooses this moment to remind her and us that all is not lost. "Mary!" Jesus says. The tone of his voice, the emphatic cry of her name calls her from her tears, and Mary knows her Teacher stands before her alive. Jesus commands her to tell the disciples that he is ascending to God; indeed, Jesus invites Mary to be the messenger of life and resurrection to all.

As we wipe away our tears of yesterday, do we hear Jesus call our names? Do we trust, yet again, in God's presence? Easter Sunday morning is a day of rejoicing, a day when sorrow becomes joy, when our names are called, and we too go forth to share the good news of the risen Christ.

God, may the alleluias of today assure us of your presence and give us the courage to hear your voice and accept its invitation. Amen.

Practice Resurrection

APRIL 6–12, 2015 • EILEEN R. CAMPBELL-REED

MONDAY, APRIL 6 ~ *Read John 20:19-23*

In the twentieth century, US Christianity placed the accent of faith on belief rather than practice. For many Christians right belief opens the door to salvation and communal belonging, becomes a way of defining identity as a religious person, a Christian. The New Testament commands readers "to believe" rightly in Jesus. Historically Christian theologies teach that no amount of action or work can achieve salvation: It is God's gift.

The concern about "right belief" can lead to a briar patch of doubt and misgiving when it runs up against scientific ways of seeing. Quickly an unresolvable debate emerges over what can be legitimately "believed," what constitutes evidence, and how beliefs fit logically or coherently into a worldview. We can ponder such thoughts endlessly.

Jesus commends to his disciples the kind of believing that leads to life—not more arguments about who is right or how to justify one's position. Belief in Jesus is participation in an embodied, practiced, incarnate (in the flesh) knowing.

Wendell Berry, poet, author, and farmer, asks his readers to reach beyond belief and "practice resurrection." Jesus invites you to reach out your hand: Experience the presence of peace, the incarnation of God, the resurrection of the dead—unbelievable things in our day and time. Hold a child's hand. Listen to your neighbor. Look into the eyes of the man selling papers on the street corner. Ask yourself: This Easter season, how shall I practice resurrection?

God of peace, you are reaching out now, inviting us to the hope of believing. Help our unbelief. Amen.

Practical theologian, codirector of the Learning Pastoral Imagination Project, and Baptist minister, living in Nashville, Tennessee

D o you dislike missing the start of a movie or speech or worship service? I do. I spend the rest of the time feeling lost, trying to catch up, wondering what I missed. That feeling of longing and desire to be in the know, to be included in the group—that feeling is epidemic in our culture. Thomas surely felt left out too.

When I feel lost or bored or like I'm missing something, I tend to reach for something else rather than simply wait. Switch the channel. Open a new tab on the computer. Play another song. Grab something to eat. Text someone. Check e-mail.

Filling that gap—the gap of longing and desire for something more—with cheap substitutes is neither filling nor fulfilling. Instead it feeds the emptiness and supports lonely isolation.

To sit still within the longing and hunger for more is a challenge for our times. Paying quiet attention to the emptiness will magnify its effect at first, increasing the dread and giving rise to anxiety that puts up defenses against such overwhelming feelings. A compulsion to fill the void overtakes mind and body. Thomas asserts that unless he sees and touches, "I will not believe." His anxiety and defensiveness are palpable.

The doors are shut in fear. The disciples lock themselves up and hide. Yet they wait together. And by some miracle, in their waiting comes the presence of the risen Christ, greeting them, "Peace be with you."

Today when you run up against fear or the longings and desires for more in your life, will you wait? Can you hold back before reaching for something to fill the gap?

O risen Christ of peace, fill our lonely and grasping hearts. Amen.

Faith communities often struggle to practice resurrection in clear and compelling ways. Maybe an example from popular culture will spark imaginations for embracing practices of communal care that embody Jesus' resurrection power.

In 2012 the Beach Boys performed their classic hit "Good Vibrations" at the Grammy Awards. The reunion performance was a miracle, overcoming a long silence from the group and their lead singer, composer, and producer, Brian Wilson.

From 1962 to 1965 the Beach Boys topped the music charts. In the decades that followed, however, Wilson withdrew from the public, struggling with a debilitating mental breakdown, drug addiction, suicidal wishes, psychotic episodes, and other physical symptoms that confined him to bed for two years. He lost significant relationships, divorced, and became estranged from his daughters. He fell victim to the manipulations of others.

Mental illness, addiction, and isolation are widespread problems, calling for new practices of care by faith communities. Genuine attention and healing for people facing these crises require practices of love and care from communities gathered in "one heart and soul." Wilson's long road to recovery began when his family removed a misguided caretaker and regained entry to his life. A community of medical professionals, family members, and musicians gathered around Wilson in the early 1990s to bring healing and restoration to his life and to return him to his creative capacities.

Wilson's 2012 Grammy performance bore witness to a man restored and significantly healed after many losses and brushes with death. Resurrection practices take many forms in response to the needy among us. The early church embraced new practices of care with the power of the risen Christ. How will we be inspired to do the same?

God of resurrection, gather us into your caring, healing work. Amen.

In the 2013 documentary *Inequality for All*, former US Secretary of Labor, Robert Reich traces the rise and fall of economic equality and inequality over the last century in the United States. Told compellingly, Reich's story shows how the inequality gap between rich and poor in America grows when law and public policies undercut investments in education, health care, and labor. The film also demonstrates the positive social and economic impact of policies that support investing in children, education, and manufacturing, and reduce the inequality gap.

One underlying issue remains troublesome for those who choose to follow Christ. All of Reich's theory and analysis, examples and counterexamples are built on a "production and consumer" model for society and economy. Here is the American dream according to Reich: Make and sell more things, boost the economy, and increase everyone's well-being. Without "investing" in the small players, inequity grows; but with capital investments in education and labor, everyone benefits and inequity remains low. The American dream, however, is out of sync with the gospel vision of Jesus, of a life together that undercuts class divisions and upends financial systems.

The gospel vision in Acts 4 testifies against a society and economy built on consuming all resources, giving no regard to the poor, and competing to win at all costs. What might happen if, in the name of Jesus, communities of faith, like the Jerusalem church, took seriously a call to resurrect generosity, life together, and living with "one heart and soul"? What would the social and economic impact be if faith communities built micro-economies of generosity and justice?

God of the poor, help us loosen our grip on the dream of consumer success and to grasp instead the power and love of your gospel vision of generosity and justice. Amen.

For years I spent a week each spring with a group of Native American women attending to the rhythms of earth, sun, sky, and sea. We became friends over time, and I learned from the wisdom of grandmothers and from the daily care of the earth by the Dominican sisters who tended to our meeting place, a retreat center on ninety acres of forest and swamp.

Each gathering brought rituals that awoke me to the needs of the earth and to my need for the earth. I walked the labyrinth and the medicine wheel (a Native path to wholeness). I lay on the ground at night, staring at the wonders of the starry sky. I sat under a twelve-hundred-year-old live oak tree and sang ancient songs. I experienced in powerful embodied ways how I was related to people—past and future—and to the earth itself and every living thing that creeps, crawls, flies, or sits upon it.

A refrain through each week's rituals came in repeating together the following words: "All my relations."

That simple liturgical phrase summoned the cosmic Christ and the interconnections of every living thing. When one rejoices, all rejoice. When one suffers, all suffer. When one mourns, all mourn. To think about these connections intently often pulled me up short. I felt humbled, even stunned to think about how all of God's creation is knit together—past, present, and future. To consider the seven generations who come after me before taking action slows down that action and shapes a different intention.

Most of my life is not marked by this sense of unity across time and space. The psalmist declares how good and pleasant it is to live in unity with our kindred, with "all our relations." What kind of resurrection and new life would it be to live in unity with all our relations?

O God, help me practice a future resurrection now, one that cares with intention for "all my relations." Amen.

Most of my life I have subsisted on admiration, all the while longing for real connection. My desire for connection, for communion, was harmed more generations ago than anyone in the family can remember. Many of us no longer know why we cannot hear, see, or touch the eternal word of life. Instead, buried in the past are seemingly eternal harms surviving from generation to generation.

We are out of touch with true fellowship, as the writer of First John calls it, getting by instead on broken dreams, cheap substitutes, and addictive behaviors. But beneath all that grasping and groping, we are people longing for connection, for communion.

Name for yourself the things you settle for, subsist on, and simply take, even though a deeper longing wells up to be fulfilled. Write them down. They are probably not things that bring you sustaining joy.

Can the word of life be resurrected? Where have you seen it alive this week?

See the word of life when one friend lights a candle for another friend laboring over a book. Taste the word of life in a meal prepared with care by villagers in a place that used to be a battlefield. Hear the word of life in the delighted laughter of a small child swinging from her mother's arms. Touch the word of life in a hand that reaches out after a bitter argument, asking forgiveness, seeking hope.

Now name for yourself the relationships in your life that lure you toward connection, intimacy, and communion. Practice resurrection today by reaching out in hope of genuine connection. In that connection you will see, hear, and know a word of life, an incarnation of the living God.

O God of joy, we long for fellowship with your spirit and presence. Give us courage not to subsist on cheap substitutes but to seek communion to nourish our souls. Amen.

Starting in third grade, my parents took me to church each Sunday afternoon to practice Bible Drill. the participants learned to locate each book in the Bible, pointing and stepping out from the line. We memorized Bible verses. Each drill lasted ten seconds. One verse I memorized was 1 John 1:9 "If we confess our sins, [God] who is faithful and just will forgive us our sins and cleanse us from all unrighteousness."

I felt relief in knowing that God would forgive me when I did something wrong. As a child I understood sin as a straight-forward moral failure: lying, cheating, saying mean things, punching my brother. The big sins like stealing, using God's name in vain, or murder were too scary even to contemplate.

As a child I thought all sins could be seen and measured and traded: I'll give you this sin, and you give me that forgiveness, like coins for trinkets at the Five and Dime store.

Much later I saw the more pervasive and complex realities of sin and self-deception. We are all implicated in sin, harmed by the corruption and failings of the world. My first grown-up lesson in forgiveness came about ten years after Bible Drill. A friend died unexpectedly and much too young. Unresolved issues between us remained. I ached for words and hugs of forgiveness, for reconciliation. I discovered that you never know when the opportunity for forgiveness may slip away.

Out of my friend's death, I began to learn two things: If we fail to forgive one another, God forgives us in Christ. And we need to practice forgiveness on all days and in all ways because we do not know when the last moment will come. In fewer than the ten seconds it takes to retrieve a verse or say it aloud, life can change.

O God of second chances and new beginnings, lead us to practice resurrection by receiving your forgiveness and sharing it freely. Amen.

A Double Take

APRIL 13–19, 2015 • MARIA KANE

MONDAY, APRIL 13 ~ *Read Acts 3:12-19*

By now, I imagine most everyone has put away Easter decorations. Any remnants of Easter in the stores are in the clearance bin. To the naked eye, Easter is over.

Except that the celebration of Easter, of Christ's miraculous resurrection from the dead, lasts fifty days. We remain in a season of awe, surprise, delight, and life—and not just at the blooming flowers and greening grass. Often, however, busyness, cynicism, and fear cloud our faith in God's power in the world and in us. We allow ourselves to speak of coincidences and accidents instead of grace, mercy, and the Spirit.

Other times we find ourselves dumbstruck, as did the crowds outside the Temple doors. They stand in disbelief upon discovering that a man they are accustomed to see begging for money is now walking without assistance. Is it magic? Is it a trick? Is it a coincidence?

For Peter and John, this is the work of God prophesied in scripture and now made manifest through Jesus' followers—ordinary men and women. We elevate the apostles to a level of excellence and authority we could not imagine ourselves bearing without acknowledging that Peter is the one who denied Jesus three times. God can use all of us to bring God's reign on earth.

The world news headlines can deaden our souls to the truth that God has not abandoned us. The fifty days of Easter remind us that resurrection happens more than once. New life and new possibilities can be realized despite our fears, doubts, and skepticism—perhaps even amidst them.

God, help us remember Peter's story and your endless mercy. Amen.

Episcopal priest, served in parish ministry and school chaplaincy; Texas native

Chances are, by the time we reach adulthood, we have been called and have responded to a variety of names other than the one given to us at birth. Some are family nicknames; others we acquire in school or college. Still others indicate how people relate to us professionally. Without even realizing it, we start to see ourselves as others see us or need us—father, mother, supervisor, teacher, student, grandparent, retiree; the list goes on. With every name comes an expectation of who we are supposed to be to others and ourselves. Yet, those names are labels and roles. To be called those names, you and I must do something, prove ourselves worthy of the name. Or, not so worthy.

But without these other roles and titles, expectations and burdens, who are you? In the depths of your soul, when no one else is around, whom do you desire to speak your name, bring life, and give you an identity that lasts forever?

It's a daunting proposition. When Jesus called his first twelve disciples, some of whom had carved out modest yet comfortable and familiar lives, he called them to more than a new job—he called them to a new way of life. They could then see themselves and their relationships to one another and God as precious, redeemed, and of endless worth.

First John 3 reminds us that first and foremost we are God's children. It's how God sees us and longs for us to see ourselves and one another. We simply trade in our love of certainty and control and reach out to God as a child learning to walk reaches out to her parent. And if she falls, she falls into the arms of grace.

What would it mean to see yourself as God sees you: beloved? How would it change how you treat yourself and others?

Change is never easy. In fact, it's often downright uncomfortable. When we are pushed away from the familiar, safe, and comfortable, and find ourselves in uncharted territory, it can feel as though God has left us in a dark room with little light to guide our way. What will happen to us? When will there be some stability?

Probably Jesus' disciples feel the same way after his death. They have heard rumors of his resurrection, and some have testified to Jesus' presence on the road to Emmaus. But what does that mean? What will they do next with their lives? Their questions are as endless as their doubts. When Jesus stands before them, grief and disbelief still shroud their eyes.

Although Jesus gives the disciples space for doubt and uncertainty, he does not let them wallow in anxiety. He is not a ghost; he shows them his hands and feet and eats fish in their presence. He then moves on to recall and interpret scripture. His being there with them brings to fruition God's plans and purposes. And in their midst, Jesus gives them a new mission. Just as they have entrusted their lives to Jesus' love, Jesus now entrusts the disciples with the message of repentance and forgiveness. They will serve as witnesses to all nations. Jesus calls them to take a second look and reimagine their lives as apostles, teachers, and leaders. As Jesus recalls the sacred words of scripture, he empowers them to see their place in the fulfillment of God's kingdom.

Sometimes our routines and comforts can blind us to the new roles or places to which God calls us. Jesus tells the disciples to look at his hands and feet, to see the grace of the ordinary that is actually quite extraordinary.

What fear or anxiety is overwhelming you and preventing you from seeing God's presence and work in new ways? Ask God to grant you the courage to see grace and not to be afraid.

The psalmist appears to be all over the place. He begins the psalm in deep anguish and ends with deep peace, entrusting himself to God's providence. How in the world does that happen? Nothing suggests that the source of the psalmist's despair has been resolved. We read no "Yes, God! You fixed it."

The psalmist cries out to God in his need and then questions those who are the source of his torment, those who shame his honor and "seek after lies." At this point, he turns to affirm his confidence in God. The psalmist exhorts his listeners to repentance as though he is God's prophet. Maybe he is. Maybe his life has moments of prophetic insight. He reminds others and perhaps himself that even when we doubt, God remains faithful. His suggestion for dealing with trouble? Ponder, be silent, offer sacrifice, and trust in God. In the psalmist's acknowledgment of God's faithfulness, he voices the laments of those around him.

If Psalm 4 calls to our minds a scatterbrained psalmist, it's only because his life of faith is not so different from ours. Perhaps in my initial reading I wanted a seamless prayer that was either full of anger or lament or joy—not a mix of all.

Pleading. Praising. Lamenting. Trusting. Exhorting. Resting. This is the blessed story of our lives. While we may yearn for perfection and excitement, Christ has redeemed our sorrow *and* our joy through his death and resurrection. Maybe moments of bliss provide benchmarks to strengthen us when we, like the psalmist, feel pressed on every side. Perhaps that is why the psalmist sleeps peacefully. Not because everything is "fixed," but because in life and death he knows that he—and all of us—belong to God.

Today let go of all worry, and rest in God's love for you.

Despite being spat upon, pierced, and left to die as a criminal, Jesus was not done. In fact, he was just getting started.

For most folks, however, the story is over. That's the disciples' fear before rumors of an empty grave. Now, after Jesus has empowered the disciples and ascended to heaven, God has used Peter to give "perfect health" to a man everyone knew as the beggar at the gate. Lest anyone doubt what has taken place, Peter makes sure they know that this is the work of the one, true, living God—the God they had come to worship. This is the same God they had abandoned and crucified.

The persons who listen to Peter acted in ignorance when they rejected and handed over Jesus to Pilate. In so doing, they have brought to fruition God's purpose: a suffering Messiah. God does not hold their evil against them but uses it to fulfill God's purposes.

God does not hold it against them, but uses it to reveal the divine longing that they become the people God created them to be. God would stop at nothing then and will stop at nothing now for us. While we may assent to such truth intellectually, we often treat ourselves and others as though that's not the case. Surely God would not be able to do such things today, we tell ourselves. Slowly doubt creeps into our lives and seduces us into a life of self-reliance. Without realizing it, our hearts and minds become closed to the God whose mercies are new every morning. Yet, even when we think we do not need God or that God could not create ashes from the beauty of our lives, God never stops the relentless pursuit and love of us. That's the glory of the cross. That's the glory of our lives.

God, every day is a chance to experience you in new ways. Help me entrust myself to you. Amen.

Growing up, I assumed Jesus' call to share the gospel meant I would travel across the ocean to a secluded village on the fringes of contemporary society. I figured I would have had extensive language training and given up my creature comforts. I watched in admiration—and perhaps envy—when I read of missionaries traveling around the world. *One day I'll be able to do that,* I thought.

Over time, I came to see that sharing the good news of Jesus is not so clear-cut. Sometimes we don't even need to use words or take action. Sometimes we just need to be with people. Most importantly, we don't have to travel very far.

When Jesus appears before the disciples and commissions them to go forth and share the joy found in turning away from self and toward God, he doesn't give them a manual or step-by-step instructions. Nor does he tell them where to go and what they are to do when they go to wherever it is they are going. He doesn't even tell them to get theological training. Jesus knows they already have what they need: the power of God's Spirit and the story of their lives.

The disciples have walked the dusty streets of Samaria and Galilee with Jesus. They have sat at the table as Jesus dined with prostitutes and have accompanied him when he touched the skin of lepers. They have experienced the fear of death and the utter shock and glory of resurrection. They have seen with their eyes and felt with their hearts the new life they are to share with others. That is more than enough to carry them, for their faith and their lives have testified to grace and love found in Jesus Christ. It's all we need as well.

What excuses or fears keep you from being the grace of Jesus to the people around you?

Ihave a friend who always reads the endings of books before anything else. She wants to know the ending because it gives her a sense of peace and calm. As an avid book reader, I have been unsuccessful in persuading her of the sheer excitement, anticipation, and thrill of not knowing the outcome. I prefer a sense of the unknown when I read a book, an aspect of my personality I don't embody in real life. Perhaps it's because I too want a sense of peace amidst the uncertainty of life. As a result, I am a master at planning, color-coordinating calendars, organizing disparate groups of people, and getting things done.

My organizational prowess has not kept me from avoiding mishaps, surprises, joys, and sorrows along the way. It has, however, done an admirable job of convincing me I am in control. The illusion of control is powerful, convincing us that as long as we are good meddlers, we can control our life's destiny.

But we can't. Because of that fact, I am starting to see the wisdom in my friend's insistence upon knowing the ending first. The writer of 1 John 3 knows without a doubt that the ending of life—the return of Christ and the establishment of his kingdom on earth—is the life for which our hearts have yearned. He concedes, of course, that we don't know what will happen in the meantime, except for this one astounding truth: We are children of God, and we shall be like him.

That doesn't tell us what tomorrow may hold or the surprises and struggles we'll face along the way. Still, that ending, oh, that ending, makes it all worth it.

God, it's so easy to get caught up in the details that we forget that you guarantee a perfect ending. Open our hearts and minds to live in confidence of such an amazing hope. Amen.

Knowing the Shepherd's Love

APRIL 20–26, 2015 • ERADIO VALVERDE JR.

MONDAY, APRIL 20 ~ *Read Acts 4:5-12*

The biblical image of people of faith as sheep resonates throughout this week's readings. The central theme is that of God as good shepherd. We may be tempted to compare ourselves literally to the animal in less than flattering ways, but the intent of scripture is that we, like the lamb, are creatures with much the same needs. We have a loving and protective shepherd to watch over us, talk and walk with us, guide us away from harm and danger, and provide the best for us. We also find ourselves drawn to the image of Jesus as the good shepherd, who during his earthly ministry performed incredible deeds, not least among them healings.

In Acts 4, we read about the ramifications of Peter and John's healing—in the name of Jesus—a man born lame. Peter and John employ the name of Jesus to heal one man, convert a multitude of five thousand, get themselves in deep trouble, and anger the religious council that oversees the Temple. Not bad for a day's work done in the name above all names.

In the midst of a people who had maintained religious commitments to God comes a new way, a relational commitment to a God who wants to be seen as shepherd—and a healing one at that. To this time and place comes a mass conversion, a healing, and a clear message of God's loving concern for all people, even us. The Good Shepherd invites us to accept or recommit to the love that God so freely offers us.

Good Shepherd, lead me to fullness of life. Thank you for inviting me into a meaningful relationship with you. May I share that invitation with others. Amen.

District superintendent, Southwest Texas Conference of The United Methodist Church, Corpus Christi, Texas

In *Mil Voces Para Celebrar*, the Spanish language hymnal of The United Methodist Church, the baptismal ritual for the naming part of the sacrament reads this way, "Every name is special and important before God. In the same way that God changed the name of Abraham, Sarah, and Jacob, the name of a person represents him or her before the community of God. A name also contains a history in and of itself. For that reason I ask you: What name do you give this child?" The worship resource committee charged with the sacraments had a long discussion over the significance of names.

Scripture affirms that no name is above the name of Jesus. In our reading from Acts, the disruption that has occurred with the use of the name of Jesus confirms that fact. The name of Jesus has healed one person and hurt others in their thinking. A man can now walk, and others find themselves emotionally paralyzed with questions about what has happened and how best to deal with this unexpected challenge. Peter knows scripture well enough to quote the psalmist, and he asserts that "the stone that was rejected by you, the builders, . . . has become the cornerstone." To the people of God, whose early history had nomadic roots and who later embraced the idea of becoming a nation of buildings that they hoped would last for ages, comes this word of a structure with a cornerstone chosen by God. The structure to which Peter refers is the faith relationship of God the shepherd with God's people, the lambs of faith.

Peter further shares that through Jesus comes salvation. For many the word *salvation* seems foreign or threatening, but at its core it is simply the invitation from God to enter into a trusting relationship.

O God, may the name of Jesus provide healing and restorative power to the needs and challenges that I face. I am your lamb, and you are my shepherd, the cornerstone of my life. Amen.

In many ways this psalm affirms the faith, comfort, and trust in the shepherd king. And we experience those same qualities. The words of this psalm share David's complete trust in the One who is always at his side. The psalm covers the full spectrum of life from beginning to end. Perhaps during his own formative years as a boy and as a boy shepherd, David acknowledged all the ways he was learning to be a good shepherd to his father's flocks, and God was doing the same with him and all of God's people. Just as a shepherd seeks to fulfill the needs of the lamb, so does God. God seeks the perfect place for rest. This may not always be a literal place in which to lie down, but the quiet and peace that surrounds us during a harried time offers rest enough.

Those who trust God to lead them find themselves in places where they can serve and be a blessing to others. And even during the difficult times when we see the lengthy shadows of fear and doubt, fear does not control us, for God is with us. David knows the power and effectiveness of both the rod and the staff—fighting off predators and rescuing lambs from hard-to-reach places. These were blessings of comfort for David and can be for us as well.

Our personal enemies may not be violent or life-threatening, but we face the enemies of apathy, despair, doubt, resignation, and perhaps a list too long to share here. The psalm says that even in the face of these, God has prepared a celebration table and we're the invited and anointed guests of honor. Ours is a journey of blessings—of goodness and mercy with God by our side—that leads us to an eternal place of joy and love.

Shepherd of goodness and mercy, walk with me this day. As I face the enemies of my life, comfort and strengthen me. May I take heart in you. Amen.

Some people desire to measure love. "How much do you love me?" is an often-asked question. Some answer, "I love you this much" and begin to name the ways they show that love. How much does God love us? we may ask, and this passage begins to answer that question for us once again. The writer of this passage believes we measure God's love *for* us by what Jesus was willing to *do* for us. "He laid down his life for us—and we ought to lay down our lives for one another." We read this shepherd theme in today's scripture. But the passage dispels the notion of only receiving love. True love is not only received, it is shared—especially with those with greater needs. This love consists not only of words but also acts of caring and expressions of assistance.

The person who experiences being truly loved lives in a way that shows love to others, even those not expecting love. The person with true love from God displays the same kind of unconditional love toward all just as Jesus evidenced that agape love toward us. We do not consider refusing the needs of a sister or brother in need. For the writer of First John, that refusal implies that a person does not possess love at all. The scriptural call is to love "in truth and action."

Another powerful image in this passage is that of our being called "little children." We see some of the sweetest expressions of love at the hands of innocent children; our call, after all, if we want to enter into God's reign, is to be childlike in our expressions of love. It may be our childlike love, after all, that is the telling characteristic of belonging to the God of love.

God of love, may I show my love more than I speak it. May I touch all in need with gestures of love. Amen.

What does it mean to have a condemning heart? It means to have a heart filled with guilt and shame, with the weight of such a burden keeping our heads and spirits bowed before God and before others. A condemning heart is filled with a sense of worthlessness so that we cannot seriously consider ourselves worthy of serving God, let alone having "boldness before God." A condemning heart creates a stumbling block to honest and open prayer. A condemning heart allows our prayer life to suffer and wither; we no longer seek time alone with our God. A condemning heart lacks proper self-love and its owner has not sought the forgiveness and righteousness needed to be the person of faith God called him or her to be. Once we are made right with God, our hearts receive again the love of God; our hearts sing our prayers. The writer states that we then "receive from him whatever we ask," because of our faithfulness in pleasing God.

John Wesley held to the importance of inward change upon receiving God's love and mercy. In Sermon 19, "The Great Privilege of Those That Are Born of God," Wesley teaches that the inward change brought about by God's Holy Spirit affects the outward expression of our existence as Christians. A heart filled with God's love will demonstrate to all the love of God.

The passage reminds us again of the new commandment that Jesus gave his disciples: We should love one another; and, in doing that, Christ will abide in us and us in him. We will be walking sermons of love both received from God and shared with others.

Gracious God, free my heart from any condemnation I may have placed in it through my own thoughts or actions. Free me to live in a way of love for all. Amen.

The psalmist's words now become flesh in this declaration by Jesus. "I am the good shepherd." We find all the qualities of a good shepherd in the person of Jesus the Christ. Unwritten but implied in Psalm 23 is the understanding that a good shepherd would willingly lay down his life for the flock. This, according to the epistle reading, exemplifies true love.

In the Gospel passage Jesus distances himself from the "hired hand" who runs away, leaving his flock unprotected and snatched away by predators. A hired hand feels no ownership toward the flock; a hired hand is just that, hired and paid to watch the flock. A hired hand clocks in and out, and leaves the sheep once he does his duty.

The good shepherd, on the other hand, feels love toward the flock. That love commitment, more than ownership, keeps the shepherd at the ready. A modern comparison would involve considering the care rendered by a person hired to dog-sit versus the care of a dog's owner. We cannot compare the care and love shown a pet by its owner to the care of one paid to watch over the animal. In the same way, Jesus' care and love compares to nothing in the world. As sheep in God's pasture, we matter and belong to God; we are known by name and need. As we walk daily with the Good Shepherd, we get to know God and God's voice. Jesus says that God knows him in the same way.

Our prayer life, our daily study of scripture, worship participation, silent reflection, and meditation: All these serve to help us learn and discern the voice of God in our lives. Prayer is especially central to knowing God if we listen after we pray. Prayer is a two-way conversation with God; we just have to listen quietly for God's answer.

Loving Shepherd, may my life become a daily walk with you. As I walk and talk, teach me to listen and to learn your voice. Guide me to faithfulness. This I pray in your name. Amen.

The appeal and demand of the gospel are universal. God intends the message of good news to reach all people in every place. Most of the New Testament references to our going forth to bear witness to God's love involve our going beyond what we know, both to people and to places. Jesus' declaration about other flocks implies inclusiveness about his message and purpose. For many of us, the "other flock" may be across the street or even across the aisle in our place of worship.

When have we reached out in love to all people with the message that transformed our lives? The biggest challenge facing the Christian faith today comes in sharing our faith with those who traditionally were not invited or welcomed into our worship centers. Many of our faith community neighborhoods have changed and gained new neighbors. Many of the old-flock members continue to drive in to church, past the new neighbors to worship a universal God, all the while blind to the new-flock possibilities.

Jesus is the one true shepherd for all people, of all flocks, both old and new. And once the church catches up with that fact, its members will begin once again to be called to a mission and purpose beyond the four walls of the buildings. Jesus laid down his life as good shepherd for all people and took his life up again as he promised in this passage, faithful to the command of God.

So we ask, What are we doing about it? We need to remove the blinders from our eyes, hearts, and hands to welcome and serve those from other folds. God's message is too precious and powerful to keep to ourselves.

God of all, open my eyes, my heart, my spirit to love and welcome all. Put me to doing all you need of me. In the name of my good shepherd I pray. Amen.

Abiding in God

MONDAY, APRIL 27 ～ *Read Psalm 22:25-31*

We turn to the psalms during times of sorrow and grief, during times of joy and delight. They provide words for our hearts when we cannot form them on our own. Today's psalm sings praise to the Lord who rules over the nations and garners remembrance from all the ends of the earth. The psalmist reminds us that this praise doesn't belong only to us in our hearts or homes or congregations or cities or countries. All the ends of the earth, all the families of the nations will worship. Praise to the Lord comes from corners of the earth we've never seen and from the hearts and voices of those we do not know.

This all-encompassing praise does not stop with the current generation either. It reaches back to those who sleep in the earth and forward to those future generations who will be told about the Lord. Those whom we never met? They praised the Lord. Those who will come after us, whom we might never meet? They will praise the Lord. Everyone will bow down to praise.

From these verses we glean three reasons for such praise: The poor shall eat and be satisfied. The Lord rules over the nations. The Lord has delivered the Lord's people. The expansiveness of this praise can overwhelm our mortal minds. So big! So many! So much! But the gift of this psalm's message comes in the reminder of our connection to one another in our praise of the One who calls us together. In all that we do and all that we are, with all that we have, we praise the Lord. Thanks be to God.

Lord, along with those from every corner of this magnificent world, I praise you. Raising my heart and voice with those from the past and the future, I praise you. Amen.

Copastor, All Saints Lutheran Church, Palatine, Illinois

Do you remember the first time you believed? Some people don't have a specific moment, so to speak. Faith has always been part of their life and rather than appearing suddenly, it has grown and changed along the way. But others do have a moment: a definitive time in their life when faith and belief clicked into place and became clear to them. Maybe it came from something they read or from a vision they had or from a message they heard—the proclamation someone else shared with them.

Today we travel along a wilderness road with Philip, where we meet an Ethiopian eunuch who is in charge of the queen's treasury. An angel has guided Philip to this place—the wilderness is usually an unsafe place, a place of temptation and bandits. The Spirit doesn't guide Philip to a place of danger but rather to a place where he hears someone reading scripture, reading the prophet Isaiah.

This passage encapsulates invitation, proclamation, and grace. The eunuch invites Philip to join him not just in the chariot but in the reading of the scripture so Philip can share his experience and the good news about Jesus. Along the way they find water, and the eunuch it would seem nearly jumps out of the chariot with excitement to be baptized: "Look, here is water!" Oh, that we should all be so joyful for the waters of grace.

Whether or not we can remember a first time for belief, we can all strive for the eunuch's enthusiasm. Long after our faith has become part of our lives, woven into all that we do, let our exclamation be, "Look, here is water!"

Lord, we come to you thirsting for your good news. Quench us with your Spirit. Inspire our proclamations so that all can hear the promise of your life. Amen.

When Philip hears the directions of the Lord's angel, do you think he wondered, *Why? Why should I go to this road that leads from Jerusalem to Gaza? It's a wilderness road! Bad things usually happen on wilderness roads! Why should I do this, you silly angel?* Well, Philip appears to be a particularly obedient disciple. Or at least he voices no recorded questions of this assignment, and as the Spirit continues to guide him to the chariot of the eunuch, Philip goes right along. Perhaps this happens when we begin to imagine what we would say in response to an angel's message.

Whether we would respond with questions of why or not and whether the editor struck Philip's initial responses from the story, the beautiful thing about this passage is that it doesn't really matter. It appears that the willingness or unwillingness of the messenger isn't the point. As always, the Spirit guides and leads. The Lord keeps Philip safe, and the focus of the story shifts from Philip's being sent to a place of wilderness and possible danger to the message Philip gives.

When Philip meets the Ethiopian eunuch, he doesn't begin preaching right away. They have a conversation, and Philip asks him if he understands. We can imagine a gentle friendship of respect and a quest for knowledge beginning on the seat in the chariot as these two begin to look at the scripture and Philip shares his proclamation.

Philip heeds first the directive to the road and then the instruction to join the chariot. Philip hears these instructions and follows them, and the Spirit continues to guide this messenger of the Lord, providing the opportunity for conversation and conversion. Where will the Spirit lead you today? What occasions for proclamation will you have?

Lord, speak through our stammerings of "Why?" and lead us to places where we can speak to your Spirit's presence. Amen.

God is love, and those who abide in love abide in God, and God abides in them." We don't use the word *abide* very often anymore, it seems. But this passage of scripture calls to our minds the power of abiding—the dwelling, standing, enduring, and remaining in God's love.

Over and over again this scripture tells us to dwell, to abide in God's love. We are to remain in the pattern of love that begins with God and moves vertically between us and God and horizontally between us and our neighbors. (Go ahead and trace that in the air. Yes, it forms a cross. That's God's love.) We embrace this pattern even when it gets difficult, and we don't really want to love those around us. But loving God means loving our neighbors.

"Love, love, love, that's what it's all about," sing the Sunday school children. "Because God loves us, we love each other. . . ." Maybe it sounds simple when we're six or seven, but the words of this scripture-based song should stay with us as we grow and struggle into relationships that need God's love more than anything. When that melody abides with us, we carry God's love into the deepest corners of our lives.

God calls us to abide in God. To remain. To stand. To endure. In God's grace and mercy and word. How do we do this? We worship in a community that proclaims God's love and mercy. We look to see God in our neighbors, and we love them as God loves us. We first remember that God loves us—a perfect love without fear.

God of love, remind me today to abide in your love and your word. Help me to love my brothers and sisters as you have loved me. Amen.

We read this passage yesterday but read it again, this time with a pencil in hand. Mark each time the word *love* or a form of the word appears. There's a lot of love in these verses!

When we read a passage that repeats a word over and over (and over and over), it can become easy to gloss over the word and forget what we're reading. *Oh, there the writer goes again with that love business*, we think. *Love . . . abide . . . blah, blah, blah.* Is that how we think of God's love in our lives? Maybe.

The truth is, that God does love us. But on any given day, how actively do we think about that amazing gift of love? Or do we skim through our day thinking, *Car trouble, hard day at work, lots of homework, dinner plans, good night.* And maybe after we pull the covers up, we pause to say, "Thanks, God. Amen."

There's nothing wrong, of course, with a short prayer thanking God for the day. We believe that God hears the prayers of our hearts as well as those of our lips. But what would happen if we took a pencil to our days and marked each time we saw or felt God's love. Would our thinking change at all? Would our litany of the day be peppered with sightings of God's presence and work in the world? Let's hope so.

Now that you've marked all the *love* in this passage, go back and read it again. Carry one of the verses with you—whether committed to memory or written out and tucked in your pocket. The love that we have from God is precious and amazing. Don't gloss over it; look for ways to highlight it in your life.

God, help me to see the ways in which your love abides around me today, and open my eyes to recognize your love. Amen.

It's spring! Freshness all around us—earth being turned, trees budding, daylight growing longer. Let the spring cleaning begin. Throw open the windows. Shake out the rugs. Clear out the closets. Whether we like to do it or not, we're pretty well versed in what spring cleaning looks like. This time of year seems to encourage the urge to make all things new, to start fresh, to cut out what we don't need in order to make room for the new.

In this passage we read that God removes every branch that bears no fruit. That sounds a little harsh. This pruning job feels pretty extreme: the nonproductive branches are bundled and tossed in the fire. But the purpose of the pruning is to make the vine bear more fruit, to make sure that the plant's energy can focus on bearing fruit.

Just as we were cleansed with the waters of baptism and made to dwell with the Lord forever, our lives are continually refreshed and renewed by the word of God—the word that Jesus speaks now abides with us. Our question today becomes, How are we refreshed and renewed to bear more fruit?

We can easily believe that bearing more fruit means doing more: adding more activities, more Bible study, more programs, more of whatever. But perhaps our calendars and commitments need a good pruning too. Maybe in order to bear more fruit, we must simplify our lives, return to basics, trim away commitments that take our time but aren't very productive.

Does your calendar need a thorough spring cleaning? As challenging as it can be to clear out a closet, evaluating our commitments can pose an entirely different challenge. Our task isn't to have a jam-packed calendar. Our call is to abide in God; in doing so we will bear much fruit.

Loving God, as I go about my day, help me prune away needless activity so that I bear much fruit for you. Amen.

The Greek root for the word we translate as "abide" is *meno*. It shows up in John's Gospel a number of times and carries with it the idea of staying, remaining, and abiding. When the Holy Spirit remains on Jesus after his baptism, that's *meno*. When Jesus proclaims that he came into the world so that those who believe in him should not stay in the darkness, that's *meno*. When we hear of the many dwelling places in the Father's house, those dwelling places are from *meno*.

Our lives are full of transitions and changes. Jobs end and new ones begin. Students graduate and begin the next phase of their life. Relationships change. People die. Babies are born. Sometimes we find it difficult to imagine a constant in the midst of the change. Today's scripture invites us to abide in God. When the world swirls around us with change, we are to abide in God, to stay put in God.

Yet, from the midst of God's abiding love, comes a call for newness and change. The branches are pruned so that they bear more fruit. These verses from John alternate between instructions to abide and discussion of our role as branches of the vine. All of it reminds us of our connection to Christ.

Out of our dwelling with God—and God dwelling with us—we grow and bear fruit. We don't do it on our own. We don't bear fruit when we aren't rooted and abiding in God's love. In fact, we would wither and die if we weren't abiding in God.

We are branches of the vine; as disciples of Jesus we are called to bear fruit while dwelling in the vine. It is the vine of Jesus from which all things grow. Thanks be to God!

God, I give thanks that you nourish me as a branch of your vine. Be with me as I bear fruit in your world. Amen.

God Leaves the Sidelines

MAY 4–10, 2015 • WILLIAM TURPIE

MONDAY, MAY 4 ~ *Read Psalm 98*

Singing is not one of my gifts, so when the psalmist invokes us to "make a joyful noise to the LORD" this is a fastball moving right past my zone of recognition. Yet I love it when a favorite song comes on the radio or in a worship service—nostalgia overwhelms me and my emotional state gets reset. As I ponder this psalm I am struck by its emphasis on creation swelling with praise for the God of "steadfast love." The poet must be recalling God's solid engagement with Israel through all of its moments of rebellion and deceit. Sadly, God's chosen people turned around only when God was the last resort. I've often acted in similar ways. For me the psalm anticipates the steadfast love that is sounded in God's promise, "I will never leave you or forsake you" (Heb. 13:5).

The poet's images depict the whole of creation bending forward with praise and emotion. As I read the words through several times, I am moved past whatever lonely morass I have crawled into, past my anguish about the future, and past my tendency to stand on the sideline. I feel compelled to participate in the swell of praise that spills over into all creation. I have to sing along—no matter how poorly I may do it. Finally, the psalmist notes God's coming judgment. It too will unfold in a special way—in righteousness and fairness. These two concepts are intimately connected with each other. Even in that time of accountability—what we will hear above all else is how righteous and fair is the God we have embraced.

Lord, help me to realize that a simple expression of praise can overwhelm my present despair and replace it with relief—even joy. Amen.

Pastor, New North Church, Hingham, Massachusetts

The expression "hang out" implies a relaxed and "laid back" attitude. I have friends I enjoy hanging out with because they put me at ease. I can laugh at myself, move with a freer spirit. I also like being around some people because they challenge me. This is what Jesus is getting at when he says, "As the Father has loved me, so I have loved you; abide in my love." We can also translate the word *abide* as "live," "remain," or "hang out."

In John 1:38, two of John's disciples ask Jesus "Where are you staying?" Jesus replies, "Come and see." The text goes on to say that they spent the whole day with him. They hung out with him. How do we spend quality time with Jesus, feeling at ease and enjoying each other's company?

I hang out with Jesus by staying in touch with the Gospels. I try to pray or meditate on Jesus' life regularly. I also try to consider and understand what Jesus is asking me to do—keeping in mind his self-giving love. This love is not based on feelings but on my conscious choice to love. To "hang out" with Jesus also means moving from what may be a laid-back attitude of comfort to one that challenges me to take on his posture of "self-giving" love.

A person calls me, and I can be thinking more about intrusions than about love. The caller asks a favor of me, and I can be thinking of the time it will require. When that happens I am not hanging out in love. This love is not defensive but proactive. It is both the reward and challenge of hanging out with Jesus.

Lord, hanging out with you is going to free me up and cost me something. Help me to appreciate both of these aspects of relationship with you. Amen.

W e often assume we are different from others and others different from us—sometimes quite different. But this passage stresses God's desire for us to understand our commonality with all of humanity. One axiom in geometry states that "two things that are equal to the same thing are also equal to each other." If you have two pieces of rope that each trace out the same length on a piece of lumber—then you know those two pieces of rope are the same length. It is common sense, and this universal rule applies to more than measurements. The apostle Peter and Cornelius, the Roman centurion, led completely different lives. One was a Jew who tried to live by the laws of his religion, which prevented association with individuals outside of his faith. Cornelius, a Roman soldier, was enveloped and beholden to his military duties and his allegiance to Rome. Yet, Peter and his Jewish associates as well as Peter's Gentile friends have the same experience of being overtaken by the Spirit of God.

Both groups wind up speaking in new languages and worshiping God with similar prayerful outbursts. If two different things are equal to something else they are equal to each other. In this case, both groups are equal before God. Both are similarly touched by God despite huge cultural differences and backgrounds. This experience signifies a game-changing moment for Peter and for the new faith that Jesus is establishing. God will work in the lives of Jews *and* in the lives of Gentiles—and in much the same way. They are equal—God is no respecter of persons. We can rejoice in our connectedness with all humanity.

Lord, help me to realize that I share more in common with those I view as different from me because you regard each of us as equals in our humanity before you. Amen.

A birth, while a hopeful experience, raises serious questions. Will this child sleep restlessly or peacefully? How will he or she respond to family love? Will the baby be fun to spend time with?

Our passage raises the matter of a birth from God. Birth—spiritual birth—is not an uncommon theme in the New Testament. Jesus discusses with the questioning Nicodemus (John 3) the possibility of a spiritual birth after a physical birth. Peter mentions a "new birth" (1 Pet. 1:3). God is giving birth to new life, new expectations. Faith can give us the chance for a restart. And that is why a spiritual or second birth is so appealing.

Some of us are looking for dramatic—even radical—departures from our past. We may be expecting too much, but there is also significant evidence that people can be transformed. It's as though they have experienced a new birth. The lives of Jesus' disciples were completely reoriented by following him. The expectation of this letter is not only that we believe but that we "love one another" (1 John 3:23). That type of love is engendered through a new birth—which could be called a spiritual birth. It is a birth in which God is present as both midwife and the source of new life—especially a new capacity to love and obey God. Jesus believed in transformation. The early church believed in change—radical change. Why not us? The transformation could be sudden or lengthy. As humans we are given the capacity to change. I know I am not where I want to be yet, but God isn't finished engineering my life. This is our hope—the hope of a continuing birth from God, which brings with it new life evidenced in a new and growing ability to love and obey.

Lord, birth can be sudden, but it usually involves a period of time. Help me to realize that you are always trying to bring something new alive in me. Amen.

Real love involves sacrifice—it is self-giving. Jesus says that he will demonstrate that kind of love for his friends by giving his life for them. I wonder about my own ability to sacrifice. Jesus' actions inspire, but they can seem remote—visible only in the paintings of Renaissance masters. I needed a more contemporary connection, and it happened for me when I spent the better part of an evening with a friend of mine who was the night beat reporter for the *Boston Globe*. As we were leaving the newspaper office, a call came in about a fire in a nearby neighborhood.

The fire trucks were already there when we arrived in front of a rundown older home with smoke still billowing out of windows on the third floor. A number of elderly people huddled under blankets on the lawn. It turned out this was not a private residence but a makeshift housing operation, which was packed with the elderly. If the fire had gotten out of control, the loss of life could have been huge.

My friend talked with the fire lieutenant and made notes for his story. When he returned to the car, he was shaking his head. He said that several of the firefighters had risked their lives to rescue the people we saw on the lawn. He also stressed that many nights these same men and women enter burning buildings to make rescues like this. They were selfless. He said, "They don't even know these people—yet they are willing to take these kinds of risks!" Their sacrificial actions move me to ask God for the strength to love and sacrifice for folks who are close to me. Hopefully I'll also grow into the capacity to let go of my life for those I don't even know. It always helps to have living examples of the sacrificial spirit we see in Jesus.

Help me, God, to realize that Jesus did not hold onto his life but freely released it for his friends and for us. May I find the strength to give my life away in both the small and the significant moments that I may face. Amen.

I was not unlike Cornelius at one time. I was seeking meaning, struggling to make sense of my life and where I fit in the world. It had been many years since I had attended church. I tried to reach out to God, but I wasn't sure God was there.

At the time my course work in college was just average, but my party grades were outstanding. Then I lost interest in the party scene as well. Just at that moment, a person who had been out of my life reached out to me. We decided to go to the movies one night; when I stopped by his home his brother and a group of friends were there discussing faith.

I found myself drawn to the discussion. Our evening plans changed. I asked questions, and the youth leader of their church began to share a very basic message about Jesus. He wound up almost quoting the Apostles' Creed, which I knew because I had memorized it once for a confirmation class. Until this moment, however, it held no meaning for me. As he spoke, the words of the creed came alive—in fact they seemed to be pulsating throughout my being. I could feel something changing inside me.

I don't know if my experience that night resembles that of Cornelius and his family, but I knew that God was speaking to me. I felt exhilarated. It was similar in many ways to Cornelius's experience with Peter because I knew God had nudged me and provided opportunities for me to be at the right place at the right time. And then, most importantly, I learned that even though the circumstances are ripe for our transformation by God's Spirit, our hearts must be ready to respond.

Lord, you show up in so many unanticipated ways. May I be open to your appearing. Amen.

The statement "his commandments are not burdensome" has to be one of the more outrageous phrases to appear in the New Testament. I beg to differ. Love that is really love for those who have acted offensively and selfishly is not easy. What is the writer of this letter proposing? I think he's talking about work! It is not easy to forgive, to love the uninterested, the deceiver, or the manipulator.

Yet, this passage offers a route to accomplish this type of love. Along with the injunction to keep God's commandments is the phrase that "whatever is born of God conquers the world." Conquering anything implies work. The word translated "conquer" comes from the Greek word that means victory. The Greeks used the word to talk about athletic competition or prevailing in a court case. The idea here is effort—discipline. We apply discipline to things like diets, playing an instrument, or maintaining an exercise routine. But do we apply it to learning how to love those who wrong us or disturb us?

I have heard recovering addicts discuss how hard they have had to work. They may have faith, but they have also set aside time to meet with groups that are healing, to get the counseling they need, to find ways to handle difficult moments by planning ahead. All this requires work. If we want to be counted with God, it helps to have faith and grace; but to conquer also demands work. I had to work hard to love her, to forgive him, but I did the work because I had the faith to believe that the work could make a huge difference. And it has!

Lord, give me the faith to believe that I can prevail and love in difficult circumstances. Give me also the ability to do the work I need to do to overcome my failings. Amen.

God's Prayer for Us

MAY 11–17, 2015 • TRICIA NOWACKI

MONDAY, MAY 11 ~ *Read Psalm 1:1-3*

I cannot imagine "delighting" in a law. I appreciate laws that serve the common good, but they do not bring me joy. Laws established by government restrict harmful actions; they do not try to bring out the best in humanity; they seek to prevent the worst.

On the other hand, the law of God does not restrict; it liberates. Today's psalm refers to the law represented by stipulations written in the Torah, the first five books of the Bible. As Christians, we approach the law in a different light, the light that Jesus shed on it. When a lawyer asks Jesus which commandment in the law is the greatest, Jesus replied, "'You shall love the Lord your God with all your heart, and with all your soul, and with all your mind.' This is the greatest and first commandment. And a second is like it: 'You shall love your neighbor as yourself.' On these two commandments hang all the law and the prophets" (Matt. 22:38-40). As Christians, we understand the commandment to love God, neighbor, and self as the most crucial. We bear the imprint of our eternally loving, communal, reconciling God; we damage ourselves, hurt others, and dishonor God when we do not live out who we truly are. If we sink our roots deep and drink from the way of love, we will flourish in the life-giving ways God intends. We will yield our "fruit in its season." We can choose our source of nourishment; we must continually and actively choose to immerse ourselves in God's law of love.

God of love, we are your children made in your image. Help us to acknowledge this fact. May we continually immerse ourselves in your law of love. Amen.

English instructor turned seminarian, Garrett Evangelical Theological Seminary; living in Chicago, Illinois

What happens when we turn from God's loving law? The psalm says we are then like chaff—the useless husk that is removed from viable grains of wheat. If we reject God's law of love, we deny our God-given purpose and deny our true selves. We become useless, purposeless; we wither.

Make no mistake about it: God's law of love and its implications in our lives is truly countercultural. Material wealth or physical comfort do not define the happiness and prosperity promised at the beginning of Psalm 1. That joy comes by being and acting exactly as we are intended to do by God, rather than our culture or society. Not one of us, no matter how righteous, can escape the literal withering and eventual perishing of our bodies, but this psalm tells us that we can choose to live beyond our finite selves by abiding in God's law of love.

Humanity's fundamental design is to be nourishing grains of wheat. The chaff, once the protective husk of the growing wheat, becomes dry and useless when the wheat is harvested; it is indigestible to most animals, and it contains no seed. It has no purpose. But the grain of wheat has many purposes—it can be used to nourish and sustain life as food, and it can produce more grain, ensuring future life. The prosperity of a grain of wheat is determined by its ability to nourish others and to sustain life outside of itself. A grain of wheat does not exist for itself—the wheat's purpose is to serve others, to promote and secure life. The indigestible, nonproductive chaff cannot do this. We choose to be like the viable grain of wheat when we heed God's commandment of love and internalize it so that all that we do reflects that law.

In what ways are you living like a grain of wheat? In what ways are you more like the chaff on wheat? Ask for God's guidance and help in becoming less like chaff and more like grain.

The disciples and the other Christ-followers find themselves in a peculiar place. Jesus, their beloved leader, has been arrested, killed, resurrected, and, just recently, has ascended into heaven. The followers once again find themselves without their teacher; but this time, they have the comfort and hope of his resurrection. Jesus has also promised the arrival of the Holy Spirit to them. But the disciples are human, and I imagine they feel a mix of powerful and conflicting emotions.

The disciples find themselves in an "in-between" time—between the miraculous events of Christ's resurrection and ascension and the promised Pentecost. The time is filled with waiting and remembrance. Such a time could have promoted idleness in the followers as they are caught up in the emotions of days past. But Peter takes this moment to urge the followers to appoint a new disciple.

By doing so, Peter reminds the assembly that God has sovereign reign. Judas "was numbered among us and was allotted his share in this ministry." God gave Judas a task, a ministry, that fell within God's providential care. God supplies tasks and resources, but the decision to choose to perform the task is that of the individual. Judas was not God's puppet. Judas chose, of his own free will, to hand Jesus over to his death.

God's foreknowledge and action do not excuse us of responsibility for our freely chosen action or inaction. Even as we are called to wait trustingly for God's action, we are not called to idleness. In every situation, in every moment, we choose to align ourselves with God's will, to employ our God-given resources for the tasks at hand.

God of all time, I trust you. In chaotic and confusing moments, I trust you. As I work to discover and carry out your will, I trust you. Amen.

This passage comes near the end of Jesus' honest yet consoling last words to his disciples as recorded in John. He has already told them that they will be scattered, alone, and persecuted. Even then he has assured them of peace because he has conquered the world. Jesus' death and resurrection lie before him, and he prepares his disciples for the difficult time they will face as they spread the gospel in hostile environments.

In today's scripture Jesus prays for his disciples. Jesus' oneness with God and his desire for his followers to be likewise unified offer the beating heart of this prayer: "Holy Father, protect them in your name that you have given me, so that they may be one, as we are one." Through this prayer, Jesus asks that God make clear the divine intentions for humanity.

Jesus' prayer of intercession illustrates the kind of loving care we should invest in our intercessory prayers. He selflessly prays for the benefit and protection of his followers. The entire prayer emanates a sense of community and reciprocity. Jesus states in various ways that what God has given him, he has given to his followers, and they have received it. The followers' reception of what he gives in turn glorifies God.

God is one and yet three—solitary and simultaneously communal, seamlessly and without end. Having been made in the image of the triune God, we find our true identity in love and community. Our souls are stamped with the reality of our triune God. Jesus' prayer makes it clear that, above all else, God desires our deep relationship with God and with others.

Gracious Creator, Loving Redeemer, and Holy Sustainer, help us to acknowledge our connectedness and interdependence. Guide us to unity. Amen.

At the close of Jesus' prayer comes a plea for the disciples' sanctification through him: "Sanctify them in the truth; your word is truth. As you have sent me into the world, so I have sent them into the world. And for their sakes I sanctify myself, so that they also may be sanctified in truth." Different religious traditions interpret the particulars of sanctification in various ways, but generally sanctification involves setting a person apart for holiness. A completely sanctified individual is fully restored to the image of God in which we all are made. These sanctified persons exist in extreme closeness with God, the source of all holiness. With this closeness to God comes an inevitable separation from worldly things. This is why Jesus says that he and his disciples do not belong to the world.

But this revelation often creates a misunderstanding about what is of "the world." God lovingly created the world, and John tells us, some fourteen chapters earlier, that God loves the world so much that God chooses to enter it and inhabit it as a human being. The worldly things are not our flesh or the beautiful vegetation or the dazzling array of creatures with which we share this earth. The worldly things are the false idols of great wealth and power, the social reality of a status quo of greed and violence, and our seemingly universal inclination toward self-preservation. The most dangerous worldly things include concepts and ways of life, not physical items.

Jesus indicates that the truth, God's word, sanctifies—sets the believers apart from the world in service. They do not leave the world but receive divine protection as they operate in the world. We too are sanctified in God's word—set apart—to do God's work in the world.

O God, open my mind so that I can distinguish your truth from the lies that surround me. As I draw nearer to you, sanctify me to do your work. Amen.

God's Prayer for Us

Right after I graduated from seminary, I applied for a job in leadership at a prominent church. I went on three grueling interviews that all went well. By the last one, I felt confident that I would get the job. Three days later I received a phone call from an apologetic pastor, stumbling a bit over her words. She confirmed that I was about to be hired, but an intern had suddenly applied for the job the day before. She had prayed about it and felt convicted that he was the right choice. I felt angry and disappointed. It took months for me to realize that I was not a good fit for the job. I then realized that I had never prayed about this possible position. I had never released the decision to God, and I had never listened for God's reply. I had simply told God what I wanted and then gone about my business.

Peter and the other disciples have carefully selected new disciple candidates, but they ultimately release their decision to God. Verses 21-22 list the primary qualification for the successor: a person who has been on the journey with them and with Jesus from the beginning. That experience will make the candidate a good witness to the works and words of Jesus Christ. Either man would have been a suitable choice. With humility, the disciples realize there is a limit to their knowledge, and they pray together for God to choose the new disciple. Their prayer begins with, "Lord, you know everyone's heart." The original Greek reference to God is translated as "Heart-Knower." Because of the disciples' confidence in God's role as "Heart-Knower," along with their acceptance of God's will, they turn to casting lots—a common practice in their day—to make their final decision.

We take responsibility for thinking through decisions, but we must also seek God's will with humility and openness. God, our "Heart-Knower," knows us better than we know ourselves.

How has God been revealed as your "Heart-Knower" in the past, and what might your "Heart-Knower" be inviting you to now?

Many people know the First Letter of John for its emphatic proclamation that "God is love." Indeed, the idea that "God is love" forms the linchpin of the entire letter. Our passage today speaks of the testimony of God's love, Jesus Christ. Jesus is the source, revelation, and proof of divine love.

This passage's focus on testimony reminded me of a colleague at my undergraduate Bible study who constantly carried around a book on the historical Jesus. He was so enthusiastic about the various "proofs" it offered regarding Jesus that he readily shared it with other fledglings of the faith. It was interesting to see various parts of the gospel "proven" by other historical documents and archeological data; but for me the proof was inadequate.

Perhaps the proof the book offered resembled the human testimony mentioned in today's text. First John speaks of God's testimony as far superior to human testimony. This does not mean that our Christian witness to others is unnecessary or of great value—it is both. But human testimony alone will not change someone's heart. Only God's testimony through Jesus Christ can do that—and then only if we allow it. If we truly have the testimony of God in our hearts, then Jesus Christ dwells within us. If we believe in Jesus' teachings, if we believe that he conquered death and birthed eternal hope through his resurrection, then his word, his actions of healing and making whole, and his profound love reside within us. And Jesus' love cannot be contained in the boundary of our hearts! This love overflows and affects all that we do. We discover the proof that God's testimony dwells in our hearts in our actions. Our loving actions in turn provide testimony to God's presence and God's love.

How have you encountered God, and what is your testimony about God? Does that testimony truly dwell in your heart? Do your actions and decisions flow from that testimony?

When the Spirit Comes

MAY 18–24, 2015 • JAMES HARNISH

MONDAY, MAY 18 ~ *Read Romans 8:22-27; Acts 1:1-5*

My nine-year-old grandson enjoys building a fire in the fireplace at my lake house. He keeps adding more wood until it burns like Nebuchadnezzar's furnace. I have trouble convincing him to wait for cooler weather to build a fire.

The final week of the "Great Fifty Days" from Easter to Pentecost finds us with the first followers of Jesus, waiting for the fire (the Holy Spirit) to fall on them. The risen Christ has told them to wait in Jerusalem for the promise that John the Baptist first announced, "He will baptize you with the Holy Spirit and fire" (Matt. 3:11).

Like my grandson waiting through the summer for the "fire season," living by faith means learning to wait. No matter how many times we have experienced Pentecost, we are always waiting, longing, praying for the fire of the Spirit to fall fresh upon our lives. That's what we mean by hope.

Paul says that waiting in hope is essential to our salvation. He asks the rhetorical question, "Who hopes for what they already see?" (CEB). If all our hopes are fulfilled, we will no longer hope. "But if we hope for what we don't see, we wait for it with patience" (CEB).

But we do not wait alone. Like a woman in labor, the whole creation joins us in breathless anticipation of the fulfillment of God's salvation. Even as we remain still, the Spirit for whom we are waiting is already present in the most deeply hidden, most inarticulate longings of our souls. Waiting for Pentecost is a little like telling my grandson to wait for fire season.

O God, teach us to live in hope that the Spirit who is already at work within us will descend upon us with fire. Amen.

United Methodist pastor, preacher, and author, Winter Haven, Florida

What are we waiting for? The question must have haunted the silent prayers of Jesus' followers during the days between Easter and the Ascension. They were waiting for the Holy Spirit, but what did that mean? What kind of Spirit would it be? When Jesus described the Holy Spirit he used the word *parakletos*. The Greek root means "one who stands beside." Translators attempt to capture the meaning of the word with a variety of names: Comforter, Advocate, Companion, Helper, Friend. With names like these, we need not fear the Holy Spirit.

Jesus promised that the Spirit would reveal the reality of sin, righteousness, and judgment; would guide the disciples into truth and turn their suffering into joy. Best of all, Jesus promised that the Spirit would take Jesus' place in their experience by becoming the living presence of the risen Christ in their lives.

In Lloyd D. Douglas's novel *The Robe*, Justus tells Marcellus, "Sometimes I feel aware of him, as if he were close by." He says he feels no temptation to cheat, lie, or hurt others when he feels that Jesus is standing beside him. Marcellus replies that he would be uncomfortable if he felt that he was being perpetually watched by an invisible presence. Justus responds, "Not if that presence helped you defend yourself against yourself. . . . It is a great satisfaction to have someone standing by—to keep you at your best."

If that's what the Spirit comes to do, then Pentecost is well worth waiting for!

O Spirit of the living God, thou light and fire divine,
descend upon thy church once more, and make it truly thine.
Fill it with love and joy and power,
with righteousness and peace;
till Christ shall dwell in human hearts,
and sin and sorrow cease. Amen.

It's one thing to hear a faithful person talk about prayer; it's a totally different experience to hear that person pray for you. Ada Blixt was past eighty when I became her pastor. She had emigrated from Sweden as a girl, but she never lost her Swedish accent. Ada didn't just talk about prayer; she prayed. Listening to the intimacy with which she talked to God could make you think that God is a Swede. I remember how she prayed for me when I went to launch a new congregation. Knowing that she was praying for me carried me through challenging times. I hope she still prays for me in heaven.

In the reading today we hear Paul praying for us. In Greek, it is one convoluted, run-on sentence. The words gush out of his soul like water bubbling up from an artesian spring. Perhaps this is what Paul meant when he said that the Spirit prays within us "with sighs too deep for words" (Rom. 8:26).

Paul begins with gratitude, which is where real prayer always begins. He doesn't fool around with petty petitions. He goes for the big stuff, praying that we will be given "a spirit of wisdom and revelation" to know Christ. He prays that we might see the hope of our calling, the riches of our inheritance, and "the immeasurable greatness of his power." Finally, Paul's prayer builds to an explosive climax with the risen Christ at God's right hand, lifted "above every name that is named" with "all things under his feet."

Paul, like Ada, offers prayer on our behalf out of an intense intimacy with God. That prayer lifts us out of the doldrums of daily life and into God's presence.

O God, may your servants be set on fire with your Spirit, strengthened by your power, gifted with your wisdom, and filled with your grace to bear witness to your kingdom in this world. Amen.

ASCENSION DAY

Both of Luke's accounts of the Ascension agree that Jesus was taken up to heaven. How on earth do we believe that? We gave up the cosmology of a three-storied universe long ago, but the imagery of up and down remains with us. We say the sun rises and sets, although we know it does nothing of the kind. We say we feel "high as a kite" or "down in the dumps." We may have rejected the cosmology, but we still explain our experiences in those terms.

The church has never tried to explain the astrophysics of the Ascension. Instead, it invites us to experience the truth of it. Do we take the Ascension seriously, and what does that mean for our lives? Today is the grand finale of the Gospel story. In Jesus, the God who is so high above us that we can never fully comprehend came down to be with us all the way to death. You can't go farther down than the grave. God raised Jesus from death, and now Jesus is taken up into heaven. You can't be more highly exalted than that.

When we affirm that we believe "he ascended into heaven," we are not speculating about intergalactic space travel; we are defining our priorities. We are saying that Jesus Christ deserves to "occupy the first place in everything" (Col. 1:18, CEB). He is exalted over everything.

When I was a teenager, the Methodist Youth Fellowship motto was "Christ above All." Fifty years later, I'm still sorting out what it means to live by that motto. Believing in the Ascension is just as simple and just as complicated as that.

O God, who took Jesus up into heaven, may Christ be exalted above everything in our lives. Amen.

A fifteenth-century Hungarian painting of the Ascension by Master Thomas de Coloswar caught my attention because Jesus isn't in it. All we see is Jesus' shirttail floating away under the upper picture frame. Mary and the disciples stare up into the sky in stunned confusion. We can hear the angel asking, "Why are you standing here, looking toward heaven?" (CEB).

Some Christians spend a lot of time looking toward heaven, either fantasizing about life after death or calculating Jesus' return. Perhaps spiritual escapism seems easier than wrestling with down-to-earth ways in which God's kingdom comes and God's will gets done in a world afflicted by economic injustice, racial prejudice, war, nationalism, and intolerance.

But Acts does not tell the story of how the apostles prepared to go to heaven. It tells the story of Spirit-empowered followers who became the presence of the kingdom of God here on earth. Jesus' "going up" prepares the way for the Holy Spirit to "come down"—to empower us to be and do what God intends. The Holy Spirit does not come down to lift us out of this world but to enable us to be Jesus' presence in this world.

I've heard an imaginative story about what happened after the Ascension—when Jesus arrives back in heaven. The angels ask how he intends to keep his kingdom work going on earth. Jesus replies, "I've left that to my disciples." Knowing just how imperfect and inadequate those folks are, the angels ask, "Well, Lord, what if they don't get the job done? What's your backup plan?" To which Jesus responds, "I have no other plan."

O God who came down to us in Jesus, come down again in the power of your Spirit that we may be the presence of your kingdom in this world. Amen.

In her poem "Renascence," Edna St. Vincent Millay listens deeply to the earth. She hears "the gossiping of friendly spheres," "the creaking of the tented sky," and "the ticking of Eternity." She feels the weight of infinity pressing down upon her. She shares the suffering, death, and reawakening of the earth and in that experience finds the "radiant identity" of God.

In the same way, the psalmist listens to creation, celebrates its immensity, feels its hunger and thirst, and acknowledges the whole creation's utter dependence on the Spirit of God to give life. Likewise, Paul hears the whole creation groaning in labor pains as it waits in hope for the coming of the children of God to free it from decay. All too often, we find ourselves contributing to the decay of the environment rather than being a part of its healing.

Pentecost is not only about the Spirit bringing new life and power to the disciples in the early church; it is about the way God's Spirit brings new life to the earth. The Spirit comes not just for people but for the whole groaning creation. The Spirit comes not just to heal broken hearts but to bring healing to the bruised and broken world. God does not abandon this earth but brings to it redemption, healing, and renewal. We are called to participate in its redemption.

Can we hear creation crying? Can we hear the groaning of a broken, abused, disrupted world that waits in hope for the coming of the men and women who serve as gardeners in God's new creation? Will the creation be saved from us or with us? Will the Spirit's work of healing be done through us or in spite of us?

O God, send forth your Spirit to renew your creation and use us as a part of the process. Amen.

PENTECOST

On May 27, 1962, the volunteer fire department in Centralia, Pennsylvania, burned some trash in an abandoned coal pit in preparation for the Memorial Day parade. The fire they started that day seeped into the labyrinthine seams of anthracite coal beneath the town. Half a century later, the fire still burns. Nothing can put it out.

Something really happened on Pentecost; something so real and yet so beyond explanation that Luke says it is "like the howling of a fierce wind." The disciples see "what seemed to be individual flames of fire" (CEB).

This "something" comes *into* the disciples not out of them. The disciples cannot explain the experience based on who they had been, but the experience empowers them to become more than they imagined. The Holy Spirit descends into their lives with an unquenchable fire.

The creative Spirit that brought order out of chaos, the prophetic Spirit that Ezekiel experienced as wind and fire, the divine Spirit that descended on Jesus at his baptism, the life-giving Spirit that raised Jesus from death, the intoxicating Spirit of the living God transforms a bunch of whimpering cowards into courageous apostles who proclaim the love of God in Christ to all people. The fire has never been put out.

On May 24, 1738, a despondent Anglican priest named John Wesley went "very unwillingly" to a small group meeting in Aldersgate Street in London. When Wesley tried to describe what happened, he wrote, "I felt my heart strangely warmed." Wesley's heartwarming experience ignited the revival that became known as Methodism in England and burns today through the churches that trace their roots to his warmed heart.

Holy Spirit, warm our hearts with a fire that won't go out. Amen.

Power and Mystery, Glory and Grace

MAY 25–31, 2015 • LEE HULL MOSES

MONDAY, MAY 25 ~ *Read Isaiah 6:1-7*

This passage is full of imagery that boggles our twenty-first-century minds: creatures with six wings call to one another across the vast throne room; the Temple's foundation trembles at the sound of their voices; smoke fills the room; live coals rest on the altar; and God is so big that just the hem of God's robe fills the entire worship space.

Incredulous, we are tempted to turn the page and dismiss these words as the fanciful imaginings of an ancient and unenlightened people. But perhaps we ought not be too quick to leave Isaiah and look for God's presence in tamer and more understandable places. After all, it is good news—is it not—that we worship a God who is bigger and more powerful than anything we can imagine. God's incomprehensibility to human minds is part of God's nature. We can't understand God; that's part of the mystery. That's what poetry is for and art and music and creative endeavors of all kinds—all serve as attempts to capture that which cannot be put into words: love, grace, beauty, power, truth. Visions like Isaiah's remind us that the God we worship lies beyond our ability to describe.

When we stand in the presence of such mystery, we may not understand God, but we can understand who we are: We are not God—we are human, capable of and prone to sin. "I am lost," Isaiah cries, "for I am a man of unclean lips!" But nearly in the same instant, the seraph touches his lips and makes him clean.

God's grace—like God's power—is mysterious and beyond our capacity to fully understand.

Almighty God, calm our fears and help us to trust in the mystery of your power and your grace. Amen.

Senior Minister, First Christian Church, Greensboro, North Carolina

It would be easier if God would just pick up the phone and call. Or send an e-mail. Or better yet, text: "Need someone to go. You?"

But that's not how it happens, at least not for Isaiah who is confronted with a mind-blowing vision of six-winged angels and the Lord on a high and lofty throne. In the midst of the vision—smoke swirling and the very floor of the Temple shaking—he hears God's voice clear as day: "Whom shall I send?"

Not many of us have had visions like Isaiah's or hear the voice of God speaking so clearly and directly. Our encounters with the Holy do not necessarily include scenes worthy of the Hollywood special effects. But does that mean God fails to speak to the rest of us? If we await a call as dramatic as Isaiah's, we may miss the forest for the trees, for God speaks in many ways.

Sometimes it's the rustle of wind through an open window in spring that calls us to be grateful for creation. Sometimes it's the "One more, Mommy?" that calls us to stop worrying about the dinner dishes and read one more story with our kids. Sometimes it's the headlines of the daily news that call to us, crying out for a prophet who will speak truth to power. Sometimes it's a neighbor, friend, church member, who says to us, "I think you'd be good at this. . . ."

Then we take a deep breath, and we remember that we are standing in God's presence—almighty and mysterious—and we say yes, I am here; send me. For as many ways as God can call to us, there are just as many ways to say yes.

Dear God, help us to recognize your voice when you call and to respond with grace and courage. Amen.

Like the images in Isaiah 6, the God of Psalm 29 holds a power beyond our capacity to imagine. We watch as full-grown trees are toppled and flames of fire flash at the sound of God's voice. It is enough to make us fall to our knees in awe.

In some ways, we take comfort in knowing that the God we worship is so fearsome, so strong, so powerful. Putting our trust in an all-powerful God means that even when we're feeling powerless, we can find strength. We can stand in the presence of God's majesty and confess our vulnerability, knowing that we are not alone. We peer into the vastness of the universe, overwhelmed at how small and insignificant we are, and we rejoice that God knows us by name.

But images like these—the thundering voice of God that breaks cedars and "strips the forest bare"—are hard to read without thinking of present-day images of hurricane damage along the coast or entire towns devastated by tornadoes. Tsunamis, blizzards, earthquakes—all acts of power and part of God's creation. How do we make sense of a powerful, mighty God without blaming God for natural disasters? The power of nature is terrifying and dangerous. Could God be there too?

Perhaps we ought to trust that the mystery of God's power is also beyond our ability to understand. Just as we cannot fathom a divine voice so loud that it shakes the wilderness, neither can we imagine the quiet whisper of a God who speaks in small, subtle, indirect ways, even as the ground shakes beneath our feet. A helping hand extended in the wake of the storm, an offer to help clean up. A shoulder to cry on, an embrace, a prayer. The power of God does not always topple trees, but it almost always takes our breath away.

Dear God, we stand in awe of your power and glory. Bring us peace. Amen.

Power and Mystery, Glory and Grace 159

It is unfair, perhaps, to quibble with a writer so influential and so long dead that he cannot defend himself. Still, we may confess to some angst when confronted with these brief verses in which the apostle Paul sets flesh apart and against spirit. For one thing, how in the world would we possibly avoid living in the flesh? Here we are, with these bodies and, in some ways, that's all we've got. These precious, fragile bodies contain our whole lives.

In this flesh, we participate in the created life God gave us. In the flesh, we share ice cream on the back porch on a summer day. We create art. We work. We embrace. We run and jump and sing. How could we live, except according to the flesh?

But Paul's point is a good one: These fleshly bodies are not all we've got, for we are also Spirit. Spirit, which sets us apart from the rest of creation. Spirit, which is life. Spirit, God in us. We are flesh, but we are also Spirit; both are gifts from a gracious Creator God.

The question then is not whether we will die in the flesh—we will, we know it all too well. In the best-case scenario, these bodies will wear out. The better question is how we will live. If we live as if we are solely flesh, life is indeed harsh and brief. We tend to neglect these bodies of ours and disregard the bodies of others. But when we acknowledge that we are also Spirit, then we recognize that we are also children of God. And if I am a child of God, then you are as well. In that cognizance, perhaps we can see one another for who we truly are. Only then can we truly live.

Creator God, we give you thanks for the gift of this life. Amen.

There is a striking intimacy in the language Paul uses to describe our relationship with God in this passage. Like a toddler running to greet his mother at the door, Paul imagines humanity reaching out to God, yearning to be embraced, cared for, and loved.

Human families are imperfect and complex, of course, but they provide an apt metaphor here. Families at their best—whether biologically formed or created by choice in any number of ways—create safe places where we are loved unconditionally, from which we can launch out into the world. Families provide us with a shared set of values that guide and sustain our lives.

So too do our faith families. We are children of God, Paul tells us, with a multitude of ancestors carrying on our tradition and handing it down to us.

From our human family, we inherit curly hair, a tendency for bad jokes, and a set of chipped china stored in the attic. From our ancestors in the faith, we inherit the stories of God's people, recorded in scripture and told throughout the ages. We inherit a peace that passes understanding, a love that knows no end, and a grace that knows no bounds. We learn from our ancestors, ancient and modern, a way of looking at the world, of living in the world that expresses our hope and our trust.

Time passes, and heirs eventually turn into descendants, which ought to make us wonder what we are passing on. What will our children inherit from us? Will we tell of the grace we've received? Will we assure them of an unbelievable hope? Will we pass on the promise that was passed on to us?

We are children of God, joint heirs with Christ, loved and accepted and welcomed home.

Everlasting God, we take our place in your family with gratitude for those who have gone before us, teaching us of your love. Amen.

We might be wise to muster up some compassion for poor Nicodemus who comes to Jesus under cover of darkness with questions that are too big for him to face in the light of day. To complicate matters, Nicodemus is a Pharisee, part of the group that opposes Jesus. He shouldn't be caught dead associating with the teacher from Galilee, but he can't seem to stay away.

The dark of night: isn't that when most of our toughest questions bubble to the surface? In the daylight, we go about the tasks of the day, burying our questions and our doubts in the chores of life. But when evening falls and the still of the night surrounds us, fear, anxiety, and doubt creep in. It is good then to have a place to turn with all our questions. Under cover of darkness, we turn to the one who calls himself the light of the world.

In the end, Nicodemus finds Jesus' answers less than satisfactory. He is right, of course. We can't be born—literally—a second time. But that's just the kind of misunderstanding that becomes so common when we try to fit the wonders of God into our understanding of how the world works. Entering into the kingdom of God—being born from above—means something else entirely. It means a new way of seeing the world, a new way of experiencing the world. It means trusting in the Spirit, in the wind that "blows where it chooses." It means looking for the light that always shines in the darkness.

Nicodemus goes looking for answers that fit a paradigm that doesn't work anymore. Maybe when we come to God in the dark of night, we had better be prepared for answers that don't make any sense but that offer us light to see the way ahead.

Holy God, thank you for listening to our questions and for being our light. Amen.

It is arguably one of the most famous passages in the scriptures: "For God so loved the world. . . . " We know it so well that fans at football games who want to remind the crowds of the good news refer to it simply by chapter and verse, 3:16. At one point or another, anyone who's ever been to Sunday school or Vacation Bible School has memorized these words. But memorizing words and living them out are two different things.

It's one thing to say that God loves the world. It's another to live as if we believe it to be true.

It's mind-boggling, when you think about it, that God could love the whole world. This whole sinful, broken, hurting world. This world where we all have different names for God, where we don't quite know how to speak to each other or understand each other. This world where we've let each other down and hurt each other in unimaginable ways. God loves *this world*? And yet, there it is, the heart of the gospel: "God so loved the world that he gave his only Son."

Perhaps those of us who confess to following Jesus Christ ought to do more than memorize these words. What if we lived as if we believed that the *world* is loved? What if we lived as if we believed that *we* are loved? Imagine how the world might change if each of us could see one another the way God sees us? Beautiful, beloved, precious, worthy of love and grace.

We can't quite comprehend what it means to love the whole world. Surely, we are mostly incapable of doing it ourselves. But we put our faith in the truth that this world is loved. This world, with all its brokenness is held dear by God, which is very good news indeed.

Almighty God, thank you for loving the world so much. Help us to be loving in return. Amen.

With Eyes of Faith

JUNE 1–7, 2015 • P. JOEL SNIDER

MONDAY, JUNE 1 ~ *Read 1 Samuel 8:4-9*

The elders of Israel paid no attention. When they said to Samuel, "Give us a king to govern us," they already had a king. The confrontation with Pharaoh in Egypt was a struggle between two kings, Pharaoh and Yahweh, to see which would possess the Israelites. The ark of the covenant symbolized God's leadership as a conquering king at the head of an armed column as it led them into the Promised Land. Moses, Joshua, Samuel represented God to the people, but no one ever called them kings or rulers because Israel had only one king: the Lord. Therefore when the people ask Samuel to appoint a king over them, their request displeases God because the leaders and the people have missed the point of their relationship. God tells Samuel, "They have rejected me as their king" (NIV).

The Israelites fail to see that, although God's presence is invisible, God's sovereignty extends to every corner of life. Their request for a king to make them like the nations is no different than our desire for practical solutions to daily problems. The Israelites do not think God is the best king for the real world of wars and alliances. We think Jesus fails to offer realistic help in our work, school, finances, politics. Which of us takes seriously Jesus' command to give to whoever asks and to turn the other cheek to repeated offenses?

God's leadership, then and now, applies to the real world. To say "Jesus is Lord" has consequences for every area of our lives. Faith is trusting and obeying God's will, even when the world's ways seem more appealing.

O God, teach me today to follow your ways. Give me strength to obey, even when other ways seem more practical. Amen.

Pastor, First Baptist Church, Rome, Georgia

The Lord's reaction to the elders' request for a king is not petty jealousy. God foresees the sorrow that the people will bring on themselves with this appeal. Thus, God instructs Samuel to make sure they understand how differently earthly leaders will treat them. God provided manna in the wilderness, but kings will demand their children to plow royal soil, reap royal harvests, and bake royal bread. God went before the Israelites as a pillar of smoke and fire, but kings will draft their children to run before their war chariots. God asks for offerings, but kings will tax everything. God's heart breaks over the poor choice the people have made.

Is this what the people desire: to exchange God's selfless love for the self-serving desires of kings? God's sad response is like a love song in which the jilted lover sings, "Who will love you better than I?" When we give our highest love to something less than God, we break God's heart because of the cost to us.

How could the Israelites—how could we—be so blind? No other rulers we serve will ever love us. They only take from us and offer empty promises. Materialism, with all its assurance of happiness, enslaves us to work for more things. Promiscuity provides only joyless pleasure. Power intoxicates but also proves addictive. Which of us ever gets enough to keep the high going? All are insensitive, demanding masters that never deliver on their promises.

Of all the rulers we can choose, only God loves us. Only God gives us what we genuinely need. Only God works for our good in all things and delivers on promises. In the promises of God we find forgiveness, the peace that passes understanding, hope, and true joy. Why would we serve anyone—anything—else?

Dear God, help me to see your love for me. Accept my loving gratitude in return. Amen.

Why does the psalmist praise God? Is it for deliverance from physical illness, or has the entire worshiping community emerged from a trial of patience or faith? All we know is the psalmist cries out and God strengthens him and delivers him.

God's rescue of the psalmist seems even more significant because of the writer's self-perception as being unworthy of God's help: "Though the LORD is exalted, he looks kindly on the lowly" (NIV). We expect the opposite. The wealthy and powerful get all the help they need. It is the billionaire's muscle and not the widow's mite that attracts assistance. Thus, in an unfolding surprise, God has not only answered the psalmist's prayer but answered a prayer for one who is unworthy. As a result of this unexpected and undeserved deliverance, the psalmist offers praise and sees God's works clearly enough to assume the whole world will someday praise God.

Praise. It is such a common word in the prayers, songs, and hymns of congregations today. What does it mean, however, to praise God? Try to explain praise to a person without a church background.

Praise differs from thanksgiving, which is offered for a specific reason or a particular gift. Praise does not depend on any single deed or gift of God. It is a prayer, chorus, or hymn directed to God out of endless wonder from our endless discovery of who God is. Praise goes beyond thanksgiving to express our amazement at God's concern for us that exceeds our expectation, merit, or imagination. Thus, praising God begins in surprise. God provides more. God is more than we had hoped or dared to imagine. We join the psalmist with a vision of a world that will someday understand—and offer praise as well.

Offer a prayer of praise today for God's surprising goodness in your life.

Who ever accused Jesus of minimizing the possibility of forgiveness? Jesus ate with tax collectors, made harlots the positive point of his illustrations, and accepted foreigners. Jesus offered forgiveness to all. So when Jesus says someone can never have forgiveness, we need to sit up and pay attention. Why does he put any category of sin beyond the reach of God's mercy?

Many have described this passage as "The Unforgivable Sin." The issue, however, is not the unforgivable sin but the irreconcilable sinner. The exact language is important. Jesus does not say God refuses to forgive anyone. He says whoever blasphemes against the Holy Spirit can't receive forgiveness. The problem lies with the individual, not with God, whose readiness to forgive never changes. Individuals must meet God's readiness to forgive by admitting their sin, their need for grace.

In this passage, the religious leaders cannot admit that God's love is at work in Jesus. Instead they describe Jesus' ministry as satanic. Thus, Jesus' reference to blasphemy against the Holy Spirit is not about God's intransigence but about the individual's obstinate refusal to recognize a need for repentance. No matter how much God wants to reconcile with a sinner by offering forgiveness, a heart that ascribes an evil motivation to Jesus' work cannot receive forgiveness because it sees no need to repent.

None of us would say Jesus is allied with Satan. That type of blasphemy poses little danger for us. Yet, don't we at times justify un-Christian actions and thus reject the possibility we need forgiveness? When we justify our refusal to forgive others because "they don't deserve it," we are closet blasphemers who refuse God's forgiveness whenever we uphold our sin as righteousness.

Dear God, help me to see the sins I have justified in my own heart—and to turn to you in repentance. Amen.

The greeting card section in the grocery store now has a category called the "simply stated" card. You send these greeting cards to relatives you find hard to love. Here we find the perfect birthday card for the brother who hasn't been home in years or the Mother's Day card for your father's second wife. The simply stated card serves as the perfect reminder that we don't live in perfect families.

The earliest Christians were a misunderstood group, often estranged from family and friends as a result of following Jesus. The choice of following Jesus meant leaving behind the people they once shared homes with. As Jesus promised elsewhere, living for him often means giving up former ties.

Thus, Mark's Gospel includes this story of Jesus' estrangement from his own family. The story begins with Jesus' family attempting to restrain him because people are saying that he's crazy. Mark then inserts the Beelzebub controversy in order to emphasize the idea of division. Next, Mark returns to Jesus' family who comes to take him home with the charge that he is beside himself. The story closes when Jesus claims his followers as his new family. The message to Christians under persecution: If leaders and family misunderstand Jesus, don't be surprised if religious leaders and your family misunderstand you. Do not lose hope, the story implies, because Jesus has claimed you as his new family.

Many of us may find it hard to imagine church or any Christian fellowship being stronger, healthier, and more life-giving than our families of origin. But in certain situations, Christian fellowship sustains life, faith, and hope for Christians who are ignored, unloved, or persecuted—even at home. For many Christians, the water of baptism is thicker than the blood of family.

Pray for Christians persecuted by family and neighbors. Pray that Jesus' true family will sustain them today. Amen.

Christians in Corinth live privileged lives. Elsewhere in the Roman Empire, believers find themselves persecuted, but Corinthian Christians have the time and freedom to argue about spiritual gifts (1 Cor. 12). Consequently, members of the Corinthian church cannot relate to Paul's suffering for the gospel. Because Paul's life does not demonstrate the same kind of material blessing they know, the Corinthians wonder if he is a true apostle.

Paul refers to Psalm 116, a psalm of deliverance. The actual quote is, "I trusted in the LORD when I said, 'I am greatly afflicted'" (v. 10, NIV). The Corinthian Christians think faithfulness and affliction are mutually exclusive, but Paul refers to the psalm to show that the heritage of trusting God in the midst of suffering is a long one. He adds, "We know that the one who raised Jesus from the dead will also raise us with Jesus and present us with you to himself" (v. 14, NIV) to tell the Corinthians that while they may not share common past experiences, they do share a common future in Christ.

We often project our own experiences on others. One Christian who speaks in tongues may think all Christians should speak in tongues. A wealthy Christian may acknowledge financial success as the most recognizable sign of God's blessing, considering the poor "unblessed."

Our experiences and circumstances as Christians differ. Outwardly, some believers may seem more blessed than others. We need not, however, judge another's present circumstances nor require them to have our experiences in order to accept them. The family of God is richer thanks to its variety. Many paths of faith experience will join and surprise us as to who is joining us in Christ's presence.

Pray today for someone whose faith heritage differs from yours, and give thanks for that individual's presence in the family of God.

These verses often provide comfort at a funeral for a person whose death was accompanied by suffering or the ravages of aging. Paul's words bring consolation to many experiencing grief: "If the earthly tent we live in is destroyed, we have a building from God, an eternal house in heaven, not built by human hands" (NIV).

The message of comfort following a death, however, is only half of this passage's proclamation. The reminder about the unseen and the eternal applies to every day we walk with Jesus. We follow Christ because we believe what was visible at the cross was temporary. Those who shouted to Jesus, "Save yourself" could not see God's eternal purposes. Death did not have the last word. Therefore, the dividing line between faith and unbelief hinges on the conviction that God was doing more in Christ than we could see at Calvary. Jesus' death, though visible, was temporary. In the invisible mystery of Jesus' death, God worked an eternal purpose.

Paul's life continued a witness to the same principle. He endured imprisonment and hardship because he believed his experiences were temporary. He staked his life on the conviction that his own famine and peril, while temporary, contributed to eternal consequences. The Corinthians enjoyed lives without burdens or hardships.

The suffering that precedes many deaths is transitory. It will pass and the joy of eternity with God looms past our forevers. But materialism is transitory as well. Its benefits are short and meaningless compared to past arguments and social slights that still engender bitterness in our memories. The temporal concerns of life are always before us. We only perceive the eternal matters when we see through eyes of faith.

O God of eternity, help me see your eternal purpose in all the circumstances of my living. Amen.

A Time to See

JUNE 8–14, 2015 • HARRELL NATION JR.

MONDAY, JUNE 8 ~ *Read Psalm 20*

The reason many people leave the Christian faith after a brief sojourn is "unanswered" prayer. I take this to mean when a person discovers that God is not Santa Claus, he or she can't find reason to remain within the fellowship of the church.

I don't believe in unanswered prayer. I believe every prayer we pray receives an answer in one of three ways: yes, no, we'll see. We have to understand and accept the fact that no is a valid answer. We also need to understand that often the thing we need most is no thing.

The psalmist gives voice to a prayer for those intangible things. Things like presence, peace, hope, assurance. These are the things that get us through those dark valleys and hard times, because these things we hold in our hearts. And these things hold our hearts; they keep us from falling into discouragement and despair.

Every prayer receives an answer. When the answer doesn't come for those things we can hold in our hands, we can count on God's being present in our heart.

Father, help me see and believe that your no will serve me better than a yes for what I want. Help me trust when I can't see the answer to my prayer. Amen.

District Superintendent, Brownsville District, The United Methodist Church, Brownsville, Tennessee

Philip joined my congregation for worship one Sunday. I don't know his last name because he didn't choose to share that with us. Nor did he choose to tell us where he came from and was ultimately heading. We only knew he wanted to get from our town to a town about twenty miles away.

A few congregants felt somewhat uneasy about the large duffel bag he lugged with him. Philip was traveling with everything he owned, and he wanted to keep it close. In order to make people more at ease, the staff assured him that we would protect his bag until the service concluded. We deposited his bag in the narthex while Philip deposited himself on the second pew and joined the worship service. Worship wasn't new to Philip. You could tell that by the way he sang—not with his voice—with his hands. Philip couldn't speak; he signed the songs.

Many people would consider Philip to be a homeless person. But on that Sunday morning, Philip was at home in our church. During the time of informal greeting many people recovered from their fear and made their way over to greet and welcome him. God moved mightily in that service of worship when the worshipers were able to move beyond Philip's appearance.

We humans place a great value on outward appearance. Samuel falls into that trap when God desires a change in leadership. Saul can no longer provide the direction God wants for the people. God sends Samuel to anoint a new king for Israel. Samuel goes, seeking the "look."

Instead Samuel meets a God who says, "Do not look on his appearance or the height of his stature, because I have rejected him [referring to Eliab]; for the LORD does not see as mortals see; they look on the outward appearance, but the LORD looks on the heart."

Lord, remind us that what we see isn't always what we get because what we can't always see is a person's heart. Help us see with your eyes. Amen.

I will always remember my first sermon at my first church. It went far better than I expected. I didn't pass out; the members didn't go clamoring to my supervisor demanding that something be done about the incompetence standing before them. They wouldn't have been wrong. That's why I was afraid of passing out in fear. I remember finishing up that sermon, having had about a month to worry about and work on it. I remembered breathing a sigh of relief until the truth walked right up and kicked me so hard I couldn't breathe. Truth said, "You have one week to get ready to do this again—and every week from now on." At that point, my fear was much larger than my faith. My doubts were more numerous than my certainties.

The next week came and went, and on and on. Grace had brought me this far, and grace would lead me on.

This God who looks on the heart does not necessarily call the qualified; this God qualifies those who are called. This God who looks on the heart doesn't focus on what we are but rather on what we can become through the presence and power of the Holy Spirit.

David didn't look like the future king of Israel. He didn't have the skill set needed to fill the role. He didn't have the age or the maturity needed to govern the people of Israel.

None of these aspects stands in the way of God's choice of David. Once we come to terms with this God who looks on the heart, we will be able to see others more clearly. We will be able to look beyond their stature, their limitations, their strengths and weaknesses. We will be able to see what the Spirit of God can do in and through a person who responds to God's call.

Lord, as we look upon our weakness, may we look to you for strength. Grant us eyes to see not only what is but what can be because of your presence and power. Amen.

I am a word collector. I like big words and little words. I like words rich in texture and heavy on the tongue. I like words that float from the lips without a care in the world. I like words that tangle the tongue. I enjoy seeing words strung together to make a powerful point or even a pointless observation.

A large part of what I do as a pastor is rummage around in my word collection and string them together to be heard or read. Words, whether we like it or not, have a powerful impact on our lives. Words can hurt or heal. They can point us in the right direction or remind us of what the point is.

The proper ordering of words serves an important function. Let me give you an example. Paul says, "We walk by faith, not by sight." These words are rich in texture, deep in meaning. If we listen carefully, we can hear the shoe soles scraping on the pavement during this walk. Sometimes the steps seem halting, hesitant, unsure. We can't see far enough ahead to put one foot in front of the other. Sometimes silence comes as we stop altogether when fear halts our movement. Sometimes we skip along with joy and excitement.

When we change the ordering of these words, we get something like this: "We walk by sight, not by faith." Honestly, wouldn't we all feel better if this were the case? Wouldn't we find this walk much easier if we could see the end of the journey, along with the numerous problems along the way?

An oft-quoted line goes like this, "The opposite of faith isn't doubt, it's certainty." In our heads we know this to be true, but in our hearts we often want certainty. Yet walking by faith is not a blind leap. Nor is it walking in the dark. We aren't walking by *what* we see ahead, to be sure. But we are walking by *who* we see ahead, Jesus the Christ. He promises never to leave us or forsake us. Keep walking.

Father, as we walk through the darkness that life sends our way, grant us the courage to walk by faith, not in fear. Amen.

I've been accused of being liberal. I am. I've been said to be conservative. Guilty. Evangelical, Pentecostal, charismatic. Yes, yes, and yes. It has been said that I am a bundle of contradictions, eccentric, and one bubble past plumb. (Or three fries short of a happy meal, or the light is on but no one is home—you choose.) Yes, yes, and probably.

If you wonder how I believe I fit all of these descriptions, it's easy. I am simply reporting how other people see me. They are probably saying the same thing about you as well. Truth is, we can't change the way other people see us. Other persons' perceptions of us shape their reality. What amazes me is how often what they see and hear from us does not even vaguely resemble what we see or hear when we look at ourselves.

I have a mirror that I look into on a daily basis to see myself and to find the words I want others to hear from me. That mirror is the Bible. When I look into it, I see not only what is but what is possible. I see not only what has been but what is to be. I see myself as God sees me. I find it a humbling experience to be sure. But it puts joy in my life, bounce in my step, and a smile on my face.

Because this is what I see: "So if anyone is in Christ, there is a new creation: everything old has passed away; see, everything has become new!" This new creation, of course, is not the face I see in the mirror nor the perception others may have. It is the life I live as I follow Jesus the Christ. This new creation that I am allows me to pray with confidence, serve with enthusiasm, worship with abandon, and live like it doesn't matter what each day may hold, because I know who holds the day.

This new creation that I am helps me realize that I may never fully understand what Christ sees in me. But in him I see home.

I am a new creation. Wow! It doesn't really matter how you see me, or how I see me, as long as I see Christ in me.

Someone once asked me, "Which of Jesus' parables is the most important?" After recovering from my deer-in-the-headlights look, I proceeded to say, "I don't know." Really, how can you go about ranking parables according to importance? Jesus told parables for various reasons, but they all have one quality in common: They provide a different perspective on reality. They invite participation because their truth is not cut and dried. I believe every parable Jesus told was intended both to shock and to inspire those who heard it.

These two parables contain an element of mystery. With all our knowledge about horticulture, at the end of the day we don't know much about life except that it is a mystery. We see the results of seeds planted and the harvesting of grain. We see the signs of life, but life itself is beyond our seeing.

The shocking aspect of these parables comes in the fact that God's kingdom has no thrones or dominions—not even one street of gold or a wall of jasper. We have no temple or church, no preacher or priest. The only sign of holiness is life itself. Perhaps that is where the holiness resides. Perhaps in this way the kingdom of God will be manifest through our lives as we bear fruit for the purpose of God's reign.

These parables also signal that the kingdom God plants belongs to God, not us. It is not under our control or power. We simply participate. Every farmer plants the seed with hope and patience, knowing that time, sun, water are needed to nourish the life that the farmer has planted. God knows that the kingdom seeds of creation will require time, patience, and nourishment from the word for the kingdom to grow. But grow it will, because it is God's. Grow it will.

Father, my impatience often causes me to run ahead, to attempt to rush the seasons along. Teach me, I pray, to watch with patience your growing kingdom. Amen.

"Can you prove beyond the shadow of a doubt that God exists?" someone once asked me. I immediately answered "No!" "Then why do you believe?" he inquired.

So why do I believe? My answer then and now is simply this: life. Life itself directs me toward God and gives me reason to believe. We humans know the exact chemical makeup of various seeds. We can manufacture an exact replica. We can place them side by side and not tell the difference.

With the planting of the seeds, the difference becomes obvious. Human-made seeds will simply melt away, leaving no trace of their existence. When we plant one of God's seeds, it sprouts, the roots go down, the plant goes up, it produces fruit. It has that tremendous mystery within; it has life.

Life is the mystery that points to God's existence. Life is the mystery that signals the existence of God's kingdom. Jesus wants us to see with the eyes of faith that this kingdom God has planted is growing. Growing! The seed of this kingdom is Jesus the Christ. The life, teaching, death, and resurrection of Jesus Christ comprise the life of this kingdom.

Christ in us, working through us, is the ongoing sign of kingdom life. When the hungry are fed, the naked are clothed; when persons accept Jesus into their hearts and decide to accept the challenge, "Follow me," the kingdom of God is alive. We Christians see the signs of life and growth and point them out for others to see. Then we celebrate this life through worship.

This world, in spite of the naysayers, is heading toward the vision described in Revelation 21, not to hell in a handbasket. "Then I saw a new heaven and a new earth; for the first heaven and the first earth had passed away, and the sea was no more" (Rev 21:1). Life goes on.

Lord, I stand in awe at the sheer mystery of life. The heavens indeed declare your presence, but a growing seed shouts, "Life!" Amen.

God's Anti-bullying Campaign

JUNE 15–21, 2015 • MICHAEL W. WATERS

MONDAY, JUNE 15 ~ *Read 1 Samuel 17:1a*

Undoubtedly, the Philistines intend to cause Israel great harm. Yes, war stirs on the horizon. The Philistines know that the opportunity to secure victory lies in assembling the largest number for battle. Israel has to view this gathering of the Philistines as disturbing. Knowing that your enemy—the greatest threat against your present well-being and your future existence—is gathering its total military force to do battle with you is a troubling proposition. Indeed, the very thought of warfare can often breed intimidation. Surely Israel faces this sobering reality as fear permeates its army's ranks.

Intimidation is a ready tool of a bully. When skillfully employed, intimidation can result in a concession of defeat before the battle has even begun. When we witness our own bullies—familiar troubles and obstacles, known heartaches and setbacks—as they begin to "gather" against us in full force, we too can feel intimidated, fearful, and discouraged about our final outcome. If we are not careful, we will give up and pronounce our certain defeat before any weapon "is fashioned against [us]" (Isa. 54:17).

Life happens, and sometimes as life happens and challenges gather, we face intimidating prospects. We can either concede defeat to bullying circumstances, or we can prepare ourselves for battle by relying on our great Defender.

God, when bullying circumstances gather against me, help me not to succumb to intimidation and concede defeat but to trust you to take care of me. Amen.

Founding pastor, Joy Tabernacle A.M.E. Church, Dallas, Texas; named among the top young leaders in America by *EBONY* magazine; author of *Freestyle: Reflections on Faith, Family, Justice, and Pop Culture* (Fresh Air Books, 2014)

We would be hard-pressed to find a bigger bully than Goliath of Gath. Literally. Goliath stood nine feet tall. The measurements encompassing his body armor and his weaponry alone are at once impressive and intimidating. Daily, Goliath bullies Israel's army, hurling insults, challenging whomever Israel selects as its warrior to fight him to the death between the camps of the Israelites and the Philistines. And daily, to these bullying insults and intimidation tactics, Saul, king of Israel, and the entire army of Israel cower in fear.

Note, however, that for all of Goliath's posturing, his proposal has effectively reduced a war between two armies to hand-to-hand combat between two warriors. His proposition for the terms of war completely changes the dynamics of the warfare. Maybe the Philistines question their ability to emerge victorious in battle with Israel's army, an army historically known to accomplish seemingly supernatural feats on the battlefield.

Goliath's manipulation of the terms of war and his use of reverse psychology work. Instead of seeing itself as a mighty army that has previously fought and won countless battles, Israel begins to see itself as individual soldiers who internalize the threats of a bully, leaving them trembling in fear. This same reverse psychology often appears effective when employed against the church today. Instead of facing our giants together as a body of believers bound together by faith in a faithful God, far too often we seek to face our spiritual bullies alone and seemingly on the bullies' terms. In so doing, we allow fear and intimidation to overcome us. This fear and intimidation often veil from our sight what our bullies see so clearly: They are no match for us if we stand together in faith.

God, help us not become dismayed at the boasts or size of our bullies but band together as the body of Christ to claim victory together. Amen.

A certain irony emerges in Jesse's instruction to his young-est son, David. Jesse informs David that his brothers are engaged in battle with the Philistine army. Nothing could have been further from reality.

David's brothers and the entire army of Israel stand posi-tioned for battle, but no swords had been unsheathed, nor bows drawn. Israel's camp is paralyzed by fear, bullied by the giant Goliath. When David arrives at camp, instead of finding a band of warriors engaged in military action, he finds an army postur-ing and performing as if it *intends* to do battle.

The Israelites line up for battle and lift a war cry. But in the end, they do not fight; the soldiers daily bow their heads to the giant's threats. David goes to the front expecting a fight. There, he encounters Goliath for the first time. David, hearing the bully's threats firsthand, shows no fear but remains undeterred.

Families and faith communities that have been bullied by difficulty and tragedy often resign themselves to posturing and performing rather than healing and progressing. Their actions and words may appear progressive, but careful analysis reveals that they are a part of a "stuck" family system.

Immersion in a stuck family system for too long encourages us to accept posturing and performing as a way of life and to mistake the passing of time as healing and progress. We accept dysfunction as the norm and resign ourselves to this paralyzed state. Those moments require fresh insight and new perspective to address our bullying troubles.

Goliath, defiant as always, makes the same threats he always made. Yet David holds fresh insight and a new perspective on Israel's bully that leads to Israel's victory, the Philistines' defeat, and an end to the fear and intimidation that crippled Israel.

God, grant us fresh insights and new perspectives to face proac-tively the bullying circumstances of our day. Amen.

In recent years, bullying has emerged as one of our nation's leading social issues. Bullying has raged from grade-school playgrounds and professional sports locker rooms to the ever-growing cyber landscapes of social media. We witness the negative impact of bullying in mass shootings and suicides resulting from victims breaking under the pressure of the relentless bullying they have experienced. In response, anti-bullying campaigns have been launched to ensure that all people feel free to live, learn, work, and grow without fear or intimidation.

Goliath relentlessly bullies Israel and, in this passage, David too. He belittles David by calling him a stick, suggesting that David's life is of no consequence. He threatens to kill David and to feed his flesh to the birds and the wild animals. Goliath curses David in the name of his gods and moves to attack him in the valley. Without question, Goliath is a bully.

This passage reveals another instance of bullying that we can easily overlook. King Saul emerges here as a bully, though his bullying is more subtle. He dresses David in his own armor, attempting to force David to embody something he is not. Saul's actions indirectly suggest that David is not good enough to walk in his calling on his own merits.

Bullying circumstances can pressure us by suggesting that who we are is not good enough, and they try to make us become something we are not to gain acceptance. If we yield to these pressures, we may never accept the person God has made us to be. We may fail to see how God has already equipped us with what we need to accomplish God's special work.

God, help me to love myself as you have made me and never succumb to the pressure to be something I am not. Amen.

Juneteenth is an important African American cultural holiday celebrated annually on June 19. It commemorates the day in 1865 when notice of the signing of the Emancipation Proclamation granting freedom to slaves in the states "in rebellion" finally reached Texas, over two years after it was signed by President Abraham Lincoln. In essence, Texas slaves were the last to know that they were free, and Juneteenth is celebrated as the official end of slavery in America. For Juneteenth, communities often gather together at public parks for cookouts and cultural presentations with celebrations now being held throughout the country and across the world. Juneteenth is a celebration of freedom!

However, Juneteenth is also a day of reflection. Many people pause to reflect upon the struggles of our ancestors during the horrible days of slavery. Our ancestors' deep and abiding faith in God's knowledge of their struggles and belief that God heard their earnest prayers gave them not only the strength to endure but the hope that one day they would be liberated from the hands of their bullying oppressors.

This deep and abiding faith finds unity with the words of the psalmist. Like our ancestors, the psalmist acknowledges his own suffering. He invites God to bear witness to his suffering at the hands of those who hate him. God emerges as a powerful stronghold, a place of refuge for the bullied and for the oppressed—a place of safety and security, especially in times of trouble.

The psalmist, like my African American ancestors, believes that God will bring judgment upon anyone who bullies and oppresses God's people and that ultimately God will bring deliverance for all people who place their trust in their Creator.

God, hear the prayers of those who long for freedom, and empower me to join you in your liberation of the bullied and oppressed people of this world. Amen.

For millennia, Christians have been bullied and persecuted. From execution by wild beasts in the Roman Coliseum to present-day sufferings in such places as Egypt, China, and India, many have suffered greatly for the faith.

In this passage, we read the words of the first noted bully of the Christian church. Saul zealously persecuted the church. He callously held the coats of those who stoned Stephen, a martyr for the faith. A supernatural encounter with the risen Christ, wherein Christ asked Saul why he was bullying or persecuting him, forever changed the trajectory of Saul's life. Saul emerged from this encounter with a new purpose. No longer would he bully Jesus and the church; he will now serve Christ and the church! Later on, he would be known as Paul.

However, Paul's new purpose means that the persecutor becomes the persecuted. As Paul journeys to share the gospel, he and those with him encounter opposition and endure gruesome bullying. Their experiences include beatings, imprisonments, hunger, and sleepless nights. They include being shunned, isolated, ignored, and lied about.

But Paul does not dwell exclusively on the bullying. He calls the Corinthians to reconciliation with God, a reconciliation that God initiates: "Now is the day of salvation!" And Paul invites a reconciliation between himself as apostle and the Corinthians: "Our heart is wide open to you." Despite his bullied existence, Paul never loses sight of his purpose and calling.

Though he has been beaten, Paul acknowledges that he has not been killed. Although gripped by poverty, Paul acknowledges that he is rich in God. And though bullied, Paul remains a servant of God!

God, bless those who are bullied and persecuted for your name's sake, and grant them peace in the midst of their struggles. Amen.

Jesus had invited his disciples on a nighttime voyage when, suddenly, a major storm arose, troubling the waters. Their vessel seemed ill-equipped for the task at hand as water began to fill the boat.

Consumed with fear, the disciples consider how to preserve their lives. Their eyes fall upon Jesus, who, to their amazement, is fast asleep. Surely the disciples ponder, *How can Jesus sleep at a time like this? We are about to die!* The disciples waken Jesus with these shocking and accusatory words: "Teacher, do you not care that we are perishing?"

The sudden and unanticipated storm bullied the disciples. At times, we too feel bullied by sudden storms, those challenges and difficulties that unexpectedly come upon us and cause us to struggle to keep our heads above water. For Jesus' disciples and sometimes for us, all hope seems lost. And sometimes Jesus, the one person we believe has the power to save us from our bullying circumstances, seems unaware or disinterested in resolving our difficulties.

But once awake, Jesus rebukes the wind and speaks to the sea, "Peace! Be still!" The wind ceases, the waters calm, yet Jesus continues in his rebuke—this time of his disciples. "Why are you afraid? Have you still no faith?"

Sometimes, we allow fear to displace faith. In our panic, we forget that Jesus is with us and that Jesus has the power to calm our sudden and bullying storms. The writer of First John reminds us that there is no fear in love. Perhaps the same is true of faith.

God, strengthen my faith to trust you in the midst of my storms.
Lead me to use my faith to overcome my fears. Amen.

Healing and Salvation

JUNE 22–28, 2015 • TAYLOR W. MILLS

MONDAY, JUNE 22 ~ *Read 2 Samuel 1:1, 17-27*

Something about the death of a special friend or relative stirs in us a desire to "say something" in the person's memory. It's as if death evokes a verbal response from us on a foundational level. So when I meet with a family to prepare a funeral or memorial service, I ask the members if anyone will want to give a eulogy following the homily that I will preach.

The deaths of Jonathan and Saul so move David that he sets forth guidelines. The Israelites are not to mention their deaths in the hearing of the enemy. No refreshing dew or rain will fall on the mountains; no oil will anoint Saul's shield any longer. It will sit and rust.

Contrast David's words with psalms of lament in the Bible. Often these psalms, while expressing a profound sadness, invoke God to act, deliver, forgive, or heal. David seems resigned to the fact that God can do nothing. David has not lost faith in God, but perhaps David's abiding trust in God assures him that he can pour out his grief.

Just as there is an appropriateness to reverent silence in the face of death, there is also a natural desire to "say something" when someone dies. I know someone who writes letters to his deceased father and keeps them in a notebook. Others might speak aloud when they visit a burial site, even if they are alone. In such ways the grieving stand in solidarity with our prolific poet David who helps us put words to our grief.

Author of Life, sometimes words are all we have in our grief. Yet it is through words, even words of profound sadness, that we can feel your caring love. Where we need silence, grant us silence; but when we need words, give us words. Amen.

Pastor, Trinity United Methodist Church, Durham, North Carolina

Sigmund Freud, the founding father of psychoanalysis, gave us revolutionary insights into the role of our parents in human development. He seemed surprised at how much his own father's death affected him. After Jacob Freud died in 1896, Sigmund wrote, "The old man's death has affected me profoundly. . . . With his peculiar mixture of deep wisdom and fantastic lightheartedness, he had a significant effect on my life. . . . I now feel quite uprooted." In a 1908 preface to *The Interpretation of Dreams,* Freud wrote that the death of a father is "the most important event, the most poignant loss, of a man's life."

No one had to explain this to David. Saul was both David's father-in-law and a strong father-figure in his life. Now both Saul and David's best friend, Jonathan, lay dead. Let's be honest: Saul would not have qualified for a "World's Best Dad" mug on Father's Day. He did not offer a strong father-figure role model by any stretch of the imagination. Yet David seems beside himself with grief. So, like many eulogies, this one focuses more on the positive aspects of the deceased.

David laments not only for himself but on behalf of the nation. He gives his people tools to get through the necessary process of grieving. The boy who slew the giant Philistine is now the vulnerable poet who will be king.

Our contemporary culture offers few opportunities to mourn publicly the deaths of those we love. A certain awkwardness accompanies a mourner who returns to work and suddenly breaks down in tears because she is reminded of the recent passing of her mother. It takes a prolific poet with a rare gift like David's to communicate the sad songs of our hearts when "the mighty have fallen."

God in triune love, we thank you for David's heart-song that gives lyrics to the grief we all experience. Give us his courage to name our griefs before you in the company of your people and thereby find your Spirit of comfort in our worship. Amen.

O ut of the depths I cry to you, O LORD. Lord, hear my voice!" Psalm 130 holds a prominent place in the Penitential Psalms (Psalms 6; 32; 38; 51; 102; 130; 143). Why would a text with such a somber tone evoke a popular response? Because we all relate to these feelings. We have all felt some deep sadness. Many of us have experienced clinical depression. We have experienced an emotional chasm so deep that we wondered, like Jesus did when he quoted from Psalm 22, "My God, my God, why have you forsaken me?"

Though not all stigma is gone, I find it refreshing to see that the contemporary church is getting better at recognizing that faithful Christians may experience depression from time to time. To experience and relate to the psalmist's feelings does not indicate spiritual failure. Great heroes of the Bible experienced mental anguish, including Jesus whose sweat fell like drops of blood before his arrest. Saints and leaders in church history left behind journals that show that many of them struggled with depression.

When people who seem to be struggling with depression approach me as a pastor, I always insist that they see their doctor and a mental health professional. But I also assure them that their depression does not represent a failure on their part as a Christian. It certainly does not anger God who, through Jesus, knows our human experience.

I will also read some psalms with them if they find it helpful. They usually take some comfort in knowing that the Bible puts words to our profound feelings. Often the psalmists give voice to their faith in the midst of their depression. Psalm 130 closes with the reminder: "O Israel, hope in the LORD! For with the LORD there is steadfast love, and with him is great power to redeem." May it be so for us.

Comforting God, assure us that you know our every thought and feeling. Meet us in the depths of sorrow. Heal those, we pray, who suffer with depression today. Amen.

Religious books with a self-help theme sell better than other kinds of religious books. People who visit the religion section are looking for the same thing they would look for in the self-help section: advice. However, Jesus did not preach self-help or how to have "your best life now." He did not try to fill people with positive thinking and mantras.

Jesus' teaching and preaching had more to do with "self-emptying." Self-emptying involves the practice of giving ourselves away just as Jesus gave himself for our sakes. We decrease so that Jesus might increase.

Paul picks up on Jesus' self-emptying and writes about the concept several times in his epistles. Today's text refers to Jesus' example. Paul reminds the Corinthian Christians of "the generous act of our Lord Jesus Christ, that though he was rich, yet for your sakes he became poor, so that by his poverty you might become rich."

Paul is right. Jesus gave freely of his wisdom, his healing power, and his very life. Now we have his example to follow. Today we can, by the grace of God, commit to a life marked by self-emptying because Jesus showed us how to do it. We will take his example over anyone else's advice any day.

Giving God,
"I am no longer my own, but thine.
Put me to what thou wilt, rank me with whom thou wilt.
Put me to doing, put me to suffering.
Let me be employed by thee or laid aside for thee,
exalted for thee or brought low by thee.
Let me be full, let me be empty.
Let me have all things, let me have nothing." *Amen.*

*Excerpt from "A Covenant Prayer in the Wesleyan Tradition"

Paul advises the church members at Corinth to finish what they have started. Specifically, he wants them to complete a financial pledge they have made to support poorer Christians, probably in Jerusalem. It would seem that Paul has a network of churches contributing to a Jerusalem urban ministry fund.

This early Christian practice is one that most churches continue today: participating in shared ministry endeavors by sending some offerings beyond the local faith community. Together they accomplish more than any one church could do alone.

And Paul explains the ethic at work here: The Corinthian Christians have a "present abundance" and can help those in need. Should they find themselves in need, others will help them—a reciprocal effort. Perhaps Paul sees that those in financial need often have an abundance of their own to offer—maybe not money but other blessings like trust and thankfulness.

Whenever my family went to visit my grandmother in central North Carolina, we would go to her church on Sunday. In the entrance to the sanctuary, I would pass a wooden model of a church building. It had a slot in the roof where worshipers could slip in a few dollar bills. The church treasurer would collect the money from this box and send it to mission projects that focused on the care of children.

Many years later I found out that in the 1970s my grandmother had commissioned my mother to make the box, paint it like a church, and (with the church's blessing) put it by the entrance door. This simple box offered the congregation a way to give beyond the local community. It still stands there today.

Generous God, always more ready to give than we are to receive, please accept our offerings for those beyond our church walls. Bind us together in shared ministry. Amen.

My favorite physician's assistant knows me by name and listens to me carefully whenever I come in. One time, however, he wasn't available. I saw a new assistant who burst into the exam room without even a courtesy knock. She didn't look me in the eye or shake my hand or introduce herself. Her first words to me were, "What do you need?"

I introduced myself and extended my hand. "Oh," she said with a limp handshake. A few moments later, she wrote me a prescription but didn't tell me anything about what to expect. Consequently, I had to ask more questions. With each question she seemed increasingly annoyed. Though my bronchitis was eventually cured, I didn't experience any real "healing."

Healing brings wholeness instead of brokenness—life instead of death. In New Testament Greek, the word *sozo* is the same word for both *heal* and *save*. The first-century mind intertwined the concepts of healing and salvation.

So when Jesus gets off the boat to head toward Nazareth, no sooner does he set foot on land than a huge crowd gathers around him. He feels power leave him and realizes that someone has touched his cloak. The woman sick with hemorrhages has touched his cloak and been healed. Hers is not just a physical problem; she is considered ritually impure. So by touching Jesus' cloak, she makes him unclean too!

Jesus asks, "Who touched my clothes?" He receives this vulnerable woman warmly, calls her "daughter," and sends her on her way with a beautiful blessing: "Your faith has made you well; go in peace, and be healed of your disease." This is more than good bedside manner. This is Jesus' power of *sozo* to heal and to save. Jesus' nature still brings healing and salvation wherever his Spirit moves.

Great Physician, thank you for the healing you bring! Receive us with kindness when we approach you in need. Amen.

Jesus has been very busy in Mark's Gospel lately. After calming the wind and the waves, he crosses over the sea to the country of the Gerasenes where a demon-possessed man begs Jesus to heal him. Jesus casts out the man's demon. Those in the neighborhood beg Jesus to leave. As Jesus gets back in the boat, the former demoniac begs to go with Jesus.

Now on the other side of the lake, a leader of the synagogue named Jairus begs Jesus to heal his daughter. As Jesus sets out for Jairus's house, a woman pushes her way through the crowd and touches his cloak. Without words she begs him for healing. Finally, Jesus gets to Jairus's house, but the little girl has died. Jesus takes her by the hand and says, "Little girl, get up!" Immediately she gets up and walks around.

Something stands out in these stories: All these folks are begging Jesus. Begging (perhaps pleading) is a literal and figurative posture that people take with Jesus that yields results. Jesus doesn't always grant the request as stated, but he doesn't criticize them for begging.

In fact, Jesus often criticized those who did not beg of him (like the haughty religious leaders or the fickle crowds). The friends who lower the paralyzed man through the roof, blind Bartimaeus who shouts at the top of his lungs, the woman who barges into the house to pour expensive ointment on Jesus: Mark portrays these supplications to Jesus as signs of faith.

Whatever our condition, we too can come before God. We can beg of Jesus. In so doing, we will find our faith rewarded.

Holy Spirit, give us the persistence and boldness to beg Jesus. Make us realize our utter dependence on him. Amaze us when we find our faith rewarded by your favor. Amen.

Balance of Power

JUNE 29–JULY 5, 2015 • MARGARET L. FLEMING

MONDAY, JUNE 29 ~ *Read Psalm 48*

This morning, I awoke, unbolted my bedroom door, turned off the security alarm, and unlocked the dead bolt on the back door to let the cat out. I live in a safe neighborhood in a safe city. Round-the-clock police and fire protection and medical assistance will arrive within minutes if I call. My security system will summon authorities for a break-in or fire. I live in a fortress.

Contrast that world with the world of the psalmist who experiences life from a position of vulnerability and powerlessness. And yet, for the psalmist, Jerusalem—specifically the God who lives in that city—are his sure defense, his mighty fortress. God's steadfast love assures everything.

The psalmist speaks of his awestruck wonder of both the city and the God who lives there. He recalls the history of attacking forces who, when they view the city, find themselves "astounded" with praise; they flee with gratitude, having acknowledged the impenetrability of the city and its God—glad to be spared.

Most of us spend our lives building fortresses of knowledge, wealth, and prestige so we can escape feelings of vulnerability. Yet our sense of power is illusory. We will experience loss in life again and again. But when we, like the psalmist, consider the "city of our God" and the God that sustains that city, we too raise our voices in praise and wonder. We too will trust in the fortress of God's power, the wideness of God's mercy, and the steadfastness of God's love.

Remembering first our weakness, let us ponder God's steadfast love.

Assistant Attorney General and Chief of the Constitutional Defense Division of the Alabama Attorney General's Office, Montgomery, Alabama

Let me be clear. I have never felt at ease with weakness. Powerlessness frightens me. I even chose an occupation where I could wield the power of cross-examination and subpoenas. My world is filled with the trappings of power: expensive shoes, judges' robes, courtrooms filled with costly marble and gold-threaded tapestries. These trappings communicate a power that seeks to dominate others. But a softer power exists that needs no forcing.

"My grace is sufficient for you, for power is made perfect in weakness." These words whisper to my heart of a better way—a way that is not impressed by wealth or confused by titles or rank. This subtle and gentle power lacks the pride and boasting of powerful political systems.

I have seen God's power revealed in this subtle and gentle way. I was once privileged to represent a woman unjustly accused. The allegations wounded her deeply, and she might have responded by becoming resentful and sarcastic. Instead, she released her pain and fear to God. The day she took the witness stand, I watched the simple beauty of the truth unfold in a courtroom for everyone to see. For hours, the opposing counsel badgered her with false accusations. The woman responded in a thoughtful and calm manner. In the end, her gentle words proved stronger than all the ranting and badgering of her accuser, and she prevailed.

The thorns of life that bring us to our knees remind us of our own weakness, as well as our need for God's grace. That sense of utter helplessness lies at the heart of our spiritual journey. We pick up our cross day by day, and if we follow in faith, it leads to resurrection power.

Dear One, when we are still and quiet, we sense that you hold us. Help us sense your presence today and be thankful. Amen.

Jesus enters his hometown and meets with approval. His teaching and "deeds of power" astound the people. But then in the very next sentence, people begin to recall Jesus' early years among them: Jesus the carpenter, the son of Mary, the brother of James. They know all about this younger Jesus—the one who grew up with them. As their remembering gains momentum, it solidifies in judgment. In this closed environment, Jesus can do no more deeds of power.

We find it difficult to hold the present moment open to the possibility of a miracle. And the older we get, it seems that the neurons in our brains wear their familiar pathways into trenches.

My own life feels like that at times. Some days, I allow my knowledge of the way things have always been to imprison my day. On those days, the people with whom I interact have lost the ability to change my life with their words; I know them too well. There is no power in such a world.

For God's power to return, my own way of being present with others must undergo a transformation. I must learn to be present to the moment without boxing it in. I must learn to see people as they are without judging them, for it is judgment that closes the box on the moment. This sort of appreciative awareness lies at the heart of contemplative practice, and it is essential to my allowing God's power back into my world.

Perhaps that is why Jesus invites us to approach God as little children—open to possibilities, not burdening each moment with fear and limiting it with expectations.

Let us open our hearts and minds to the endless possibilities of the day as we pray, "Come, Lord Jesus."

David, the forgotten son, the one out tending the sheep when Samuel came seeking the future king—this same little shepherd boy has become the shepherd of a nation. God instructed Samuel not to be misled by David's small stature. Mortals "look on the outward appearance, but the LORD looks on the heart" (1 Sam. 16:7). David—the young boy who faced Goliath, the musician with the capacity to lose himself in dance before God—this overlooked little boy was anointed by Samuel, and God's Spirit made a home with him.

Years later, people see the fruit of the Spirit that resides within David. The fruit of God's inner anointing has become manifest, so that even those mortals who look on the outward appearance now see in David what God has always seen. After Saul's death, the Israelites come to the northern city of Hebron. They affirm David's leadership and anoint him as their king.

Several characteristics distinguish David's leadership as king. He rules as a shepherd who protects the flock and looks out for its well-being. Only this type of leadership could allow for the unifying of two geographical bodies of the Northern and Southern Kingdoms (a unity that lasts until the death of Solomon). And this king is one chosen by Yahweh, which creates a bond between God and David and God and the people. It is a covenant relationship. God sends God's own essence—God's very Spirit—to make a home. In that fertile ground, God nourishes the seeds of compassion, courage, and self-forgetfulness.

These qualities take time to grow in us. The holy seeds planted by our loving God are in the process of growing. And the fruits of God's Spirit in us will naturally, over time, show themselves, even to those who look only on outward appearances—a witness to our covenant with our God.

Let us remember that God is with us and within us all, shaping us and molding us. Give thanks.

Outside, the sky forms a soft gray dome. The sky has no shape, no cumulous billows for the sun to break through. Just gray—solid and dull. The sky mirrors the weather of my soul. These days, I am being led where I do not want to go, and a sense of helplessness permeates the landscape.

My aging mother's health is declining. No amount of prayer or doctors' visits will change that. My sense of powerlessness where she is concerned is acute.

But I take comfort in knowing that Jesus found himself powerless at times. He wants to heal, but he cannot. Circumstances do not favor his desire for healing: He is "amazed at their unbelief." Jesus does not lose heart, however, nor should we. He moves on in his mission, sending out the twelve two by two. They go out with little, relying on the hospitality of those in the houses they stop in. Those who do not welcome them and refuse to hear receive the dust of the disciples' sandals as testimony. Jesus does not try to force people or circumstances to be other than they are.

Aging happens. We all must grow old and eventually die. Circumstances in my life are not how I would like them to be at the moment. But I can choose to dwell on my disappointment; or, like Jesus, I can accept matters as they are. I can release myself from the prison of my expectations, relax my notion of how things should be, and open myself to the possibilities that the present moment holds.

The Lord of all hopefulness can transform and bring healing to tragic life moments if we will welcome them as they are and allow their hidden beauty to emerge.

Open our eyes, Dear One, to behold your beauty in unexpected places today. Amen.

Growing up, I could not boast about personal weakness. Instead, I shaped myself into a person of strength. I put together this "false" self the way a toddler might assemble a puzzle by using only half the pieces. I selected the pretty pieces —the qualities about myself that my parents, teachers, and friends liked and admired—my so-called strengths. Those pieces of myself that I judged as weak or lacking, I kept hidden away in the box.

Paul's detractors in Corinth are looking for visible signs of power from Paul to confirm his true apostleship. But Paul is not playing their game; he chooses to boast in his weakness. He has "a thorn . . . in the flesh." Despite praying for its removal three times, relief does not come. And yet, only through this weakness does Paul experience the power of Christ.

According to Paul, when I deny the weaker parts of myself, I deny my true strength. Each of us possesses strengths and weaknesses, but we tend to value the strengths, thereby denying the power of Christ that comes through our weaknesses.

Those parts of ourselves that we regard as weak, when strengthened by Christ, can offer gifts to the community at large. Take my friend Sammy who lovingly addressed incarcerated youth despite his severe speech impediment. Sammy's courageous delivery kindled the hope hidden in those young hearts, becoming a doorway for God's Spirit to enter.

Let us give thanks for weakness and for Christ's power to bind us together in the community of love.

Sometimes my life feels like a cluttered room filled with so much junk I cannot tell one item from the next. In that room, most of the items of activity seem as valuable as the next: watching a movie, taking a walk, putting a puzzle together. All are distractions, each with some redeeming benefit or other, be it physical or mental. I find them all, and none seems particularly significant. None, except one. In that room of clutter, the one endeavor that stands out above all else is prayer. But I must choose it or not choose it each day.

For me, prayer is a time of total vulnerability and utter surrender. Those qualities make this endeavor seem a little scary. But it offers me a place to go where I find my connection to a strength that is humble, gentle, and yielding. In this place I can sense that I am slowly changing, becoming more and more open, like the gentle Spirit.

I can glimpse this Spirit in others—in the humble attitude that takes no offense at insults; in the flexible frame of mind that bends like a willow in the wind; in the good heart that takes no note of others' wrongs; in the open schedule that accommodates others' needs.

"And David became greater and greater, for the LORD, the God of hosts, was with him." David's covenant with God expanded the power and influence of his anointing. That bond between God and us can expand our power and influence as well. I can choose to start the day with an exercise routine, a to-do list, a plan for addressing each thing in my cluttered day as one way to approach life. But a better way presents itself, a way born in surrender to the One whose will is superior to our own, whose strength is made perfect in our weakness.

O God, we surrender ourselves to you. Do with us today as you will. Amen.

Participants in God's Plan

JULY 6–12, 2015 • JOHN VAN DE LAAR

MONDAY, JULY 6 ~ *Read Ephesians 1:3-8*

Our lives are not random. We inherently sense that our lives are part of something bigger than ourselves. This conviction lies at the heart of the letter to the Ephesians.

From the very beginning of his correspondence, the apostle calls his readers to offer praise and thanksgiving for God's activity in their lives and for the invitation to participate in God's saving activity in the world. In Christ, God has chosen us to receive every spiritual blessing, to enjoy God's presence, and to know the security of being God's children. But God has also liberated us from our worst selves and forgiven our failures. God's overwhelming love and generosity reveal a startling truth: God values us highly and has done everything necessary for us to find a life of meaning and abundance through deep intimacy with God.

These words must have brought great comfort and encouragement to the Ephesian Christians, who lived in a center of commerce, Greek culture, and the worship of the god Artemis. Living out their faith would not have been easy, and they may have begun to wonder whether it was worth the price. Like these early Christians, we too may struggle as we live out of sync with the values and goals of our society. We too may wonder whether our faith is worth the price, and we may question whether our lives make any real difference. But as we remember all that God has given us and the lengths Jesus was willing to go for us, we can find the hope and courage we need to stay faithful and to embrace God's gifts.

Thank you, God, for giving me a life of meaning and purpose in union with you. Amen.

Methodist minister; founding director of Sacredise.com, a liturgical training and publishing ministry, Cape Town, Republic of South Africa

I'm just one person. What difference can I make?" How often have you heard these words? You may even have said them yourself. From a human perspective our contribution seems so small when compared to the massive challenges our world faces. But when we catch a glimpse of God's perspective, the picture changes dramatically. Paul proclaims a startling and exciting truth: God has revealed God's plan to us! Everything is working toward a glorious and liberating goal!

Because Jesus' return is taking longer than the Ephesians have expected, they begin to doubt the working out of God's plan. But the apostle reminds them of God's ultimate dream. All things, heavenly and earthly, will be brought to wholeness and unity in Christ, and we are part of God's saving purpose. This vision of new life is our inheritance in Christ, and God calls us to proclaim its glory to the world. We have received the gift of God's Spirit to empower us and give us a foretaste of the life to come.

It seems incredible that God would ask us to share in this amazing dream, but that's exactly what the apostle expects us to believe. The Holy Spirit guarantees the truth of this call and the power we need to fulfill our part. If we read the rest of this letter we would discover that the daily details of our lives are the raw material through which we bring God's plan into being in our small corner of the universe. And when we realize this, we discover the joy of knowing that our small lives make a difference.

Spirit of God, constantly remind me of your dream and empower me so that my life can contribute toward bringing it into being. Amen.

If you have ever seen a parade, you know how it feels to get caught up in the fanfare and the exuberant joy of the moment. If the procession promoted a beloved celebrity, a victorious sports team, or a prominent world leader, it may even have felt a little like worship. Keep this helpful image in mind as you read Psalm 24 because it served as a liturgy whenever the ark of the covenant entered Israel's central place of worship.

The psalm begins with proclaiming God's absolute rule over creation. God is the one who conquered the chaos of the waters and established the earth, so the entire world belongs ultimately to God. This idea has significant implications for God's people. Those who live with integrity in the community (with clean hands, free of innocent blood, or false testimony against another) and who seek God (with pure hearts free of idolatry) are blessed because they proclaim God's goodness and glory through their lives and help to manifest God's rule on the earth.

Finally, the psalm calls for the gates of the city to open so that God—believed to be riding on the ark—may enter in. This last section of the psalm, which may have been sung responsively, declares that where God is acknowledged as the One who reigns over all, God is present.

This psalm's call continues today. God remains the sovereign ruler of creation, bringing order where there is chaos. God still seeks those with clean hands and pure hearts to participate in revealing God's presence, grace, and justice to the world. If we answer this call by worshiping wholeheartedly and living with integrity, our lives manifest God's reign to those around us.

I open the gates of my heart to you, O God. May your presence make me a person of clean hands and a pure heart. Amen.

Conflict is never easy. Although we try to avoid it, as we embrace the values of God's reign we will inevitably find ourselves in opposition to anything or anyone that harms, oppresses, or rejects others. When this happens, we may draw comfort from John the Baptist's story.

Herod Antipas, in an intricate web of family connections, has married his brother's wife. John the Baptist, who called God's people back to God's ways, cannot retain his integrity and stay silent about the king's immoral actions. But, in speaking out, he brings about his own arrest and wins the hatred of Herod's wife, Herodias. Nevertheless, something about John's goodness and courage gains Herod's respect, and the king can't stop listening to him. It makes you wonder if Herod had not made his rash, probably drunken, promise whether John may have made a greater impact on this man's life and what the results might have been.

When we choose to follow the way of Jesus, we will sometimes find ourselves in situations where we have to choose between silence and integrity. Our silence may keep the peace and protect us from the consequences of offending those in power over us, but we will lose part of ourselves. Standing against injustice and the abuse of power demands courage. It will often cost us dearly, but it will also demonstrate our integrity and our commitment to God's alternative way of living. If we answer God's call to participate in God's plan, we will have to prepare ourselves for these conflicts and learn to experience God's life and grace in the midst of them.

Give me the courage and integrity to stay faithful to your ways, O God, even when it brings me into conflict with those in power. Amen.

The values that drive us are best seen not in what we say but in what we do, in the fruit of our lives. Herod Antipas is probably trying to win the support of the people by continuing his father's project of rebuilding the Temple. But his real values are far more selfish and expedient. When he wants to marry his brother's wife, not even God's law can stop him. When John the Baptist challenges him, he arrests the prophet. And when his wife, by manipulating his foolish boasting, threatens John's life, he is too weak to oppose her and has John executed. These acts reveal Herod's priorities, and he finds himself haunted by his own sinfulness. When he hears about Jesus, he immediately thinks that John has returned to call him to account.

Both John the Baptist and Jesus offer a strong contrast to Herod's destructive values. While their deaths differ in detail, the causes are the same. Those in power refuse to hear the call to justice, peace, and love; they destroy the prophets who challenge them. Yet, both John and Jesus willingly give their lives for God's dream because they know it is the only way to bring about a world of true shalom—well-being, equality, peace, justice, and love—for all. Their commitment to these values still resonates through history and still brings shalom into the world.

What values drive our lives? What is the fruit of our priorities, not just for us or for our loved ones but for our neighborhood, our nation, and the world? How willing are we to lay down our lives to participate in bringing God's shalom into our world? The gospel demands answers to these tough questions.

May my values and the fruit of my life help to bring your shalom into the world, O God. Amen.

Why do we so often know what to do but fail to do it? Why do we believe one thing but live something different? Perhaps part of our struggle comes in thinking that the problem is in our minds, when it is really in our hearts. When the mission of Christ truly captures our hearts, we cannot help but participate in God's plan. But if our hearts remain unconvinced, no amount of intellectual reasoning will motivate us for very long.

Although he had become king of Israel and had almost everything his heart could desire, David still longed for the return of the ark of the covenant to Jerusalem after its capture by the Philistines. David's heart is convicted of the need to focus energy on the worship of God, so he goes to great lengths to restore the ark to its rightful place at the center of Israel's life.

His wife, Michal, feels less convinced. She, being the daughter of King Saul, has probably experienced the influence of Samuel and other prophets. As a daughter of Israel, she has been raised in the worship of God. Yet, when she sees David's unrestrained devotion, she despises him. In spite of all she has learned and experienced, her heart remains unmoved. She has become cynical and judgmental.

When we allow cynicism and negativity to take root in our hearts, our commitment to God's dream will slip. We cannot sustain a life of simplicity, service, and sacrifice by constantly questioning God's plan. But when we open our hearts to celebration, praise, and thanksgiving, we chase away destructive attitudes and strengthen our commitment to God's way.

Capture my heart, O God, with your dream, and let it drive away any cynicism or negativity. Amen.

King David is not a perfect person. His motives are often mixed, and he makes destructive choices that have long-term consequences. Yet, he never wavers in his devotion to God's purpose for his life. He acknowledges his role as God's servant and God's call on him to participate in a plan that is far bigger than himself.

The ark of the covenant symbolizes and signals God's presence and favor with God's people. When the Philistines capture the ark in battle, it is a major national catastrophe. But after a number of bad experiences, the Philistines decide to return the ark to Israel. It ends up in the home of Abinadab, where it stays for twenty years. When David finally manages to bring the ark to Jerusalem, his joy overflows and he responds with extravagant worship of God and extravagant service to his people. No matter how important and powerful David has become, he longs to cooperate with God's purpose and to unite his reign with God's sovereign plan.

God promised there would always be a descendant of David on the throne of God's people. The Gospel writers all declare that Jesus fulfills this promise. Now, we who follow Jesus are called, like David, to submit our lives, our motivations, our dreams, and our priorities to the higher vision of a world of justice, peace, and grace under the loving rule of God. To the extent that we do this, we too become part of the fulfillment of God's purpose in our world, and we participate in bringing God's healing and unity into the universe. It's a great dream, but our contribution comes in the small acts of extravagant devotion and service we offer each day.

I submit my dreams, my priorities, and my life to the greater dream of your reign, O God. Amen.

At Home in the Household of God

JULY 13–19, 2015 • RICK SUMMY

MONDAY, JULY 13 ~ *Read 2 Samuel 7:1-14a*

His enemies finally at bay, the significant and sometimes self-inflicted troubles of his life for the moment both behind and before him, given a chance to rest, King David sits back and settles into his favorite soft sofa, looks around at his house hewn from the finest cedar, and has a thought: *See now, I am living in a house of cedar, but the ark of God stays in a tent.*

David decides to build God a house. Why, do you suppose? Perhaps he is simply grateful to the God who always has his back. Maybe he feels guilty: David in a house of cedar and God in a nomad's tent. Could it be that he is searching for the perfect outsized, over-the-top project to impress the people—and maybe God too?

David is king after all. It's good to be king, but even the king has his place. And it is not David's place to build God a house, Nathan discovers. For starters, God says, I never asked for a house. Apparently God is not interested in settling in like the king. Besides, David—king or not—is God's servant and not the other way around. And just in case either David or Nathan has forgotten, God reminds Nathan that it is God who has taken David from pasture to palace.

God seems to be putting David in his place. Only, hang on. It's God at work here. God is not simply reining in the current king but has a plan for the future. David will not build God a house, but God will build David a house, a lineage based, as was David's kingship, on God's own steadfast love.

Kings and commoners alike, sometimes just when we think we've got a plan of action, God gives us something far greater instead.

Senior pastor, Atonement Lutheran Church, Wyomissing, Pennsylvania

It seems odd that God will not permit David to build God a house. David has been victorious. It's a time of peace. He is now king over all of Israel and has settled down in a nice cedar house. Isn't it time for God to settle down too? Apparently not.

For one thing, God, through Nathan, reminds the king that it is God who has given David his success. It's God who has given him rest from his enemies. It's God who raised him from a shepherd of sheep to the shepherd of Israel. It's God who will make his name great.

God is the subject of the sentence; David is the object of the sentence, the instrument upon whom God acts and through whom God works. King or not, well-meaning or not, David does not get to change the order of things. God will not be tied down, contained, controlled.

Besides, God is more concerned with other houses. God will not get a house just yet, but God's people will. "I will appoint a place for my people Israel and will plant them, so that they may live in their own place," God tells Nathan.

And, of course, David is going to get another house too, a kingdom-line that will be established forever, for the sake of the people. God is more concerned with God's household, with God's own people, than with a house of God's own.

Even today we cannot contain God in the churches we sometimes call God's house. God is present in our churches but is also present in our homes and places of work, is present with and through us wherever any of the members of God's human household stand in need.

God does not settle down, house or not. That's good news for us who sometimes settle too easily.

Dear Lord, thanks for your relentless willingness to go wherever we are and for gracing us with the challenge and care we so desperately need. Amen.

The psalmist says, "If they violate my statutes. . . . " But we know better. It really is just a matter of "when"—*when* David's descendants will forsake God's law. *When* they will violate God's statutes. *When* they will not keep the commandments.

When it comes to human beings, even the descendants of King David, there is no if, and, or but about it. It's a matter of when. When it comes to human beings and our responsive obedience to God, it is only a matter of time before we fall short.

In human relationships, falling short is often fatal to the relationship. Many marriages fail when one or both partners stray physically, emotionally, or both. Friendships crack over unspoken expectations of time and attention. Siblings can bark and bite. Families usually fail to hide the symptoms of dysfunction. With human beings, when one or more of us falls short, things often fall apart.

By contrast, when it comes to God, our inevitable "when" does not lead to a response of "if" on God's part. With regard to David's descendants, the psalmist says that disobedience will take its toll. Actions have consequences. But the relationship between God and the descendants is never threatened—no cutting off or casting out. God's steadfast love and faithfulness remain. God's holiness is inviolable; the promise remains unbroken.

Along this line, we receive assurance that this is true for us too. Not "if" but "when" we cause or allow harm or stand by while others are hurt, even then our relationship with God is not at risk. God's loving relationship to us is steadfast, "established forever," which leads, perhaps, to a more faithful response when we . . . .

Lord God, when we fall short, you do not abandon us but keep your promise of steadfast love. Encourage in us a more faithful response to your call. Amen.

The author calls the readers of Ephesians to remember. To remember when they stood on the outside looking in. To remember when they were aliens and strangers. To remember that the good old days weren't always good. The epistle writer calls them to remember what once was not, to recall what they lacked, so that they might rejoice all the more in what they have been given in the now. *Now* they have been brought near. *Now* the dividing wall has been broken down and the hostility that went with it has been overcome. *Now* they are no longer strangers and aliens but citizens with the saints and members of God's household.

Christ mends what was separate and broken into a single whole. It is Jesus who brings near those who were far off. Jesus, through the cross, reconciles and makes peace. It is Jesus through whom everyone gains access to God.

Those who were at cross purposes have been made one by the purpose of the cross. Most of us, at one time or another, have probably been left out too, have been on the outside looking in. A beloved sibling left us behind. One for whom we longed chose another. We weren't picked for the team. Whatever it was, I bet we still remember.

While the scale of the Ephesians reading is larger, the opportunity to redeem the difficult memory of exclusion remains. The work of Christ still operates.

Remembering our own experiences, then, may we, welcomed by Christ as members of God's household, rejoice in what the Lord has given us now. And let us give thanks for being included in the one new humanity called into being by the cross.

Redeeming Lord, you who welcome us all without regard to background or experience, help us to rejoice in the gift of welcome you have given us and to share it with others. Amen.

It all started with David's decision to build God a house, but that got turned around in a hurry. The next thing you know, God is making David a house, not out of cedar but built on the promise of a kingdom. Psalm 89 asserts the unconditional nature of God's steadfast love and faithfulness; the behavior of David's descendants will not deter God's promise.

In Ephesians, the cross of Christ expands the house imagery even farther. Not only does the cross remove the dividing wall between Jew and Gentile but, built on the cornerstone of Christ Jesus and the foundation of the prophets and apostles, the household of God opens to all humanity.

The good news is that a physical structure made by human hands, a house of mortar and stone, still cannot contain God—no matter how awesome or beautiful such a structure might be. Despite the importance of Solomon's Temple, Israel discovers that God is not contained even there. The God of Israel packs a bag and travels to be with God's people even while they are exiled in Babylon. The image of the curtain of the Temple being torn in two at Jesus' death is yet another way of saying the same thing. God is not contained.

But that does not mean that we don't know where to turn. Ephesians tells us that the faithful "are built together spiritually into a dwelling place for God." We, the people, have become God's house.

Now that the wall of division has been dismantled and the enmity between Jew and Gentile obliterated through Christ, there is no place or no people among whom God is not both present and at home.

Reconciling Lord, we give thanks that you make your home among mortals. Blessed by your presence, grant that we will live guided by your grace. Amen.

The law of inertia goes something like this: a body in motion tends to stay in motion, while a body at rest tends to stay at rest. The apostles have been in motion since Jesus sent them out two by two. They have gone from house to house. They receive welcome in some places; they shake the dust from their feet in others. They stay on the move: proclaiming the good news, casting out demons, anointing with oil. In our reading today, they have returned, both exhilarated from the good work and a little road weary.

Being a messenger is great, but it can take a lot out of you. Following Jesus can make for a frenetic lifestyle of constant motion. In response, Jesus decides to break the law of inertia. He invites the twelve to take a little time off—to stop moving and rest awhile.

The plan doesn't work out exactly. The time of rest lasts the length of a boat ride. The crowd recognizes them and hurries on foot, arriving ahead of them.

I'm pretty sure I would have been frustrated. But Jesus has compassion. He knows that those in the crowd need a person in whom they can find a home. And so he breaks the law of inertia again and goes back in motion to meet need. God's like that.

For us, following Jesus does not mean that we can always be like Jesus. Even if we think we know what Jesus would do, it doesn't mean that's what we are called to do. Not always.

Sometimes we simply find a home in our need for rest, to be on the still side of inertia, to be reminded of who is God and who is not. Otherwise, we wear out and have little to offer anyone. In my experience, compassion is among the first gifts to go in such circumstances.

Patient Lord, thank you for the good work of being your disciples and for calling us to the rest we often need so much. Amen.

Jesus lived on the fringes. As far as we know, at least during the part of his life revealed in scripture, Jesus has no particular place to call home. He feels at home with tax collectors and other sinners. But he also shares meals in the homes of the religious authorities.

We read that Jesus values time spent in prayer. With the possible exception of the time in Gethsemane, he feels at home when in conversation with the one he calls Abba. But when the people crowd in on him, even when he intends to find rest and renewal with his disciples in a deserted place, he does not send the crowd packing but demonstrates God's deep compassion. The shepherd is not at home with leaving the sheep alone.

The conclusion of our reading tells us that people came from everywhere—villages, cities, farms—so that those in need might get close enough to touch the fringe of his cloak with the hope of being made whole. The one who lived on the fringes apparently can heal others by their merely touching the fringes of his garments.

From the fringes then, Jesus reminds us that we will not find God in the palace of a king or in any building we can make. The church may be God's house, but it is not God's home. We may not find God in any one particular place. Instead, God finds us in many particular places—in the church, in any place we might find ourselves, even in those places where we try to hide—places, all of which because of God's presence, are home.

Gracious God, you make your home among your people and find us wherever we roam. Even as you bless us by your presence, help us trust that by your loving grace you will welcome all your children home. Amen.

Reordering Our Priorities

JULY 20–26, 2015 • WALTER L. KIMBROUGH

MONDAY, JULY 20 ~ *Read 2 Samuel 11:1-5*

The acquisition of position, power, and greed has led many to sin and self-destruction. Leaders in all walks of life who succeed in winning people's admiration can become victims of sin because of greed through positions of power. It seems as if leaders make sinful decisions because their power supports whatever actions their hearts desire.

One pastor, an effective communicator with tremendous charisma, cast a vision and secured a large following. The church prospered under his leadership. But when the pastor was named in a sex scandal, things changed. Loyal supporters began to fall by the wayside because of his sinful mistake.

Stories of this kind exist across all denominations and faith groups. Persons who acknowledge a call upon their lives are expected to live on a higher plane. When a call has been placed on the life of a pastor, it is like living in a house of glass. People see clergy when their actions are honorable or dishonorable.

David, king of Israel, wields great power. He enjoys position, power, and prestige. David serves under appointment by God rather than election by the people. He takes advantage of his high position, and greed enters into his spirit. The greed causes him to fall from grace into the sin of adultery.

When have you been tempted to sin when you've held a position of power? Do you know someone who has fallen from grace due to the sin of greed? If so, how did you respond to that person and his or her action?

God give us the strength to resist the temptation to sin and the wisdom to seek your forgiveness when necessary. Amen.

Retired pastor, North Georgia Conference of The United Methodist Church, Atlanta, Georgia

Several decades ago the people of the United States and the world were caught up in amazement over the discovery of what has been called Watergate. People at the highest level of politics were accused of corruption. Instead of being honest and confessing their sin, those involved made an all-out attempt to cover up the sin with a lie. One lie requires other lies, and the truth remains the same. As a result of the cover-up, the highest ranking political leader in the United States resigned his office.

King David faces charges of adultery and fathering a child with another man's wife. After learning of the pregnancy, he encourages the husband to sleep with his wife. When the man refuses out of abiding commitment to his fellow soldiers, the king arranges for his death in battle. David engages in a cover-up attempt, and despite his power, he fails.

The truth will usually prevail, freeing the liar from the crippling effect of the lie. Whenever a person testifies in a court of law, he or she takes an oath to tell the truth and the whole truth as the person knows and understands it. A half-truth becomes a cover-up and consequently a lie is told. Integrity needs to become a standard of conduct embraced by all people who are followers of Jesus Christ.

Have you ever had to give testimony in a court of law with the admonition to tell the truth? Or have you witnessed someone blatantly lying as a cover-up instead of telling the truth? Remember, the truth can set us free.

Help us, God, to speak the truth faithfully at all times and in all situations. Amen.

Iremain constantly amazed by the response of family and friends of persons who die suddenly and tragically. They present the deceased as having been a model citizen who loved and supported everybody. Often, the truth reveals not a model citizen but an ungodly life. Persons who live as if God does not exist are foolish.

Psalm 14 gives voice to fools who say in their hearts, "There is no God." They have no moral accountability, so everything is possible. Without God's existence, they give themselves over to self-idolatry and actions with no limits. Their lives fail to bring pleasure to God's heart. They act as gods unto themselves and decide their own destiny. The perception of power tends to corrupt their ability to think rationally. The self becomes the center of attention, while God, along with everyone else, drops to a lower plane. Fools and evildoers fail to live in harmony with God's will, not having the sense to make wise decisions.

The opposite of the fool is the wise one who acknowledges God's action in the world. The Lord sides with the poor and stands in the gap for them. God brings deliverance and the restoration of fortune to the people. Evildoers end up experiencing terror for their ways, but "Jacob will rejoice; Israel will be glad." God will not disappoint the righteous.

King David is probably the right person to record the words of Psalm 14. His life embraced both the good and the bad. He behaved in both a foolish fashion and a wise one. But even while corrupt, he became a blessing for others. Perhaps you have not always been good; perhaps you fell short of the glory of God but repented of your sins and accepted the gift of salvation. David's life might very well define your journey.

Thank you, God, for looking beyond our faults and ministering to us at our points of need. Amen.

After serving for forty years as a pastor in The United Methodist Church and currently serving in my second year as a retired supply pastor, I can honestly say that one of the most disturbing experiences I have encountered in a local congregation is a divided house. Too many of our congregations are not only divided but splintered.

In some congregations, the persons who call themselves Christian face such a vast divide that healing becomes impossible, and the church splits. All the while we sing, "They will know we are Christians by our love." I have experienced people in the church who seek power and recognition. They become combative to protect their position of leadership and are even unwilling to relinquish the position to a blood relative.

Christ's presence needs to surface as the focal point within congregational life rather than any member or group. The epistle writer emphasizes the church's unity rather than its division. The author asks that the readers grow in spiritual strength—in understanding and love and in the knowledge of the depth of Christ's love for them. Momma Gilstrap, one of my favorite church members, consistently preached that what the church needed was love. As we bow before the Parent of all, we acknowledge our connection to all others in the human family—but our connection to God is primary. We can then see and experience the movement of God in all our congregations. The vitality of the church will become contagious, for the people will come into a loving relationship with their Lord.

On a scale of one to ten, with ten being the highest, how would you rate your capacity to show love within the church of Jesus Christ and in the world?

God, grant us the capacity to love one another. We bow before you, seeking strength for the work of love you have set before us. Amen.

I experience worship as a high point in church life—the time when the people come together out of diversity into a spirit of oneness. I am most appreciative when all the people become participants in a great symphonic chorus. The Doxology invites the people to stand and give praise to God. This is grounded in the position that God is worthy of all praise, honor, and glory. Worship, therefore, is not only the high point in the life of the congregation; it is also a unifying force among a diverse and sometimes divisive people.

A great joy for me in my pastorates was to look out my office window and see people walking rapidly toward the entrance of the sanctuary for worship. What a high moment in the life of families and individuals who gather on a weekly basis as participants in worship!

The author of the epistle, in writing the conclusion of chapter 3, leaves us with these immortal words, "Now to him who by the power at work within us is able to accomplish abundantly far more than all we can ask or imagine, to him be glory in the church and in Christ Jesus to all generations, forever and ever. Amen." This remains an often-quoted scripture even to this day. It speaks to the power and authority of God realized in Christ Jesus. For it is in worship that we are liberated to be all that God has called us to be.

Commit the doxology above to memory, recite it often, and be blessed by it. Then, share the good news with others to the end that they too will be blessed.

Thank you, God, for the apostle Paul, who gave us so much through the leading of the Holy Spirit and by your grace in Christ Jesus. Amen.

A local chapter of the United Methodist Women served an evening meal prior to their monthly meetings. The husbands came for the meal. This practice developed into a church-wide potluck supper. Everyone brought a dish to share. No matter how many people showed up for the meal, the food never gave out. In fact, there was always plenty of food left. This remained the case even when the crowd outgrew the capacity of the fellowship hall.

Jesus feeds five thousand people with a boy's lunch. They have followed Jesus from afar because the power and profundity of Jesus' teaching and preaching amazes them. It seems that time slips away from them; the hour grows late. The people need food, so Jesus instructs the disciples to feed them. They perceive this as an impossible request. They forget that with Jesus all things are possible.

Jesus takes charge. He organizes the people into manageable groups, offers a blessing, breaks the bread, feeds every person, and has twelve baskets left over. It's a miracle—a miracle with two small fish and five pieces of bread. In Jesus' hands all things are possible. A miracle happened then, and miracles happen every day by God's grace.

Consider the great things that have transpired in your life; were miracles taking place? When has God brought you through trials of life without your own ability to make a difference? Maybe a miracle took place. They happen every day; expect yours.

Thank you, God, for the miracles of long ago and the miracles of today, especially the miracles in our lives. Amen.

Any journey that takes you to the feet of Jesus is worth the investment of time, money, and emotion. Destination can determine the success or failure of the journey. You want to end up at the desired place; otherwise, you feel lost and disappointed. Jesus' life story testifies to what it means to be Christian. His boundless love is available to all.

Jesus' disciples row across the lake without Jesus. They have gone three or four miles, navigating through the darkness of the night. In every direction all they see is water. They hear the moving of the waves and feel the gentle breeze. Then they see what obviously is a mirage. The wind picks up, and Jesus appears to them walking on the water. Walking on water is a skill quite outside the ordinary.

Our Lord, being anything but ordinary, walks on the water. With no GPS navigational system or even an auto club map but led by the Spirit, Jesus leaves the shore and goes walking on the water in the middle of the night. He catches up with the disciples in the boat and joins them.

The disciples expect Jesus to join them and yet are fearful when he shows up! He assures them of his identity: "It is I; do not be afraid." He guarantees their safety, and the boat comes to shore. What a mighty God we serve. Jesus exhibits no self-serving greed in his life, only the power of gracious love. Thanks be to God.

What is it about your relationship with Jesus that makes you fearful? How does Jesus come to you, bringing calm and safety?

Thank you, God, for your assurance of our well-being. Give us the grace and strength to model our lives after Jesus. Amen.

The Bread of Life

JULY 27—AUGUST 2, 2015 • DAVID RAINEY

MONDAY, JULY 27 ~ *Read 2 Samuel 11:26–12:13a*

The prophet Nathan tells King David a story about a rich man stealing from a poor man. When David reacts to the obvious injustice, Nathan courageously declares, "You are the man!" Nathan's call to confession moves David, but the story speaks to us all about our own sinfulness and hope for redemption.

That the Bible has preserved this exchange is notable. After all, David, the most revered king in Israel's history, is a political powerhouse whose leadership and faith inspire his people. He is the shepherd boy who took on Goliath, the poet whose songs filled Israel's hymnbook. The authors of scripture could have downplayed or deleted David's capabilities for great evil and deception. Instead, the scripture lays it all out, as if to say, *If even King David can engage in such sinfulness, surely we have sin to confess. And if God forgives David's sin and redeems his life for further service, surely that is the case for us!*

Nathan remains David's friend through all his indiscretions. Who knows how long David might have woven his tangled web if the Lord had not used Nathan to intervene. Nathan confronts David with the truth. To his credit, David confesses, "I have sinned against the LORD." He realizes that in sinning against Bathsheba and Uriah, he has wounded the God who loves them all.

David's story goes beyond simple embarrassment to pain and tragedy. We note that David's confession does not erase the consequences of his sinful acts. But the good news is that everyone—David, you, and I—can receive grace and continue to live.

O God of grace, I hear your call to confession. I thank you that my sin does not have the last word. Amen.

United Methodist pastor, Nashville, Tennessee; husband and father of three adult sons

In the story from Second Samuel, Nathan calls David to confession. The note in my Bible introduces Psalm 51 as David's prayerful response to God. "I know my transgressions!" It is the song of a sorrowful and humbled heart, one that feels unclean and distant from God. Perhaps David's deep sense of relationship with God allows him now to experience such pain and distress. David readily acknowledges the evil of his actions, actions that he knows warrant God's judgment.

The psalm is a lament, and yet it does not convey fear or despair. Hope fills its words. David cries out for mercy as one who trusts that God's very nature is that of mercy. He believes in a God of steadfast love whose love can wash him clean, put a new and right spirit within him, teach him wisdom, restore his joy.

Psalm 51 comes as a gift to you and me as people of faith. It gives us words to confess our own sin and express our own sorrow, words to cry out from the depths of our own sense of separation. It also carries us with David into the presence of God's steadfast love where we personally can be washed, forgiven, and restored to the joy of God's salvation.

At the top of my daily prayer list I have written a quote regarding Abba Pior, one of the desert fathers: "Every single day he made a fresh beginning." I have found this simple statement so helpful because it reminds me of a basic message at the heart of our faith—David's, yours, and mine. Every single day, whatever we have done or left undone, whatever has happened to us or to those we love, God's grace invites us to make a fresh beginning.

Create in us clean hearts, O God, and put a new and right spirit within us! Amen.

Psalm 51 records an individual confession that we traditionally associate with King David. While David's transgressions
and our own are often personal in nature, the Bible speaks to the
collective nature of our sinfulness as well. David's confession
became meaningful to Israel because it symbolized the sin and
redemption of the whole nation. In David's forgetfulness of the
commandments, in his greed and arrogant misuse of power, the
people of God recognized sinful realities that loomed larger than
any one person's transgression. They prayed that God would put
a new and right spirit in them as a people. As liturgy, Psalm 51
became both a collective and an individual confession.

The Bible reminds us that we too get caught up in sin that
is bigger than the individual misdeeds of any one of us. We all
participate in systems that are hurtful to others based on realities such as race, nationality, gender, language, religion, sexual
orientation, and economic status. We may not personally intend
evil, but neither can we claim innocence. As communities,
nations, and churches we may not will evil, as Paul says, but we
still do it. Collective confession gives us the opportunity to come
clean about this. And it gives God the opportunity to change us.

In my grandparents' day few people worried about harming
the environment. For most of human history we've made modest
impact on God's good creation. In recent decades, our impact has
changed. Now our shortsighted practices are influencing land,
water, and air in ways that will affect generations yet to come. If
we can confront our transgressions, the Creator may yet teach us
wisdom and sustain in us willing spirits.

When we next participate in a Communion service, let's
notice that the prayer of confession and pardon is in the plural!

*Merciful God, . . . forgive us, we pray. Free us for joyful obe-
dience, through Jesus Christ our Lord. Amen.* (A Service of
Word and Table II, *The United Methodist Hymnal*)

I grew up eating corn bread made with buttermilk and baked crisp in a well-seasoned iron skillet. After I left home I called mom for her recipe. I was hungry for the staff of life! Over time I have learned about other kinds of bread and the joy not only of eating bread but of making it and serving it to others.

When Jesus tells the crowd, "I am the bread of life," he chooses a familiar and compelling image. Most cultures eat bread in some form. It is the most basic of all foods. To speak of "bread" goes to the heart of things or, more accurately, to the stomach of things—our deepest needs and hungers.

Jesus knew personally about hunger of all sorts. After all, he began his ministry in the wilderness. Maybe that's why his heart went out so readily to the hungry people he saw around him. He wanted so much to give them bread! He also understood the temptation to feed our hungers with that which does not ultimately satisfy or save.

Earlier this week we read about King David. As it happens, Bethlehem, the city of David, literally means "house of bread." David acknowledged his relationship with God as the true bread of his life, but he found himself vulnerable to feeding his human hungers in other ways. His misuse of power had disastrous consequences—for him and others.

We all hunger—for companionship, for control, for meaning, for relief from pain. Tempting possibilities abound, promising to meet our needs; but Jesus warns that they will not ultimately satisfy. They may even destroy.

For what do you most deeply hunger today? How are you being tempted to satisfy that hunger?

Lord Jesus, you know what it means to be hungry. Help us resist the temptation to feed our hungers in ways that are destructive and do not satisfy. Be our daily bread. Amen.

This week's Gospel lesson follows the day that Jesus has fed the multitude with loaves and fish. Jesus looks up, and the crowd is back. He's not surprised really. Maybe they are hoping for another miracle—and he can't blame them. But he doesn't want them to miss the point. His primary offering is not bread for their bodies but bread for their spirits—the bread of God's love that will feed their hearts and sustain their hope in the days to come.

The crowd indicates interest but wonders aloud, "What must we do?" Surely they have to take action, "perform the works of God"—in order to receive such a meal ticket! They do not yet understand that Jesus wants to *give* them this bread—not because they have earned it but because they need it, and he loves them. He himself is the bread, the bread of heaven, the bread of life.

Like the crowd in the story, we sometimes have a hard time grasping Jesus' words. He invites us to come to the table and be fed. In time we will find there is plenty to do: loving, healing actions. And we will desire to do those things—not to earn a place at the Lord's table but in grateful response to having been included and fed ourselves.

At a gathering of church members who had provided a lunch for homeless guests, pastor and homeless advocate Charlie Strobel remarked, "You know, vending machines can feed people. It's our privilege to share a meal." He went on to explain that in a true meal people share not only food but the bread of loving community.

"Break thou the bread of life, dear Lord, to me." Thank you for the joy of sharing your bread with other people who hunger. Amen. ("Break Thou the Bread of Life," Mary A. Lathbury)

Several letters attributed to Paul compare the church to the human body. Paul points out that just as a physical body has different parts, so it is with "the body of Christ." Church members differ from one another in many ways; but when all is well, the parts work together for a common purpose with sympathy, harmony, and graceful unity.

Today's reading expresses Paul's concern about the church's unity. He implores members to live up to their calling: to be humble, gentle, and patient; to bear with one another in love. Given sinful human nature, Paul knows this is easier said than done. He makes his appeal on the basis of what they have in common. They have one Lord and life by one Spirit. They share one faith and baptism. The many gifts among them come from one Giver, Christ himself.

Paul's words serve as a timely reminder to the church. Unless we, the members of the one body, intentionally remember the source of our unity, differences can undermine both our experience of community and the effectiveness of our mission.

As we all know, church meetings can become contentious and stressful. Difficult issues and personalities remain inevitable. Meetings may begin with prayer but then lose their spiritual center and direction. As a pastor I did not expect or want uniformity in the life of the church, but I did pray for unity.

One day I felt moved to light a candle at meetings. The candle served as a visible reminder that Christ sat at the table with us. I sensed this helped us talk with one another more lovingly and openly, appreciate one another's gifts, and stay focused on the desires of the One who had called us together.

"We are one in the Spirit, we are one in the Lord, and we pray that all unity may one day be restored." Amen. ("They'll Know We Are Christians by Our Love," Peter Scholtes)

Paul uses the familiar image of the human body to help us understand some important aspects about the church, the "body of Christ." In this passage he speaks of the body's growth.

To a certain extent growth is about size, of course. In the natural order of things, a baby doesn't stay a baby for long. A child eats more food, requires bigger shoes, and hears doting relatives exclaim with delight, "My, how you've grown!"

Growth, a natural progression, excites people and churches. Yet Paul's concern is not so much on how many members a congregation has. He wants the church to grow, but even more he wants the church to "grow up." He desires mature disciples who reach "the measure of the full stature of Christ."

Someone has observed, "Growing older is mandatory; growing up is optional." As anyone who has attended a little league baseball game knows, the eight-year-old players on the field often behave in a more mature fashion than the parents in the stands. Physical maturity doesn't necessarily mean emotional maturity. Likewise, longtime church membership or a large congregation does not necessarily reflect spiritual maturity.

Paul suggests several qualities that reflect a "grown-up," spiritually mature church. One is when members and leaders use their gifts to build up the community of faith rather than promote themselves or their own personal wishes. Another involves resisting being swayed by everything they hear. Instead, the members strive to grow up into the mind of Christ, the one who is the head of the body. In a mature church, members grow in love, in the ability to work together, in their inclusiveness and compassion. Even difficult words are spoken with respect and kindness—everything supports the body's growth in love.

Lord Jesus, help us to grow—and grow up—in your spirit. Amen.

Loving God through Troubling Times

AUGUST 3–9, 2015 • JANE HERRING

MONDAY, AUGUST 3 ~ *Read 2 Samuel 18:5-9*

The story of Absalom's rebellion is on the verge of its tragic climax. These dramatic and murderous events are part of a series of disasters that began with David's adultery with Bathsheba and the murder of her husband. Now father and son will meet on the battlefield. The day of battle between David's seasoned army and Absalom's conscripted soldiers has come.

There is no happy ending to this story. Unlike the prodigal son, Absalom will not return home to make amends and become part of the family again. Battles are deadly, not life-giving.

Absalom's story warns us of our vanity, of self-righteous revenge, of greed for power and control, and of obsessing over others as the source of our problems. While we may not have deadly armies to set marching in battle against our enemies, our emotional battles with ourselves and others can be spiritually deadening.

What threatens to deaden you spiritually? How can you be honest about the battles you wage and turn to God instead?

Holy God, cut me free of anything that threatens my moral and spiritual well-being. Put my feet on your path and walk with me. Give me the strength and hope I need to grow in stature and in grace with you. Amen.

Hospice chaplain with a lifelong interest in spiritual formation; retreat leader and writer

David expects obedience and gives Joab explicit orders not to harm Absalom. Joab refuses David's command and has Absalom killed in order to save the kingdom. Joab sees through David's inability to make hard choices at this time. In painful mourning David cries out, "My son, my son." David wishes he had been killed in Absalom's place. Of course David mourns the death of his son.

In contemporary language, the time for David to treat Absalom with "tough love" has come and gone. The damage is done. Without healthy boundaries, we can damage ourselves and the ones we love.

We are meant to cherish one another, to respect and care for our familial and social relationships, but we must also remember that no one belongs to us. Even our children belong to God, not to us. We express God's love to one another, but we belong to God, not to other humans. It seems that David made an idol of his love for Absalom. It is easy to do in romantic relationships, familial relationships, as well as in friendships and professional associations.

Sovereign God, help us love one another as you would have us love. Prevent us from making idols of one another, and sanctify our loving relationships to be life-giving reflections of your grace. Amen.

In many spiritual assessments used by hospital chaplains and hospice spiritual-care coordinators, measuring gratitude toward God is one way of assessing the spiritual vitality of patients. The psalmist expresses great praise toward God and undergirds this praise with a deep sense of gratitude.

In current positive psychology practices, gratitude is considered one of the most powerful positive forces in the lives of healthy, resilient people. People with an attitude of gratitude overcome tragedy more easily, are more likely to reach out for help, and will likely experience a greater sense of well-being. Gratitude doesn't mean a naïve denial of life's difficulties. Rather, gratitude understands that life can be full of suffering and unfairness but intentionally seeks to name those things that bring measures of joy and moments of beauty.

The psalmist identifies himself as the poor, oppressed soul delivered by God. Are we not all the poor and oppressed? There are many kinds of oppression. If we do not suffer from physical poverty, we may be awash in the meaningless luxuries of a consumer society that leave us spiritually impoverished. God is for us, offering liberation from oppression of all kinds. When we experience liberation from oppression, physical suffering, emotional suffering, or spiritual suffering, a natural expression of our gratitude is praise of the Lord. We want to share this experience with others, and so we encourage others to "taste and see" the Lord's goodness for themselves.

Creator God, thank you for the beauty and joy in our lives. We say yes to your love. Train our hearts and minds on your goodness and mercy. Guide us to share your love with others. Amen.

This passage exhorts us to have concern for what we say, how we handle our anger, for any type of thievery, for making an honest living, and for building one another up rather than tearing each other down. Ultimately, we are not to grieve the Holy Spirit, by which we are marked as Christians, but to act toward one another as Christ acted toward us in forgiving us.

We have been made new by the forgiveness of Christ. Ugly behavior comes from within us, not only from traumatic events we have been unable to resolve within our own hearts but from the depths of our primal fears of abandonment, our fears that God cannot really love us. We are forgiven and by the grace of God we can extend this forgiveness to the world around us.

As we mature in Christ's forgiveness of us, our growth is made evident in the way we live, the words we say, and the actions we take. Our lives become manifestations of this forgiveness. We speak in ways that support faith in ourselves and others. Our actions become expressions of Christ's love.

Forgiving God, make us sensitive to the ways in which you have made us new. Allow us to recognize ourselves as your beloved children and to live our lives as such. We rejoice that we are sealed by the Spirit. Amen.

My husband has a habit of saying he will do something I ask him to do and then not doing it. Taking out the trash, moving clothes from the washer to the dryer, feeding the dogs. Why doesn't he just tell me he can't do what I ask? He wants to be the person who does what he says he'll do. He wants to help with all of life's chores, but he forgets or gets distracted by the other two million responsibilities he must handle. Does knowing his good intention keep me from getting annoyed? Sadly, no.

My annoyance is one way in which I fail to be like Christ. Because I counsel people as a chaplain and have been exposed to many kinds of people in many situations, I know I am not alone in my failure to imitate Christ. We humans are wild and varied in the many ways we fall short of modeling Christ. It is far more natural for us to behave as abandoned, ill-tempered children than dearly loved children.

What would it look like for me to walk in the way of Christ the next time my husband agrees to pick up dinner on the way home from work but comes in empty-handed. I could huff and puff as usual, or I could smile, offer a hug, and give us both the time and space to make another plan for feeding the family. A sense of urgency seems to accompany my irritation. Christ, on the other hand, offers eternity. I can breathe in Christ's love and ask for help at any moment.

God of eternity, give us patience to grow in your likeness. May we not forget that we are made in your image, that your love lives within us. Help us show this love in all we do and say; help us experience the peace and joy of this reminder as a reality. Amen.

A friend of mine who traveled to the Scottish island of Iona says she heard there a eucharistic blessing that went like this: "Jesus was always the guest. In the homes of Peter and Jairus, Martha and Mary, Joanna and Susanna, he was always the guest. At the meal tables of the wealthy where he pleaded the case of the poor, he was always the guest. Upsetting polite company, befriending isolated people, welcoming the stranger, he was always the guest." I felt my heart deeply moved when my friend shared that with me. Jesus was always the guest.

Here is the second half of this blessing from the Iona Community: "But here, at this table, he is the host. Those who wish to serve him must first be served by him, those who want to follow him must first be led by him, those who would wash his feet must first let him make them clean. For this is the Table where God intends us to be nourished; this is the time when Christ can make us new. Jesus Christ, who has sat at our tables, now invites us to be guests at his."

To receive Jesus' bread of life, we must serve and be served. The bread that will meet our soul's hunger and the water that will satisfy our soul's thirst is Christ. When we can be the host, we must serve. When we find ourselves in need, we must be willing to be served. Radical hospitality means we know that Jesus works through us to nurture others in times of need and that Jesus works through others for us when we find ourselves in need.

Nurturing God, help us be fed by you and nourished by you. Help us then do your work in the world. Amen.

This passage in John contains one of the "I am" sayings that are a hallmark of the Fourth Gospel. The metaphors Jesus uses to explain his person and his mission symbolize that which is most necessary for abundant living—and eternal life. When Jesus says "I am the bread of life," he is telling those gathered that he can fulfill their deepest and most basic needs. He can satisfy their true hunger. He can sustain them for life and beyond.

Those who hear Jesus' words begin to complain: How can he be the "bread that came down from heaven" when they all know Jesus as the son of Joseph and Mary? Jesus then tells them not to complain. Their complaining calls to mind the Israelites who wandered in the desert whose hunger was met by manna. They lost sight of God's promise. Jesus goes on to say that they ate manna and died. But the bread of heaven allows those who believe to live eternally.

Ultimately, Jesus explains that the bread he gives for the life of the world is his flesh. The words of this verse evoke both the Incarnation and the Crucifixion: the gift of Jesus' life that sprang from God's love for the world as well as the death of Jesus on the cross, also an expression of God's love. In Matthew 12:32, Jesus reminds us that when he is lifted up, he will draw all people to him. This is the power of the cross.

When we, like the people Jesus addresses, quit complaining, we can hear Jesus' message of redemption and glimpse the Promised Land. God's gift of love in Jesus will draw us and sustain us in a relationship of love.

God of life, may we not forget that we are made for eternal life in you. Thank you for the nourishment you provide us, body, mind, and spirit. We rejoice in your gifts to us! Amen.

To God Belongs Eternal Praise

AUGUST 10–16, 2015 • TITUS O'BRYANT

MONDAY, AUGUST 10 ~ *Read 1 Kings 2:10-12; 3:3-14*

God comes to meet us. God comes to us in our limitations and weaknesses, in our failures and misunderstandings. Solomon discovers this aspect of God's character early in his reign. The royal historian who authored the books of the Kings of Israel notes how Solomon demonstrates his love for the Lord by following David's example—except for his practice of offering sacrifices at pagan places of worship. We know Solomon as a wise man who gives way to the folly of marrying many wives and worshiping many gods. This story indicates the roots of both his great wisdom and his foolish idolatry.

Yet the most striking character in this story is not Solomon at all (or even David) but the God who comes to meet Solomon. God does not wait for Solomon to straighten out every aspect of his life. God has no interest in Solomon's knowing all the right answers or gaining a deeper level of maturity. God meets Solomon exactly where he is—questioning, uncertain, inexperienced, vulnerable, making mistakes, worshiping with pagans.

God meets us in the same way. God is not looking for the holiest of saints to grace with divine presence. God does not wait for us to earn divine favor. God wants to join in our lives exactly where we find ourselves, just as we are. Do you feel hampered by indecision, lost in uncertainty, or weighed down with guilt? God will come to meet you, bringing divine presence—not because of your greatness but because of God's.

Gracious Lord, thank you for joining us in our ordinary, everyday, mistake-filled lives. Open our eyes to see you at work and our hearts to feel your presence. Amen.

Research writer, Hope for the Heart, Plano, Texas; attends Gateway Community Church, Wylie, Texas

Do you ever play "What if" games? Normally, once a year I find myself drinking too many sodas and indulging in too many French fries. My expanding waistline seems to coincide with the McDonald's Monopoly promotion when I am enticed by the possibility of peeling back a small sticker and experiencing life changes due to a windfall of Monopoly money. I start imagining what I would do "if" I won.

Imagine being in Solomon's position. He has just won the grand prize. The omnipotent ruler of all states, "Ask what I should give you." Solomon's response reveals the quality and character of his heart. He does not ask for power to dominate his enemies. He does not desire riches to satisfy his appetites. He only asks God to equip and enable him to serve others. He wants wisdom to administer justice. When Solomon faces this startling question from his Maker, his first thoughts are not for himself but for his people.

We may never have the same encounter with God that Solomon had, but we all answer the same question. We reveal what we want by the way that we live. What does our manner of living reveal about our deepest desires?

If we want unconditional love, we choose to love those who seem unlovely and are entirely "different" from us. If we want contentment, we cease trying to accumulate more and more "stuff." If we want to experience peace, we resist the impulse to control and dominate others.

How would you respond if God asked, "What do you want?" Every choice you make, every word you speak, every goal you set—the sum total of your life answers that very question. What has your answer been, and how would you like to change it?

Father of wisdom, shape our lives to reflect your values. Amen.

God acts in many and varied ways. Sometimes the actions are surprising and unmistakable. At other times, the quiet actions work in gentle harmony with everyday life. In some seasons of my life I have been unable to discern God's hand at work. But even when I am too busy to notice, God is working—always gracious, glorious, and great.

This psalm is an acrostic following the Hebrew alphabet from beginning to end. Each line begins with another letter. From A to Z (or Aleph to Tav)—God reaches out to us, demonstrating greatness. From the beginning of our lives to the end, God extends this grace to us, working for our good.

The psalmist has experienced God's working throughout his life, from beginning to end. The setting for this recounting of God's nature and activity is the worshiping congregation. The priest says aloud all the reasons to praise and thank the Lord: for food and guidance, for the possession of the land they now inhabit, and for their covenant with God. God establishes, performs, and redeems. Clearly, the "fear of the LORD is the beginning of wisdom."

What has God been doing in your life? Take time to review God's provision and guidance for you. If you are passing through an uncertain time and are wondering if the Lord is at work in your life, then hold on to the belief that since God is always working graciously among God's people, surely God is at work in your life.

Praise God's faithfulness, and share your experience with someone else. A friend may notice God at work where you have missed the activity.

Magnificent God, thank you for your goodness, provision, and guidance. Grant me faith to believe you are active in my life, even when I can't see your hand. Amen.

The apostle directs us to consider thoughtfully the choices we make. Earlier in the chapter, Paul reminds us (and the Ephesian believers) that we were once part of the darkness, slaves to our own desires—consumed with greed, lust, and foolishness. Now, we are part of the light.

Light contrasts with darkness. In today's reading, Paul directs us to embrace the positive choice in the three contrasts this passage lays out:

1. To be wise rather than unwise,
2. To be understanding rather than foolish, and
3. To be Spirit-people rather than drunken people.

Being wise means knowing who we are and where we are. We are children of the light who live in the dark. In our days, evil often seems to have the upper hand, but we are part of a new community founded by Jesus Christ. Our every breath is praise and thanksgiving to God.

In every situation, we wisely choose to follow the Lord's will instead of self-serving desires. In the past, we stumbled in the dark. Now our guidance comes from relationship to the Lord.

Drunkenness is an attempt to fill an empty, wounded soul with temporary pleasure or distraction from pain. We can be drunk with wine or just as easily intoxicated with the pursuit of more possessions and greater wealth, power, and politics—or impurity and pleasure. If we are to stand out from the crowd, we must be filled with the life that God gives. We must become Spirit-people who thirst for goodness, righteousness, and truth; we desire to share those qualities with others.

When we join with the family of believers, our lives become a song of praise to God—a never-ending expression of gratitude for all that God is and has done.

Holy Spirit, fill me so that I will know your will and do it. Amen.

The book of Ephesians was written to help a group of early Christians establish their identity as beacons of light in a dark world. Terrorism, warfare, violence, impurity, unbridled greed, hatred, and division—these are the distinguishing marks of our time. There is no question that these days, just like those of the Ephesians, feel very dark at times. The real question is, "How will we respond?"

Some voices in our Christian community tell us to run in fear. They warn us that things have never been this bad before and will only get worse. They encourage us to find safety within sealed fortresses of ideology where we hear only the echo of our own grim thoughts.

Other voices direct us to change these evil days by seizing power and imposing our will on those who are evil. Political activism (on the right or left) suggests to us that we can force the world to conform to our ideal of what is "Christian" by using the methods of the world: control, power, and coercion.

Paul's call to us is to understand the Lord's will so that we can buy back these days from slavery to darkness and evil.

Stanley Hauerwas has argued, "The first task of the church is to make the world the world, not to make the world more just." Sometimes, we can become so concerned with making the world "more Christian" that we fail to notice that the church has become just like "the world," taking on worldly characteristics and methods of domination and division, power and control.

The Lord's will for us is neither to run away from nor to fight and conquer the world. Instead, our calling is to be God's presence of goodness, righteousness, and truth. This is how we can "redeem" evil days.

Holy Spirit, help me understand that your will is not to make the world look more like the church but to make me (and your church) more like Jesus Christ. Amen.

In today's Gospel reading, Jesus follows up the miraculous feeding of the five thousand with a few loaves and fish by inviting his followers to a far greater table. When we celebrate the Lord's Supper, we participate in gospel living and give expression to the essential elements of the Christian faith.

We come to the table empty-handed, expecting to receive the gifts of God. There is no distinction between rich and poor, weak and strong, good and bad. We approach on an equal basis of need.

At the table, God comes to meet us. The miracle of the Incarnation is that God became human. In the person of God the Son, Jesus Christ, deity forever united with humanity. The bread and the cup remind us of the flesh and blood of Jesus. Just as the bread is broken and the cup poured out, so Jesus' body was broken and his blood spilled at the cross. Eternal life comes at the expense of death on a cross. His sacrifice ensures our life. The nourishment we receive at the table strengthens our bodies, and our spirits are made alive by the life-giving presence of Christ within us.

The table does not belong to any person, group, or denomination. The table is the Lord's, and all are invited to come. Christ's presence spreads into the world through those who receive him.

Each time we celebrate the Lord's Supper, we not only remember what Christ has done but we look forward to what he will do in the future. When his kingdom comes and his reign is fully realized, we will join him in the great feast. We may be broken and in need now, but we trust him to make all things new. Christ has died, Christ is risen, Christ will come again.

"Bread of heaven, feed me till I want no more." Amen. ("Fill My Cup, Lord," Richard Blanchard)

Jesus often utters surprising, even shocking, statements. He doesn't say these things for their shock value but for their teaching value. His teaching turns much about Jewish religious and social life upside down.

We may find Jesus' teaching difficult to understand. In his day, disputes and arguments raged over the meaning of his words. Sometimes we still engage in fruitless, contentious arguments and ignore the heart of his teaching altogether. His disciples often questioned him about his instructions, and even then they often missed the point.

If Jesus were to join us in weekly worship and stand to speak, his words would be no less shocking to us than to his original audience. His teaching can upend the value system of our lives and challenge the priorities of our world. Yes, even for those of us who never miss a Sunday service!

Jesus claims to be the bread from heaven that gives eternal life. Listen to his words, "Very truly I tell you, unless you eat the flesh of the Son of Man and drink his blood, you have no life in you" (NIV).

"Unless you eat. . . ." Eternal life requires a commitment from us. Jesus offers himself as the life we desperately long for and need. However, we will never experience it . . . *unless*.

Entering God's kingdom demands our participation and action. The gift of life in Christ can no more be forced on the unwilling than food can be shoved through clenched teeth. Receiving Christ through trust in his message and his finished saving work claims our lives. We belong to him. We are responsible to participate in his life today and to put the ethics of his coming kingdom into practice now. How are you actively involved in Christ's reign?

Lord, inspire me to respond to you with ever-growing faith. I trust in you, and I am yours. Amen.

Communion with God

AUGUST 17–23, 2015 • KRISTEN E. VINCENT

MONDAY, AUGUST 17 ~ *Read 1 Kings 8:1, 6, 10-11*

In seminary my ethics professor asked us to write an argument to support the significance of coming together for worship. My own Sunday morning routine seemed mundane, hardly significant. But the assignment—inspired by my professor's thought-provoking lectures—changed my way of thinking. I sat in church one morning and looked around at the congregation. Like me, they had gotten out of bed and embarked on their morning routine before coming to church. For some, the morning activities were slowed, weighed down by depression, grief, anxiety, or loneliness. Still others were conflicted about whether to come to church, wanting instead to sleep in, play golf, get caught up on work, or do something else entirely. But here they were, sitting in their pews. They had chosen to come and worship God. Their reasons for coming would vary. Very few, if any, would name the real reason we are here: God called, and we responded.

That is what makes gathering for worship significant: Whether we realize it or not, we are responding to God's call to come into God's presence to praise and worship God. In today's passage, Solomon calls the nation of Israel and its leaders to assemble. It is a momentous occasion: They are dedicating the new temple in Jerusalem. Everyone gathers to watch as the priests carry the ark of the covenant into the temple for the first time. At that moment, the glory of the Lord fills the temple with a great cloud. God is here in this place. That is significant, indeed.

Loving God, you have called us to reconnect with you. Help us listen and respond. And in so doing, help us inspire others to respond as well. Amen.

Frequent speaker and writer on prayer; author, *A Bead and a Prayer: A Beginner's Guide to Protestant Prayer Beads*; Oxford, Georgia

Unless I am in the midst of a crisis or other extenuating circumstance, I like to begin my prayer with praise. It just feels right. Prayer is a time when I am conscious of being in the presence of the Lord. Being in God's presence naturally elicits praise. I see this in today's passage. As he imagines himself in the Lord's presence, the psalmist offers praise to the Lord in effusive, ebullient words.

My favorite line of this passage is the last one, where the psalmist exclaims that "happy is everyone who trusts in you." I think that is so true. Praise directly results from trust. We cannot praise God if we do not trust God. Think back to the garden of Eden. The Lord gives Adam and Eve everything they need. All God requires of them is trust and praise. Yet, they listen to the snake, who implies that God is not trustworthy. So they disobey God's command and become disconnected from God.

Once we acknowledge God's trustworthiness—a stance from which we rely upon God for everything and affirm that God will ultimately save us from sin and death—then we will reconnect with God and offer praise.

Like the scene in Revelation, we will find ourselves among the throngs proclaiming God's worthiness "to receive power and wealth and wisdom and might and honor and glory and blessing!" (Rev. 5:12). Again, the words are effusive, ebullient.

Creator God, you are worthy of praise, for you are trustworthy. I trust that you loved me enough to create me in your image. I trust that you love me enough to meet my every need. I trust that you love me enough to bring me into your glory one day. And for that, I give you praise. Amen.

Last year my church created a prayer team: volunteers who stay connected by e-mail and phone. Each week, the team leader compiles a list of joys and concerns and forwards it to the prayer team volunteers. The church assistant also includes a printed list in the Sunday bulletin.

The creation of the prayer list itself is hardly earth-shattering; many churches have one. What I find remarkable is its power. People learn more about one another when they share their joys and struggles. They offer support and seek updates on conditions. They look out for one another. Even when they meet a stranger, if that person shares a concern, the church member offers to add it to the list. The list grows, and so do the connections.

The prayer list's power also evidences itself as visible, concrete proof that God is at work in our lives. God invites our prayers and petitions. Accepting that invitation acknowledges our need for God and provides an opportunity to witness to God's work in our lives: lifting us up, bearing our burdens, offering us grace when we least expect it. The list grows, and so does our faith.

Paul would have loved the prayer-list concept. Indeed, he would love any way that people lift up the needs of themselves and others in prayer. As we see in today's passage, he believed that we should offer prayers and petition "all the time" and "for all believers" (CEB). He recognizes prayer as a full-time job that feeds our faith and our connections to God and one another.

What prayers and petitions do you have to offer God? Whom can you pray for? Who is praying for you?

For most of my adult life I have resisted the sabbath. There was too much to do, and I did not need to rest. Resting seemed like a waste of valuable time; better to stay on the move and accomplish something.

But in recent years I have become more attuned to the movements of the Spirit through prayer, worship, study, and community. Those practices have helped me to nest at the altars of the Lord. I have learned to close the computer, put down the broom, or let the overflowing laundry hamper wait while I relax, rest, and restore my energy levels, both physically and spiritually.

I now realize the benefits of quiet nesting. I am calmer, more fulfilled, able to be fully present for the blessings that life has to offer. With this gift, I understand that the ability to rest requires trust: trust that God is in control, enabling the world to continue to revolve on its axis without any help from me. I can just be. And in being, I can connect with God.

Today's reading describes the joy and pleasure that comes from resting in God. Here our yearnings for communion and presence find fulfillment. God both hears and sees. We are invited to relax in the Lord's courtyards. Here I imagine gurgling fountains and luscious, landscaped gardens, with hammocks swaying in the breeze under enormous oak trees. This place is one of peace, a place where all of creation—even the sparrows and swallows—come for rest and renewal, to "be" with God.

How will you honor the sabbath? How will you rest and be renewed by God? What do you need to leave behind or set aside in order to be with God?

The Eucharist is my favorite part of the liturgy. The powerful words boldly declare that the Lord is with us; the appropriate response is the offering up of our hearts in thanks and praise.

I also enjoy observing Communion. I hear the rustling of paper and the murmurs of parents guiding their children down the aisle. I see the elderly man who walks more slowly these days, the woman who looks as if she hasn't slept well in several nights. I watch as the people lift up their hands to receive the bread and the cup. It is all so ordinary that we often miss the significance of the act. We forget that we are tasting the body and blood of the God who chose to live and die and live again for us.

I think Jesus addresses this issue in today's passage. The day after the feeding of the five thousand, a crowd gathers around Jesus. Remembering the previous day's miracle, they want more. Well aware of this, Jesus calls them on it. "You are not here for the miracles," he says. "You are here because you were well fed yesterday, and now you are hungry again." In other words, they do not expect Jesus to save; they just want another meal.

Jesus realizes the people don't understand the significance of what he is doing for them. But it does not matter. Whether they understand him or not, he will die for their sins. And he will invite them to participate in the Resurrection. Our salvation does not depend on our ability to comprehend this mystery. It depends solely on God's boundless love and God's desire to be connected with us eternally. That is good news!

Gracious God, thank you for your love. Thank you for offering it to us freely. Help us to accept it and be grateful. Amen.

It is easy to feel connected to God when life is going smoothly. We go to church, we find time for prayer, we recognize the blessings in our lives, we give thanks. It is much harder, I think, to feel that connection when life becomes challenging. In the midst of grief, fear, pain, and confusion, we may feel abandoned by God and wonder where God is. We begin to feel alone, forced to fend for ourselves. Today's reading is critical to our faith.

The thriving church in Ephesus is experiencing some difficulties, some real-world problems, including conflict and division. Paul challenges the church to be strong—but not strong in its own resources. The church relies on God; specifically, he encourages the church to ground itself in God "and his powerful strength." Using familiar military metaphors, Paul challenges Christians to "put on the armor of God." This includes the "belt of truth," the "breastplate of righteousness," and the "shield of faith." This metaphor certainly makes the point that we can draw strength and protection from our faith in God. The all-powerful God will uphold us when we deal with difficult situations.

Even more powerful is the idea that God is with us. We sense God's presence with us as close as the breastplate on our chest or the shoes on our feet. During hard times, we may feel that God is far away or has abandoned us completely. But God is closer than we think.

It is good and proper to feel connected to God in the good times. More so, it is good and proper to feel connected to God in the tough times. God is with us. Thanks be to God.

Look back at the dark times in your life. Can you see how God was with you even when you may have felt alone? How can you put on the armor of God?

Solomon has called the nation of Israel together to dedicate the temple in Jerusalem. It was large, ornate, painstakingly handcrafted. It took seven years to build.

I imagine the dedication of the temple as a grand celebration. After all the hardship the Israelites have experienced—slavery, desert wandering, rebuilding their homeland, enduring attacks from foreign armies—they now have something to celebrate: a beautiful place to call their own; a holy place to house the ark of the covenant and to gather for worship. Surely everyone comes to the dedication dressed in their finest.

For me the most interesting aspect of this story is Solomon's prayer. In dedicating the temple he prays a lengthy prayer in which he praises God and thanks God for the gift of the temple. God has fulfilled God's promise to Israel in bringing the people to this moment in time.

But as the prayer goes on, Solomon shifts his focus away from the Israelites. He begins to pray for "a foreigner, who is not of your people Israel." He asks God to listen to the prayers of people from other lands. They will hear of this wonderful temple and want to travel to see it. Solomon hopes that when they do, the sight will move them to pray to the God of the Israelites. At this powerful moment in history, Solomon could justifiably have maintained his focus on the needs of the Israelites. After all, they built this great temple. They are God's chosen people. Instead, he sees the opportunity for evangelism and prays that the temple will connect others with God as well.

Most gracious God, your love for us is abundant. Help us recognize that such abundance is meant not only for us but for others as well. Help us find ways to share your love with others, and in so doing, may we become one in you. Amen.

Words of Life

MONDAY, AUGUST 24 ~ *Read Song of Solomon 2:8-13*

"The time of singing has come."

Much singing goes on around my house. My daughter especially is a little songbird. She will repeat the latest tune or melody over and over as she dances around the house in her ballet dress. Her passion and joy are palpable. These songs seem to get "stuck" in a loop within her heart and mind, being repeated over and over again. That's how it is with a tune; it captures you. The words and the tune come together and draw us into their rhythm. They speak to our heart.

In this text, the woman sings of her "lover" coming to announce a new season. The winter has passed. A new season is present; "the time of singing has come." "The old things have gone away, and look, new things have arrived!" (2 Cor. 5:17, CEB). I delight in this interaction because it serves as a metaphor of our relationship with God. God sings to us, calling us each day to a new season of singing and dancing. God offers mercy, forgiveness, and grace each morning. God offers words for our hearts to sing over and over—to ourselves . . . and to the world around us.

As you begin this new week, give yourself permission, maybe even instruction, to usher in a season of singing the words of life sung by our Creator. Sing songs of grace, mercy, love, and forgiveness, because you are God's Beloved!

Gracious God, thank you for your song of grace. Enable our hearts and lives to sing in tune with your grace. Amen.

Christ-follower, husband, dad, pastor, teacher, golfer, Duke fan, living in Atlanta, Georgia

TUESDAY, AUGUST 25 ~ *Read Psalm 45:1-2, 6-9*

"A marvelous word has stirred my heart" (CEB).

Have you ever seen a happy couple? In their love for each other, they give expression to God's love for creation. This song of love and admiration acknowledges the virtues and actions of the king. It does not give way to sappy emotional gushing; rather, it details a response to loving actions and kind works. Psalm 45 dovetails with yesterday's Song of Solomon text that reminds us to sing God's words of grace and life. What marvelous words have you heard? What works of God have stirred your heart?

Creation—God spoke all that we see and know into existence through *words*. To pause and marvel at the wonder, beauty, simplicity, and complexity is a gift.

Strength and power—God is able. No one is like our God. God provides strength and power to the weak and powerless. (Isa. 40:28-31).

Righteousness and fairness—The "speaker" of Psalm 45 asserts the king's commitment to justice, not just to power and dominion. The good king gives life and motivates us to act for good.

Truth and humility—Love is kind and truthful. God shows the kind of love that will be our plumb line for living and serving. God comes to us in Jesus, through humility and truth-speaking, stirring our hearts and transforming our lives.

God speaks marvelous words of life that stir our hearts, inviting us to trust and hope for what God will do next. God has done great things, and God's words enliven our world. Today, may you receive these marvelous words and live accordingly.

God of grace, stir our hearts with your marvelous words of life this day that we may serve you and our neighbors with grace. Amen.

"Grace has been poured out on your lips" (CEB).

Lips are a wonderful creation. They help us form sounds and words. Our words convey power; they can be life-giving or life-taking. How many times have we been wounded by a harsh word from another person?

We long for words of grace. In my life, I am drawn continually to the people who offer grace-filled words; my life is fuller and richer because of them.

In this passage, the psalmist alludes to the qualities of the king. The king has lips of grace and has acted in a way that is consistent with his heart. The king evidences his driving passion and desire through the words he speaks to others.

The king's scepter is one of equity. He seeks righteousness and justice. *Therefore* marks the link between justice and prosperity—an understanding of well-being that comes with righteous rule. God anoints with the "oil of gladness."

Grace comes from God, showing that God blesses and affirms actions that align with God's desires. This psalm challenges us to affirm God's grace that surrounds us. What grace do you see? Are you aligned with that grace? If so, may other people say, "Grace has been poured out on your lips."

Loving God, be patient with us as we grow in your grace, and set before us the call to live accordingly. Amen.

"This people honors me with their lips, but their hearts are far from me."

Paying lip service to something or someone has never been a good idea. Having been so heavily marketed to in recent times, people have very fine-tuned "authenticity" radar. People generally spot the truth-teller from the one "giving a line." It seems our culture is full of false pretenses and open-ended promises, all in the effort of keeping up appearances.

Today's text serves as a counterbalance to yesterday's readings from Psalm 45. Remember our theme this week: "Words of Life." Today we stop and reflect on ways we are *not* living into God's words of life. The religious leaders of Jesus' day say the right words and take the right actions, but something is missing or askew.

Take young boys, like my son. My wife and I tell him to take a bath. He goes through the motions of filling the tub, getting in, splashing around, and then getting out. He, like most nine-year-olds, doesn't seem to understand the need for soap and shampoo within this process. My son thinks that somehow we won't notice the stench, which reveals the "heart" of the matter. Yes, he obeyed the rule—get in the bathtub. But the intended result does not occur—get clean!

Today's challenge is intense: We are to honor God with our hearts! Paying lip service to God's way while holding on to selfish intentions or hidden agendas is unacceptable. God cannot be fooled. Let us today search our lives for the desires of our hearts. Do we long for God's words of life or for our feeble substitutes?

Forgiving God, receive our confessions of hardened, empty, fearful hearts. We want to live into your best, but we need your help. Amen.

"From the human heart. . . . "

The human heart is amazing! Pumping oxygen-enriched blood to our various extremities, the heart is central to our body and keeps us alive. But our hearts can become sick and diseased, both literally and figuratively. Saint Augustine, one of the church fathers, compares this heart disease of humanity to that of a person bent over inward toward themselves. This inward versus outward focus creates trouble within our human hearts.

Jesus highlights this problem and identifies the characteristics of such hearts. I am troubled by the list because he seems so unreserved and judgmental. Jesus is supposed to be kind, gentle, meek, and loving. Hasn't he already given instruction somewhere else about speaking with love and compassion? He can't really be talking about *my* heart, can he?

Only one response to these charges is a worthy one: confession. Tell the truth. Speak aloud the things that are real. Make public those thoughts, desires, and facts we seek to keep private. Confession makes forgiveness and restoration possible. When we acknowledge the inadequacy of our words and allow the words of life to stand side by side, we are humbled by the gap of difference between our human hearts and the divine heart.

So, will you allow the core of who you are to be guided by human words or divine words of life?

Loving God, forgive the sin that has so diseased my heart. Fill my heart with your words so that my life reflects your truth and love. Amen.

"He chose to give us birth by his true word" (CEB).

Yesterday we considered Jesus' piercing words that call us to confession so that our relationship to God can be restored. Today James reminds us of our *new* birth in Jesus. Here James echoes the understanding in John's Gospel of Jesus as the Word made flesh who lives among us and gives us new life. James employs the image of God the Great Planter who prepares the soil, plants the seed, and nurtures the growth. As James writes, we are the first fruits of everything God created. Wow!

But I don't always feel that way. Many days I feel like the leftovers at the bottom of the seed packet. James offers us the hope for this new birth: "Be quick to listen, slow to speak, slow to anger." *Listen* to the word of life. In listening we make ourselves available and ready. We are engaged to receive. We can hear and remember.

Too often we quote to ourselves (sometimes) and others (often), "Be quick to listen and slow to speak." Sage advice. Now, can we live it? Listening takes practice and focus. Listening offers us the chance to understand what we believe. And yet, as we read farther, we learn that James considers listening (or hearing) as subordinate to doing. We must hear and *do*.

Psalm 1 portrays the image of a tree planted by streams of water, receiving its water from deep roots. In this new birth, we welcome "the implanted word that has the power to save [our] souls." May our roots grow deep into the words of life given to us in Jesus the Christ. May we welcome the word planted deep within us.

Wonderful God, thank you for new birth and new beginnings. Open my heart, eyes, and ears to your wonderful words of life that nourish my soul. Amen.

"You must be doers of the word and not only hearers who mislead themselves" (CEB).

Most professionals in the field of communication indicate that well over 60% of our communication is nonverbal. We don't need to say a word before others will catch on to what we want to communicate. James understood this concept long before our modern scientists studied it. He posts the clarion call to let our actions speak louder than words. This can come only when the word of life lives in us.

We've journeyed together this week and explored the characteristics, power, and greatness of God's word for our lives. The conclusion comes from James's key concept in verse 26: "Control what they say" (CEB). As a United Methodist, I am proud to be part of a connectional community that is active in faith, showing our beliefs through our lives. But how do we as Christians keep matters in check? How do we remain faithful? How do we avoid being misled? We need others who hold us accountable for our actions.

We need to receive these words from James within community, so we enable one another to be hearers and doers for the kingdom. Today you will join other disciples in worship, fellowship, and service. Today—and every day—is your chance to be the words of life for someone else.

One United Methodist discipline is the work of Holy Conferencing, when we listen and receive the word of life from others' perspectives and engage those perspectives for our own growth and holiness. Today, watch, receive, listen, and hold with holiness the lives of your brothers and sisters in Christ. Then you will become the community of doers defined by the words of life and led by the Holy Spirit.

Faithful God, bring the words of life within our community as we gather together today in your presence for worship. Amen.

A Share in the Household of God

AUGUST 31–SEPTEMBER 6, 2015 • ELAINE EBERHART

MONDAY, AUGUST 31 ~ *Read Proverbs 22:1-2, 8-9, 22-23*

He stood outside the donut shop of my building at the university, wanting a dollar or a cup of coffee. His name was William, and we talked each morning before I left to deal with e-mail, calendars, and meetings. He would be absent for days at a time and upon his return would tell me that he had been sick.

Most mornings I bought him a cup of coffee when I bought my own. Sometimes I was busy and gave him a dollar. And sometimes I was too late to do more than wave. Whatever I did, I always had a sense of guilt. Was I doing enough?

Dennis, a colleague, and I shared the same office coffeepot. Though our paths didn't cross often, we sometimes stopped to say hello when crawling over each other in the tiny break room. I saw him talking to William one day, taking my place as the coffee buyer. I asked him about the situation when we got to our office. Yes, he knew William. He knew he had a drinking problem; they talked about the lost days when he would go on a binge. Dennis tried to get William a job at the donut shop. He talked to the manager and took William to meet her. William wouldn't apply, but Dennis was working on him, he said.

What accounted for the difference in the way we talked about William—Dennis with his determination that William get a job, I with my fear of not doing enough for him? We were both concerned about William, but I saw William as someone I felt obligated to help in just the right way. Dennis saw William as he saw himself, someone who needed others to make it through life's challenges, large and small.

Thank you, God, for those who teach us to help and those who teach us to accept help. Amen.

Member, Pilgrim Congregational Church, Birmingham, Alabama

The writer of Proverbs warns against robbing the poor merely because they are poor. Those who don't heed that advice will have a hard time because God pleads the cause of the poor and afflicted; and that same God will despoil the life of those who despoil the life of God's chosen.

We rob the poor by ignoring them when they ask for a dollar and by pretending that we don't see them when they offer to clean our window for change. We rob the poor, sometimes without thinking, when we forget the donation for the rescue mission campaign or the cans for the food bank drive. We rob the poor in these small individual ways, but together our harm is much greater.

We rob the poor when we allow check-cashing businesses to thrive in poor neighborhoods, charging exorbitant fees to cash paychecks. We rob from the poor when we cannot find ways to connect the working poor with traditional financial services so they aren't victimized by an industry that makes their economic progress impossible.

We rob the poor when we build subsidized housing over sites of former chemical businesses. Oily liquids that can't be identified leach up in the yards where children play. The raised levels of cancer and other diseases come as no surprise. Only when a television camera shows sludge draining from a playground does anyone question the apartments' location. Even then, few residents are relocated.

Giving cans of food is important, but we are called to address those who despoil the lives of our brothers and sisters. Advocacy in areas of public policy can seem overwhelming, but perhaps it is the avenue of the most help. What if our only choice was to live with our children in the apartment over the chemical dump?

How are the poor robbed in your community? How can you and your church address the problems?

Istruggle to understand the psalmist's worldview. He has known political occupation. Except for the days around September 11, 2001, I have never thought about the possibility of another country invading mine. He writes as one entitled to land through a covenant between God and his ancestor Abraham. He knows that if intruders conquer the land, they will not dwell there long because God has promised the land to the just. I can't view my country as particularly chosen by God while others are not.

I don't have to return to the psalmist's time to broaden my perspective. Innocent people in recent years have lost their homes and lives to tyrants concerned only with amassing more power and money. The fighting in many countries around the world leaves children without parents and with bombed-out shells of family homes. In other parts of the world, parents live in fear of their children's abduction. Landowners are routinely thrown off their lands and if allowed to remain, crops are burned.

The psalm writer affirms that those who trust in God will not be moved, just as Mount Zion cannot be moved. God will lead away the evildoers while doing good to those who are upright in heart. More important, God will surround those who trust in God as mountains surround Jerusalem.

What does it mean to live with uncertainty about my survival and know that God surrounds me as mountains surround Jerusalem? I won't presume to speak for people in other countries whose experiences I can't imagine. But when I think about the possibility of facing overwhelming loss, assurance of the Creator's care makes life bearable.

Your care surrounds me as mountains, O God, and I am comforted by your presence. Amen.

This text discomforts me. I can't quite reconcile the Jesus who was sent to the nations and who bids the children come to him with the Jesus who calls this woman and her people dogs. Calling someone a dog was probably a racist remark in Jesus' day, used to malign the Syrophoenicians and their ancestors, the Canaanites. Why would Jesus use this term to reject a woman who bows at his feet earnestly seeking help for her daughter? Scholars offer no firm answer. Some contend that the word *dog* here refers to a family pet or lap dog, which softens the blow of Jesus' words a bit. Others disagree: to label a woman a dog was to revile her.

Whatever the meaning of Jesus' words, the conclusion of the story is the main focus. The Syrophoenician woman willingly bows before a man who is her cultural enemy because she believes he may help her daughter. Then Jesus dismisses her, telling her that the children must be fed first. But she responds from her place at his feet with an audacious claim, "Sir, even the dogs under the table eat the children's crumbs."

The Syrophoenician woman does not ask for the privileges of a family member. She will take her place under the table with the dogs, but she asserts her right to a share of the household food. She is at once humble before one who holds her only hope and bold to ask for what she needs for her child. Surely Jesus has time enough for her daughter to offer one crumb of his power!

Jesus, moved by her response, grants the woman's request; she receives much more than crumbs. He sends her home to find her daughter well.

O God, with humility and boldness I ask for the fullness of life that is found only in you. Amen.

Through the crowd some people bring to Jesus a man who can neither hear nor speak. Jesus takes him to a private place, puts his fingers in the man's ears, and touches his tongue. Looking toward heaven Jesus says, "Be opened." As quickly as he says it, the man can hear and speak plainly. Jesus sends him on his way and instructs those with him to tell no one.

With a word and a touch, Jesus restores the man to life and to his community. The man can now participate in worship since he no longer violates the purity laws. Daily tasks will be his again. He will not depend on someone else's schedule to pursue activities that require listening or speaking. He can enjoy the fullness of life through hearing and speech. He can listen to the sounds of nature, music, and crying. He can whisper, argue, and sing.

We can imagine that the man and his entourage maintain their silence—until they get past the city limits. Then they buy a loudspeaker for their wagon so more people can hear what has happened. They hold an impromptu meeting in a market along the road. When they reach a larger town they rent out a stadium and announce to growing crowds that Jesus does everything well. Jesus opened a man's ears, and the man speaks again.

Jesus has urged the man and his friends to tell no one, but they can't remain silent. The change they have witnessed is too dramatic. And isn't the removal of any impediment that keeps us from fullness of life dramatic? When we witness it, aren't we astounded beyond all measure?

We who have known the transformation of our lives can't be quiet. We who have witnessed healings large and small that have enabled us to be more fully human can't maintain silence. Thanks be to God.

Consider the ways you have been healed to live more fully.

Many of us learned about social boundaries in our high school cafeterias. We sat at tables depending upon what sport we played, or if we played at all. We sat at other tables if we were deemed popular or unpopular. Sometimes we sat at a table because of our race or the language we spoke at home. If we were studious, we chose one area; if we had more or less money, we sat in another. After our short lunch period, we went back to class where we didn't have the safety of our little group. Our best chance to cross a social boundary had just passed. Around those tables we could have examined our labels face-to-face if we had talked to someone new. Teenage social boundaries are difficult to cross.

Adult social boundaries are not much easier to negotiate. Now we wonder how to reach out to the woman downstairs who doesn't speak English. Driving onto the ramp of the interstate, we see a man with a sign asking for food and work. We can't imagine how to cross our social boundaries to include him in our lives. A man and his partner visit the church today. Will we be the first to cross a social boundary to welcome them?

James urges his hearers to honor the poor in accordance with God's plan. We invite poor and other oppressed people to our tables and ask to sit at theirs. As in high school, we find it tempting to stay in the comfort zones of our neighborhoods, our biases, and our past experiences. If we can cross our social boundaries and care for those who have been dishonored by our world and even by our churches, we will fulfill God's command to love our neighbors as ourselves.

Allow me to cross my social boundaries, O God, so I may come to understand that all are invited to your table. Amen.

SUNDAY, SEPTEMBER 6 ~ *Read James 2:14-17*

Christian belief and action are linked inextricably. Informed by the Spirit, belief in Christ's love motivates love of neighbor. Experiences in the love of neighbor reinforce belief in Christ's love. When this cycle of belief and action occur in community, it deepens both communal faith and outward ministry.

Many teenagers reared in The United Methodist Church spend a week each summer on mission trips. Whether at a mountain location, in an inner city, or on a barrier island, the jobs are usually the same. Teenagers and adults repair homes and churches. They lead Bible schools for children. The work usually is both strenuous and fun.

Sometimes, a teenager experiences her first cross-cultural exchange on the trip. After meeting people who seem strange to her, she wonders why she decided to come. She promised Jesus that she would do anything to serve him at the closing service of the fall retreat, and she signed up for the trip while her belief was strong. Her belief isn't holding up well after two days in a strange land. She feels afraid of the people she came to serve.

Enter her community of adults and teenagers, many of whom have made this trip before. Their belief has called them to love the neighbor. Listening to an elderly man through a window as they replace the boards on his porch reinforces their belief. They know that he has gifts to share with them that are as important as the work they will complete on his house.

Tomorrow someone will notice that young woman and will ask her to join the group going back to work on the porch. The man's gift will remind her of her belief, and her group will help her put her belief into action.

Transform my faith, O God, into one that actively seeks to love you and my neighbor. Amen.

Words of Wisdom

SEPTEMBER 7–13, 2015 • LAWRENCE M. STRATTON

MONDAY, SEPTEMBER 7 ~ *Read Proverbs 1:20-33*

The image of a woman summoning her listeners to heed wisdom, which she personifies, has a charismatic power. These words evoke cinematic images of a majestic woman crying out on busy street corners, city squares, and city gates where society's economic, social, and political life intersect.

Wisdom's question in verse 22 presumes that the simple love being simple, that scoffers enjoy scoffing, and that fools hate knowledge. She wants to change their minds and attitudes, drawing in hypothetical listeners and readers who yearn for wisdom's counsel. But not everyone. Wisdom laments that she has called and stretched out her hand, only to be refused and ignored. As a consequence of this rejection, she will not answer; despite their diligent pursuits they "will not find me." The reason for her cold shoulder: They "hated knowledge and did not choose the fear of the LORD," ignored her counsel and despised her reproof, which results in the bad fruit of misdeeds. Wisdom then juxtaposes the negative assessment of how waywardness kills the simple and how complacency destroys fools with her positive assurance that "those who listen to me will be secure and will live at ease, without dread of disaster."

Our gracious God gives us the ability to understand. We can choose to "give heed," to return to God. When have you heard God's call and refused to heed? How do you experience Wisdom's call?

Lord, help me seek your wisdom this day and evermore. Keep me on the path of wisdom, confident in your love. Amen.

Director, Stover Center for Constitutional Studies and Moral Leadership; Assistant Professor of Ethics and Constitutional Law, Waynesburg University, Waynesburg, Pennsylvania

This psalm tells its readers what they already know, namely that the heavens bear witness to and preach the wonder, goodness, and power of God.

Psalm 19 proclaims that the heavens and the earth reflect God's presence everywhere. Despite lacking the speech of humans, "the heavens" and "the firmament" pour forth speech and declare knowledge. Their collective voice and words proceed throughout all the earth to the end of the world.

Echoing the wonder of creation in Genesis, the psalm's imagery moves from the broad array of stars in the heavens and the solid ground of the earth toward the sun. The heavens are a metaphorical tent in which God has set the sun. The psalmist poetically describes the sun's movement across the sky, as a bridegroom comes out of a wedding canopy and as a strong runner advances through the course with joy. The sun rises and moves across the heavens and "nothing is hid from its heat," the psalmist continues.

By extolling God's glory in the heavens with the movement of the stars, the psalm hints that the earth and all creation reflect God's wondrous order. The apostle Paul quotes Psalm 19 in Romans 10:18—"Their voice has gone out to all the earth, and their word to the ends of the world" to support his point that God has manifested divine glory to all people.

Read these verses, then put down the Bible. Go outside to sit and view a marvelous vista. Pay attention to God's preaching through the heavens!

Dear God, whenever we might feel as though you are distant, help us to ponder Psalm 19's message that the heavens declare your glory. Comfort us with your presence, and surround us with your grace. Amen.

The psalmist shifts from the sun's circuit across the heavens to the perfection of the law of the Lord. The perfect law revives the soul. The surety of the Lord's decrees make the simple wise. The Lord's precepts are right and therefore make the heart rejoice. The Lord's commandment is clear, which enlightens the eyes. The fear or reverence for the Lord is pure and lasts forever, and the Lord's ordinances are true and righteous.

After describing the perfection of God's law and precepts, the psalmist extols their high desirability, beyond fine gold and the sweetness of honey. The psalmist then moves from the high value of the law of the Lord to the law's authority to give warning and the benefits of following God's law.

The psalm's grand description of the heavens, sun, and desirability of God's law leads to personal introspection: "Who can detect their errors?" The psalmist yearns for forgiveness, "Clear me from hidden faults." The psalmist expresses concern over personal shortcomings and then asks for the Lord's protection from others.

The psalmist closes with the famous prayer that pastors often use before delivering their sermons: "Let the words of my mouth and the meditation of my heart be acceptable to you, O Lord, my rock and my redeemer."

Psalm 19 thus begins with God's glory being proclaimed in the distant heavens and ends with an individual's security in God, "my rock and redeemer."

Lord, help me look to the heavens and firmament to see your handiwork. Clear up my hidden faults so that I may better follow you and live according to your perfect law. Amen.

James's text provides a strong warning about the importance of words; namely, we should watch what we say! The book of James has a way of getting under people's skin. None other than Protestant reformer Martin Luther called the letter an "Epistle of Straw." Luther thought James contradicted the apostle Paul's principle of justification by faith alone when James wrote, "So faith by itself, if it has no works, is dead" (2:17).

James's call to choose our words carefully can be unnerving, especially for teachers who find his warning striking. "Not many of you should become teachers, my brothers and sisters, for you know that we who teach will be judged with greater strictness."

The reason for James's admonition resides in the weakness of the human condition. As Patrick J. Hartin writes in his commentary on the epistle of James, "Sins of the tongue are the hardest to avoid."[*] Because teachers do a lot of talking, especially those who teach in the church, they are at greater risk of misinterpreting the law and tradition; therefore, teachers will be judged with heightened scrutiny.

James uses two commonly recognized metaphors to describe the tongue's destructive power. Just as riders control horses with bits and a ship's pilot steers an immense ship with a tiny rudder, James observes that although the tongue is small, it is capable of great exploits. When have your words brought great hurt? great enjoyment and pleasure? How do you rein in your willingness to set a forest ablaze by idle words from your mouth?

Gracious God, give us your wisdom so that we will be quick to listen, slow to speak, and slow to anger. Help us to teach and say the right thing when you would have us speak. Amen.

James Sacra Pagina Series, vol. 4; Collegeville, MN: Liturgical Press, 2009, 173.

The tongue "sets on fire the cycle of nature" and in the strongest language James can muster, he says that the tongue "is itself set on fire by hell." He notes that "no one can tame the tongue." The poison of the tongue negatively affects the individual, society, and even cosmic levels of existence.

With the tongue, "we bless the Lord and Father, and with it we curse those who are made in the likeness of God." This verse offers hope. James advocates an integrity of faith, word, and action as he describes the contradictions of the freshwater spring pouring fresh and brackish water, a fig tree yielding olives or a grapevine figs, or salt water and fresh water.

Created in the image of God, whom we praise, we agree with James as he paints an unpretty picture of the consequences of destructive speech and declares, "My brothers and sisters, this ought not to be so!"

Many of us regret words we have spoken to family members, friends, or colleagues at school, church, or work. In retrospect, we may wish we had not made certain statements, no matter how apt they may have seemed at the time. How do we make amends for words spoken besides saying, "I'm sorry"?

James offers no resolution to the difficulty of taming the tongue but encourages us to rein in our speech. John Calvin suggests that this passage about taming our tongues encourages our meekness in the face of our own tongue-related infirmities so that we might forgive others whose words injure us: "He acts unjustly who denies to others the pardon he needs himself." This merciful attitude inclines us to follow James's advice in the next chapter, "Draw near to God, and he will draw near to you" (4:8). May we speak words of blessing.

Lord Jesus, guard our tongues so that we speak wisdom in the context of your love and grace. Help us to be merciful toward others, particularly with regard to their speech. Amen.

Who do people say that I am?" The disciples' answers read like an equivocal poll summary, as they offer a range of responses: John the Baptist, Elijah, one of the prophets. In today's era of focus group surveys, we can almost hear the percentages related to each response.

Jesus then asks the direct question, "But who do you say that I am?" Peter answers, "You are the Messiah."

Jesus confronts all of us with his question: "Who do you say that I am?" In two thousand years of subsequent history the answers and definitions extend beyond John the Baptist, Elijah, and one of the prophets. Many say that Jesus was a wise teacher, a revolutionary hero, or other symbolic figurehead whose life and death divides history. Peter's heartfelt answer, "You are the Messiah," affirms Jesus as the fulfillment of Old Testament prophecy, the person Mark calls "Son of God" (1:1), the anointed one.

Mark reports that Jesus immediately tells Peter and the others to keep quiet. With this strong command to keep Jesus' messiahship a secret, the disciples will begin to appreciate the significance of Jesus' identity. Perhaps from a practical standpoint, proclaiming Jesus' divine identity too soon will infuriate Roman and Jewish officials. Or perhaps Jesus moves quickly to counter the disciples' expectations about the Messiah—notions that the Messiah will be a political or military leader. We also risk making erroneous assumptions about Jesus. Who do you say Jesus is? How does his identity play out in your daily living?

Lord Jesus, help us to see more clearly what Peter acknowledges, "You are the Messiah." May our response to your question also spring from our hearts. Keep our focus on you, Lord Jesus, and help us to see and understand you. Amen.

After Jesus commands the disciples to tell no one that he is the Messiah, he gives them some grim news: the Son of Man will undergo suffering, rejection by the elders, chief priests and scribes, be killed, and after three days rise again. Peter is not partial to Jesus' interpretation. He takes Jesus aside and rebukes him. Jesus then rebukes Peter in the strongest possible words: "Get behind me, Satan!" Jesus' rebuke suggests that by seeking to prevent Jesus from fulfilling his mission, Peter actually promotes the principle of evil. Jesus tells Peter: "For you are setting your mind not on divine things but on human things."

Peter gets the right answer about Jesus' identity, but he does not connect the Messiah to rejection, suffering, and death. We as Jesus' followers also share in this apparent contradiction as life's existential pressures and alienation surround us.

Yet the harshness of Jesus' rejection and suffering, as well as his strong rebuke to Peter, is tempered by his earlier promise that he would "after three days rise again." This paradox of the cross being juxtaposed with Christ's resurrection lies at the heart of the Christian faith. Mark's Gospel wants to affirm that our faithful response to life's inherent difficulties and severe challenges is to follow the path of Jesus and to set our minds on divine things, "for the sake of the gospel."

We know that Peter, *petros* in Greek, meaning "rock," becomes the Rock of the church, despite many stumbles and denials. At this point, Christians find great hope as they too take up their cross and follow Jesus.

Lord Jesus, help us to set our minds not on human things but on divine things as we take up our cross to follow you. Shape us so that you will not be ashamed of us when you come "in the glory of [the] Father with the holy angels." Amen.

Wising Up

SEPTEMBER 14–20, 2015 • NATALIE A. HANSON

MONDAY, SEPTEMBER 14 ～ *Read Psalm 1*

Psalm 1 sets the stage for all the psalms that follow. Happy are those, it says, who delight in the law of the Lord. *Delight* here means "to value, to take pleasure in, to engage, to wrestle with, to explore"—to live into all that God offers. And while *law* includes the commandments, it also refers to God's direction and teaching. So our delight comes not just in rule-keeping but in what theologian and scholar Walter Brueggemann calls "playful activity"; in being unafraid to experiment, to take God's direction, to try God's teaching on for size. Brueggemann writes about our becoming "Torah-shaped persons," who learn by doing and who throw themselves into exploring God's directions for living, deeply and often. The more we engage, the more we are nourished and molded. Happy are those who wrestle with God's teachings and—in the wrestling—are shaped in God's image!

Remember learning to ride a bicycle? You can watch other people ride, but until you try it yourself, you don't begin to learn. Then, as you learn, the time comes to take off the training wheels, trust the bike, feel your balance, and fly! You may sustain a few scrapes along the way, but once you get the hang of it, you know that balance forever.

Wisdom begins with the desire to engage. We grow wiser through active relationship with God. We are shaped as we explore God's teachings. Righteousness is less about keeping a rule than about the spirit and direction of our living. That's what the psalm says. No wonder this is Psalm 1.

Holy One, if I choose one direction for my life, let it be toward you. As I choose, help me choose joyfully, fearlessly. Amen.

Pastor, Christ First United Methodist Church, Jamestown, New York

A capable wife who can find?" Really? This question in Proverbs 31:10 is snarky! Yet this is the nature of Proverbs: Its insights can be acidic, comforting, funny, scary. Proverbs captures some of the same qualities that catch our attention in quips on our T-shirts: "What goes around comes around." "If you're too open-minded, your brains will fall out." People have always favored edgy, clever, pithy sayings—even if they're a little mean.

So we understand this about the style of Proverbs, set it aside, and look to see if something more important is being said.

It is. The author describes not simply the virtues of a capable wife but the characteristics of wisdom itself. Verse 26 says that the wife "opens her mouth with wisdom." In verse 27, translated as "she looks well to the ways of her household," that first Hebrew phrase ("she looks well to") is pronounced *sophia* (tzo-fi-ya). *Sophia* is the Greek word for wisdom. It's probably an intentional pun. Wisdom is "in the house," so to speak! And what does wisdom do? It "does not eat the bread of idleness." Wisdom is not passive but attentive and active.

Now the many tasks that lead up to verses 26 and 27 are put into context: The wise one goes to work, acts with savvy and kindness, takes responsibility, dispenses justice and mercy, serves and honors those around her. Wisdom is not something to be possessed as an achievement or an academic exercise: It is meant to be lived.

There's our message. Not that we are never to reflect or contemplate or spend time listening to and learning from God; but when we have learned something, that's just the beginning. The learning becomes real when we act upon it. We grow wise as we apply God's word in our daily decisions. We can't leave wisdom sitting in the corner.

Lord of this day and of each day that comes, help me apply your grace and wisdom in everything I do. Amen.

James lists seven characteristics of the "wisdom from above." The phrase *from above* means "original"; thus it is wisdom that's been around since the beginning, wisdom from the Source, wisdom that teaches us God's original intent for our lives.

This wisdom is pure (meaning holy and worshipful), disposed toward peace, gentle (meaning patient), open and willing to yield (to God's direction and to each other's needs), full of mercy (meaning compassion) and good fruits (meaning goodness in action), undivided (meaning whole and unambiguous), and sincere (without hypocrisy). Where persons live out of these values, true community exists. When persons live out of these values, we find the beginning of God's kingdom on earth. James writes that those who, out of this wisdom, make peace are sowing amazing seeds whose fruits are righteousness and harmony.

On the other hand, bitterness, envy, selfishness, and ambition are anti-wisdom characteristics. When people act out of these impulses, community collapses. We see disorder, meanness, conflicts, and disputes.

So there is a "flavor" to all we say and do that tends either toward the bitter or the sweet, the life-breaking or the life-building. The flavor affects the taste of absolutely everything—especially in the sphere of relationships. We humans are wired to give much more power to the negative than the positive. We apparently need to receive seven words (or more) of affirmation to balance the bitterness of just one criticism. So the "wisdom from above" implores us, for the world's sake, to choose the other flavor; to let compassion and patience and goodness saturate all our actions, all our relationships, through and through.

God of all wisdom, if we're going to flavor the world with anything, let it be with your love. And if we've got any meanness or bottled-up rage on our shelves, help us clear it out. Amen.

Wising Up

In Buffalo, New York, is a major cancer research center called Roswell Park. Over the years they've become skilled in growing different kinds of human tissue, starting with a tiny sample of cells placed in a petri dish. Before introducing the cells, the researchers fill the petri dish with a medium that contains everything the cells will need to flourish and grow. If the medium is contaminated or wrong, the cells will die.

The letter of James describes a "medium," a culture, in which wisdom has died. The community faces conflict. People give expression to the war inside their hearts and minds by warring on the outside. In fear, greed, and pride, people are not talking but taking. Instead of working together, they're working each other over. The outcome is loss and poverty for all on every level.

James calls the people of this culture "adulterers," but he's not really talking about sexual infidelity. He's talking about being double-minded: about holding back from commitment, trying to live in two directions at the same time. When we think we can embrace the world's wisdom *and* God's, we are torn apart—and we tear each other apart in the process.

But there is a medium that can nurture wisdom in us, a culture in which we can develop wholeness of heart and integrity of life, and that culture is built of mutuality and trust. Mutuality begins with the understanding that we are most alive when we are connected—when we let our guard down and take the first steps toward each other and God. Even before we take those first steps, God has been drawing near to us all. Trust believes that even in the worst of falls, we'll be caught; that the experience of falling and being caught, the experience of needing, receiving, and offering grace will be the making of us. Wisdom grows as we build communities of mutual honor and trust.

Grant me this day, dear Lord, singleness of heart, an overarching, undergirding love for you and yours. Amen.

Charles Cousar, writing about this portion of the Gospel of Mark, says that in their continual misunderstanding of Jesus, the disciples become mirrors in which we see ourselves.

Before this, the disciples have shied away from what Jesus tries to teach them about their power to address the world's hunger. When Jesus walks toward them on the water, they fear his difference. They have almost claimed Jesus' true identity but hesitate at the thought of his death—and maybe their own. They experience glory on a mountaintop.

Then, after all this less-than-stellar discipleship, the disciples brashly argue among themselves about who is the greatest! Can you imagine that? The answer is, "Yes, we can"—because we're just the same. Even in the church (maybe especially in the church), we shy away from responsibility. We fear those who are different. We want to be brave, but we're afraid of sticking our necks out. We'd rather things be nice all the time. Sometimes we're so afraid of failing that we won't let ourselves be challenged. We can so focus on defending our version of the truth that we won't ask the questions that might help us learn from each other. Just like the disciples.

And just like the disciples, in our haste to appear wiser than we really are, we end up looking foolish. Ouch.

The good news is that if we'll use it, the mirror is a great learning tool. The good news is that no matter how afraid and dysfunctional the disciples are, Jesus never gives up on them. The good news is that Jesus lived and lives so that folks just like the disciples, just like us, may be free from fear to live a truly abundant life.

So maybe it's time to wise up.

Don't give up on me, Jesus; don't let go until I release my self-defeating fears, until your kingdom begins to blossom in me. Amen.

At the height of the disciples' misunderstanding of Jesus, rather than chiding them, he offers a concrete image of the kingdom. He brings a child among them, takes the child in his arms, and tells them that anyone who wants to come out on top will have to start at the bottom. He says the first must be last. He says leading is serving. He notes that welcoming such a little one means they are welcoming him and, through him, welcoming God into their lives.

Jesus is saying that if we're going to understand the way God works, we have to turn the world's understanding of power on its head. He calls for a reversal of roles, status, and expectations . . . for a purpose.

That purpose is not merely for exchange, not merely to flip positions, as if the rich becoming poor and the poor becoming rich changes anything in the long run. No, the purpose of reversal is to explode barriers, to sweep away false assumptions, and to create identity among all God's children. If the disciples can walk beside and identify with those who are lower on the power pole, it will transform their understanding of justice, community, and the value of each person. Only then will they encounter the extraordinary, unifying power of the kingdom of God. They might even experience glory.

A contractor has to "see" the architect's vision before building. Chefs need to know the taste of a dish before they begin to cook. We need the experience of God's life-transforming kingdom before we can help build it in the world, and so we become servants to all. We choose to stand beside those without power who are marginalized, invisible, to earn their friendship and to let ourselves be changed. What the world views as upside-down, we welcome as wise; we know it opens the door to life.

Abba, if I've grown distant from any of your other sons and daughters, help me run to close the gap. Amen.

Earlier this week, we considered the "Torah-shaped person" who is molded and changed by engagement with God. Psalm 1 contrasts the outcomes for the righteous with the outcomes for those who tread other paths. Scoffers are not intentionally wicked, but they are certainly fragmented, centerless, confused. This way of life is like chaff, the husks of the grain left over after threshing. This life is weightless, groundless, prone to being blown about with every shift of the wind.

On the other hand, the law-shaped person feels constantly refreshed and renewed, fruitful in the world, watched over by God. The psalmist draws these sharp contrasts to make a point, but the psalmist knows—and we know—that it's not that simple. Human beings are famously inconsistent. One day we know God as an intimate friend; a few days later we feel God is a million miles away. One week we feel like a tree planted by the waters. The next week we feel as if we're lost in the desert. In one season of life we feel confident, centered, capable; then our world shifts and suddenly we feel like chaff, blown by the wind in all directions. That's life.

With this in mind, we can read this psalm less as a judgment on different lifestyles than as a prescription and a hope for us inconsistent folk. When we're lost, there's a direction in which to go. When we're empty, there's a well that never runs dry. When we're confused, there's a wisdom that never fails us.

We're reminded of Jesus our Christ, whom we call the living water, the way, the Word, the abundant vine. We recall him offering grace again and again, despite our inconsistencies. We yearn for that grace to fill and enliven us. We long to look out through grace's wise eyes. We want to live Christ-shaped lives.

Because you came so close to us, dear Christ, we trust we may come close to you. Draw us so near that we reflect your light. Draw us so near that when others meet us, they see you. Amen.

For Such a Time as This

SEPTEMBER 21–27, 2015 • TIMOTHY JAMES JOHNSON

MONDAY, SEPTEMBER 21 ～ *Read Esther 7:1-6, 9-10*

A close friend is retiring from a prestigious university. However, before she retires, she believes God has called her to address rampant social injustices in the institution, and she feels divinely appointed to expose these unjust circumstances.

Esther's story takes place during the captivity of the Jewish people in Babylon. The setting is the royal city of Susa, from which King Ahasuerus rules over the Persian Empire. Lives and fortunes rise and fall by mere pronouncements of the king's word. The antagonist is Haman, a powerful and ambitious man who intends to destroy the Jewish captives. The protagonists are Esther and her cousin Mordecai. Esther has been elevated as queen, but she has hidden her Jewish identity. Mordecai appeals to Esther to use her position as queen to neutralize Haman's plan. His appeal to Esther is this: "Perhaps you have come to royal dignity for just such a time as this" (Esth. 4:14).

After a three-day fast, Esther courageously goes unannounced to the king's court (a potential capital offense) and invites him and Haman to a banquet where she brings to light Haman's evil plot. Today's scripture reading offers the moment of truth. Esther reveals the wicked plot. King Ahasuerus is infuriated, and Haman is sentenced to death.

But the true drama here is that God puts people—even captives of low status like Esther— in places to serve as instruments of God's righteous plans. This week's meditations explore the truth that God uses ordinary people to do extraordinary things.

God, give me understanding and courage to be an instrument of your plans for peace and goodwill on earth. Amen.

Ordained Baptist minister, Emeritus Professor of Social Work, Roberts Wesleyan College, Rochester, New York

We generally mark birthdays, graduations, and anniversaries with celebrations—the manner in which most people benchmark their lives' progression. The core of these events calls the past into the present, which renews the value of what was significant in the past for moving into the future.

Historical events, both tragic and joyful, also provide cause for remembering and celebrating—but on a national scale. In today's scripture, Mordecai initiates an annual celebration of God's deliverance of the Jewish people from death in Babylon. The celebration of God's deliverance through Mordecai and Esther has deep roots in Jewish religious culture. Jews celebrate the occasion, called Purim, annually in March. At its core, Purim extols God's grace in the appointment of Esther and Mordecai as divine agents of deliverance of God's people from grave danger.

Many of us are familiar with a scientific experiment with light: An image or beam of light directed at one mirror, if reflected at just the right angle onto a second mirror, gives an infinite repetition of both the second mirror and the image. Mordecai's letter instructs that the Jews celebrate Purim by giving gifts of food to others and giving food to the poor. These acts of grace on the part of Jewish captives create an infinite mirror image of God's grace.

God appoints each of us to be an agent of grace. Each of us receives responsibility to move forward God's acts of kindness, justice, and love. We celebrate God's deliverance in gratitude by expressing concern for others' well-being as we do justice and love kindness.

Teach us, O Lord, what it means to be called your agents in today's world. Teach us how to transform your grace into personal acts of love, justice, and peace. Amen!

Among memories of my childhood church was the practice of "raising hymns." An old a cappella tradition from my African American Southern roots, it occurred during preservice devotional periods. Someone would spontaneously sing out a line of the song. The congregants would pick up the tune and repeat the singing of that same line. This call-and-response method of singing joined congregants together in worship and prepared them to enter a higher spiritual plane.

Scholars believe that Psalm 124, a "song of ascents," is one of a group of psalm songs sung by worshipers on their way up to the temple in Jerusalem. In the psalm, a lead singer begins the testimony with "If it had not been the LORD who was on our side" and then calls for the worshipers to respond with the testimony, "Let Israel now say." The psalm song testifies to God's grace in vanquishing Israel's enemies. Testifying leads worshipers to praise God by blessing the Lord who protects. The psalm ends with reaffirmation of dependence on God, "Our help is in the name of the LORD, who made heaven and earth." Imagine the spiritual frame of mind of the worshipers who have sung this psalm responsively before entering the Temple for worship.

Palm 124 will have brought to the singers' minds some of the great conquerors of the faith: Moses, Joshua, Deborah, Abigail, Samuel, David. Psalm 124 reminds them of the constancy of God's delivering grace.

Psalm 124 should encourage each of us and our worshiping communities to testify publicly and often to God's saving grace. Remembering God's grace by recalling God's divine appointment of people in our past provides divine resuscitation for our own callings from God.

Lord, we remember and thank you for the mothers and fathers of our faith who lived out divine appointments in their lives. Amen.

For Esther, Mordecai, and the Jewish people, the threat of annihilation is past. Mordecai records for posterity the sad train of events along with the joyous sequel to which they led. The threat of death has evoked sorrow and mourning, but deliverance of the people leads to gladness and joy.

When Esther first hears that Mordecai sits at the king's gate wearing sackcloth and ashes, she tries to alleviate the symptoms by sending Mordecai a change of clothes. He rejects them. Mordecai's divine appointment for that time is to help Esther own a solution for the impending destruction. Esther is called to place her life on the line. (See Esther 4.) This is Esther's appointed time. Because Esther becomes a hero in the solution, the days of feasting and gladness are hers to own, along with Mordecai.

All of us could wish to live free of tragedies and sorrows, but in the matter of living we will always face woe. Yet in the face of trouble, the psalmist writes of the transformative power of God to change sorrow into joy: "Many are the afflictions of the righteous, but the LORD rescues them from them all" (Ps. 34:19). From Esther and Mordecai and countless other Bible stories, we note that in the midst of troubled times, the Lord makes divine appointments that change sorrow into joy. God uses people as instruments of change.

Are we listening for God's call in the midst of our own life's troubles and sorrows? Do we hear God's call to be agents of transformation as we offer ourselves to break down any barriers to abundant living for others?

Lord, give us ears to hear your call, tender hearts to respond to others' sorrows, and transformative courage that changes sorrow into joy. Amen.

Shortly after completing high school, I worked at a dairy in the refrigerator storage building. The environment was dank, cold, and unpleasant; my coworkers were rough-hewn men. One coworker was particularly profane and insensitive. One afternoon while working with this man and utterly despairing of him and the job, I heard him begin to sing in a remarkable baritone voice, "There's Not a Friend Like Jesus." My dismal experience became holy ground. From that encounter I realized that God does not limit divine appointments to those who actively seek them. They also come by God's decision to accomplish the divine will for a particular time and circumstance.

Jesus has commissioned the disciples to proclaim the kingdom message and cast out demons. Imagine the shock of these newly minted disciples when they encounter a person who is *not* a follower of Jesus casting out demons in his name. The passage implies the disciples' failed attempt to have the man cease and desist. Unsuccessful in that endeavor, they seek Jesus' counsel. Jesus, ever the revolutionary, gives a shocking answer: "Whoever is not against us is for us." I figure this took the wind out of the disciples' sails. But then Jesus takes the matter even further, indicating that even the lowly act of giving a cup of water in Jesus' name merits reward.

Whether our calling leads to astonishing acts like casting out demons or the mundane act of giving water in Jesus' name, every calling from God has sacred significance. God uses surprising circumstances and unlikely persons to accomplish God's will. How wonderful it is to be surprised by God's voice speaking in unlikely places and in unexpected ways.

We thank you, Lord, that you use unlikely people in unlikely ways to accomplish your will. Amen.

Earlier in the week, I used the metaphor of infinite mirror reflections to describe the aggregate impact of God's people reflecting God's grace. Today's scripture focuses on the polar opposite of this metaphor. It deals with the consequences of being a stumbling block to faith, being "ungracious." It contains a sobering message of dire consequences expressed in language that confronts us with unwelcomed and frightening ideas: being drowned, cutting away body parts, unquenchable fire, and consignment to hell. The scripture creates tension and great discomfort in us.

Jesus relays the message to his disciples and to us that as God's people the way we live in the world is a sober and weighty responsibility. It carries with it rewards or consequences. Jesus speaks of placing "a stumbling block before one of these little ones." "Little ones" may refer to those young in the faith, all the "Christ following" adherents to which Jesus' message led. In biblical metaphorical language we hear Jesus saying in effect, "Better to maim yourself than cause another person to stumble."

Again, the familiar metaphor of people of faith as salt is put forth to describe how we are to live in the world. Implicit in the scripture is the summons to season the world with God's grace. We are appointed to the preservation of God's creation and of those who serve God. Setting aside our doubts about hell-fire language, we acknowledge that God is love, and love covers a multitude of sins. We recognize this outpouring as grace. How does living out our divine appointment as the people of God keep us from causing people to stumble?

Gracious God, where I find stumbling blocks to faith, help me build bridges of love and grace. Amen.

Faith goes beyond believing; rather, the good news of the gospel is inextricably bound with communal living. James calls us to actualize our faith. Today's reading presents prayer and singing as two staples used in communal expression of faith. The communal importance of songs and singing resonates with words from Ephesians that God's people should "be filled with the Spirit, as you sing psalms and hymns and spiritual songs among yourselves" (5:19).

We benefit from the divine appointments of others. Note James's instructions in case of sickness: "Call for the elders of the church and have them pray over them, anointing them with oil." In the case of sin, James presents communal confession as a sacred act of faith that leads to reciprocation with communal prayers. He offers Elijah's use of prayer to exemplify the power and effectiveness of the prayers of the righteous.

We began the week by reflecting on the divine appointments of Mordecai and Esther to save their people from destruction during the Babylonian captivity. Mordecai wore sackcloth and ashes and wailed. Esther fasted. We can assume that in these rituals, prayer was embedded as a segue to answering God's call.

Imagine a job posting by God: Wanted! Persons to fill divine appointments. Responsibilities: rescuing victims of social injustice—including the poor, sick, hungry, women, children, immigrants, and those who live alternate lifestyles. Also wanted! Persons to fill divine appointments to rescue perpetrators of social injustice. No experience necessary. A willing heart is essential. Equipment provided: power and effectiveness through prayer. Please respond.

God, may we not limit your call to the extraordinary and miraculous. Remind us of our call to fill divine appointments within our everyday lives. Amen.

Signs and Blessings from God

SEPTEMBER 28–OCTOBER 4, 2015 • BROMLEIGH MCCLENEGHAN

MONDAY, SEPTEMBER 28 ～ *Read Job 1:1, 2:1-3*

Job is devout and faithful. Because of his righteousness, he gets plucked out of obscurity and placed in the midst of a heavenly dispute. In the opening verses, the Lord and the heavenly court debate how to recognize true devotion. "Obviously, Job loves you, with all your blessings," says the divine district attorney. "Let's test him, and see how he feels then."

Job is an amazing fellow—there is none like him, says the Lord. Many of us have witnessed or experienced suffering, but how many of us continue to live in accord with our principles when the going gets tough? How many of us believe that God is punishing us, even if we don't believe in that sort of God? How many of us grow angry at God and turn away instead of passionately engaging and looking for understanding?

Job experiences unjust persecution. He laments, and his cries teach us an important lesson: Unjust suffering exists. This directly contradicts modern-day prophets who blame suffering on its victims, who blame nations with predominantly non-Christian populations for the natural disasters on their soil, who blame women for sexual assaults against them.

Unjust suffering exists. Our righteousness will not protect us. But when we encounter suffering, we can know that it does not come at the hands of the Creator. We can affirm that God is with us, whispering, speaking. We are not alone, and we are not always to blame. This knowledge can lighten our burdens.

O God, we do not understand the workings of the world, but we know that you are present in its midst, speaking, challenging, and comforting us. Amen.

Associate for Congregational Life, Rockefeller Memorial Chapel, University of Chicago

Today Job acquires some loathsome sores. Not only does Job persist in his faith, but he sits down and tries to remedy the situation—or at least scratch his many itches. Job can handle whatever the Lord or Satan throws at him, as long as he has a potsherd.

As Job sits in the ashes, his wife becomes the first in a long line of Monday-morning quarterbacks to offer commentary on his suffering. "Curse God, and die," she says. This is the exact response that Satan tells God to expect in verse 4. People will give all they have to save their lives. After being struck down, all Job has left is his integrity and his life. Satan and his wife think he ought to give even that up. What's the point?

Surely this temptation to resignation and faithlessness is not what Job wants to hear from his only remaining family member. I don't hear malice in his wife's injunction though. I hear the voice of a spouse who's trying to make matters better for her husband. To find resolution or peace—even if it is the easy way out.

Marriages and other relationships are complicated: We don't always say the right thing or even know what the right response is. In those times, we need to listen well to the expressed needs of the hurting one and hold those in concert with who we know this person to be. Job's wife may have spoken out of love, but she forgot how much Job values integrity. If we're suffering, it can be hard to hear the wrong thing from a loved one; but knowing they're trying as a gesture of love can make all the difference.

O God, help us to find words of grace and healing when speaking to the needs and hurts of those we love. Amen.

Bullying is a tremendous problem in the United States. Too often when kids get picked on, they internalize the criticisms lobbed at them. *I'm slow. I'm stupid. I'm ugly. I'm all wrong. I will never fit in.* They loathe their tormentors but would give anything to gain their approval.

The psalmist has experienced pain and would give quite a bit for deliverance. But he clearly desires vindication from the Lord and chooses no part in reconciliation with those who have wronged him.

We find strength and hope in this psalm for those who have suffered abuse. The psalm delineates the division between evil-doers and the righteous. It affirms that even those who have been hurt can continue to "walk in [their] integrity."

In the Christian tradition, we speak regularly of the need for reconciliation, for peace in the community. Dr. Martin Luther King Jr. reminded us that "there is no peace without justice." The hope for the oppressed does not reside in setting aside differences and joining their oppressors—at least not until *after* justice has been wrought. For the bullied child, justice isn't being welcomed into the group of bullies. It's in knowing that God is present, knowing that God is just. It's in figuring out how to cling to integrity—to your true identity as a holy child of God—and standing firm against those who treat others so poorly.

Kids who are bullied need places to feel safe and protectors to honor their worth. Teachers, parents, and supportive peers are essential. But so too is the affirmation of the steadfast love of God and a welcome into the place where divine glory abides.

O Lord, may your steadfast love and presence assure those in need of hope and grant them courage to be steadfast in their integrity. Amen.

Much of our remembered knowledge of the letter to the Hebrews is inaccurate. It's not a letter; it's not written to Jews; it's not by Paul. In the first century after Christ, both Jewish and Gentile Christian communities existed. Both experienced persecution under Roman emperors, and such hardship might have tempted followers of the new faith to return to their old traditions and beliefs. The author attempts to embolden them and to suggest that following Christ is the natural progression of Jewish tradition.

Hebrews presents Jesus Christ as the fulfillment of the scriptures: the "heir of all things," "superior to angels." The first line reminds us that the relationship between Christians and Jews—in the first century and today—is more complicated than we might realize. "Long ago God spoke to our ancestors in many and various ways by the prophets, but in these last days he has spoken to us by a Son." The author addresses the matter of first and last things: "long ago" and "in these last days." Jesus was present at creation and even now "sustains all things."

God speaks to people and communities in different ways over time. Christians filter their understanding through a lens of the life, ministry, death and resurrection of Jesus, who is the "reflection of God's glory."

That's good news: God still speaks. God has spoken through the ages "in many and various ways," through the prophets, through Jesus' life, and still today. The relationships among the people who claim these texts as sacred are ongoing, and we hear the Lord's voice in different ways. When we speak with our brothers and sisters—Jews, Christians—may we recall the way Jesus welcomed all in the work of interpreting the word of God.

Lord, teach me to hear and know your voice. Amen.

What does it mean to be human? This passage, which quotes Psalm 8, seems at first glance to suggest that what makes us human is our status as little lower than angels, to which many things are subject.

What makes us human? I shared an apartment in grad school with a PhD student in anatomy, and he and I frequently discussed this. We share so much DNA with other creatures. Dolphins have language, chimps use tools; animals have families and social hierarchies. My roommate didn't mean to suggest that we weren't awesome—we're made of the same materials as stars, after all—but little is clearly distinctive about our species.

The way we think about humanity often affects how we think of the work Jesus does as the Christ. What is humanity's great need? What do we need to be saved from or saved for?

One quality that unites us across our species is the fact that we experience suffering and death, and we feel threatened by the meaninglessness of these experiences. That may seem like a less than inspirational reminder from the author of Hebrews, until we realize he is reminding us that Jesus, the one who is even higher than the angels, willingly subjected himself to suffering and death and the threat of meaninglessness. Jesus became human and suffered. Jesus became human and died. Hebrews points to the singular nature of Jesus' redemptive suffering. Only one who was human could die, and only one who was God could die in sacrificial love.

We are not alone, even in our darkest moments. Christ is exalted; we will be exalted with Christ.

Christ our Lord, help us know we are not alone, that you are brother of all in the human family. We are members of one family, and we stand and fall together in the light of God. Amen.

Huge percentages of marriage end in divorce. While few people desire it, I can see its necessity sometimes—because of hardness of heart. But the story of a marriage, even one that ends for good reason, shouldn't be dismissed.

When I sit down with couples preparing to be married, I always remind them that no matter how holy the moment in which the marriage begins, I cannot grant them the ability to read each other's minds. Good communication—sharing what's on minds and in hearts—is critical to making a marriage work.

Jesus is right (unsurprisingly) about marriage. Something happens in a long-term, committed relationship. Scientists refer to it as pair-bonding. We might call it marital love or the creation of a new entity—two people bringing to birth a marriage.

That marriage might produce children or a home that welcomes and grounds a family and community. It might produce other creative endeavors or as the United Methodist *Book of Worship* suggests, "Grant that their love for each other may reflect the love of Christ for us." If that relationship ceases to reflect the love of Christ, if it's not grounded in mutual care and respect and hope, it may well need to end. That's a painful and serious issue. Divorce signals the death of a marriage—not the death of a person, but a death that requires grieving nonetheless.

In this moment, Jesus demonstrates that the legality of a relationship is not always the primary focus for faithful people.

O God, who blesses our relationships and shows us how to love, abide with us. Help us to know that whether we are engaged in the work of joy-filled creation or mourning a broken relationship, you are present with us always. Amen.

What does it mean to receive the kingdom of God as a little child? Does it mean we receive a great gift and then ask for something else ten minutes later? Does it assume that the kingdom of God is all about us?

I am the mother of two small children. I adore them and their foibles, but I am fairly certain Jesus doesn't mean that we're supposed to be self-absorbed (even in developmentally appropriate ways) or unable to see the big picture or long-term consequences of our actions.

This morning, my three-year-old fell, scraping hands and knees. I picked her up, kissed the boo-boos, wiped away tears, whispered affirmations into her hair.

She sniffled, "I fell because I was running too fast!" She's learning cause and effect.

My kids are fearless about some things, in a way that makes me worry sometimes. They are not anxious. They do not understand limits—their own or others'—very well. And so they tend to run as fast as they can for the thrill and joy of it; make as many friends as they can, because friends are great. Steal as many hugs and kisses as they can from mom and dad before bed because signs of love are important and wonderful. They live and bask in abundance.

As their mother, I want to protect my daughters from all manner of ills, just as I try to protect myself. But Jesus calls us to join them in their abundance so we might know the abundant joy of the kingdom of God. We can't open ourselves to God if we close ourselves in fear, if we restrain ourselves from the glory for which God created us.

Saving God, we know our redemption does not lie in safety and security. Give us the strength to follow you into a life of uncertainty, risk, and the possibility of great joy—into eternal life. Amen.

Trusting God in the Land of Emptiness

OCTOBER 5–11, 2015 • J. R. DANIEL KIRK

MONDAY, OCTOBER 5 ~ *Read Job 23:1-9, 16-17*

Job is a faithful companion for us through life's valleys because Job knows that life with God does not give us easy answers. Job knows that God is powerful over all things, and so he can complain to God about what he thinks God has allowed to happen. Job also knows that he has been faithful to God and that God will vindicate him if given the chance.

But God is nowhere to be found. The darkness that causes us to call out, "Why, God?" is often made deeper by God's silence.

Job prods us to keep crying out in the darkness. When we have the boldness to say that God is just but our world is not, when we have the boldness to cry out to God and demand that God heed the voices of those who demand that God's righteousness be made known, we play the part of the faithful righteous.

In the pursuit of humility, we must ensure that we do not give up on the idea that goodness exists on the earth and God should honor it. We too easily give up on the idea that the suffering we see or experience is unjust. Or we too easily give up on the idea that our God wants to act to make all things right. Job stirs us to remember that the very means by which God has chosen to make God's presence known in the world is divine response to the cries of God's people.

In the end, the injustice that Job experiences as "God's heavy hand" and Job's "I cannot perceive him" are one and the same. God is made invisible by the injustice of the world, but divine glory is displayed in justice, grace, and mercy.

Almighty God, display your justice, so that all may see you and know you. Amen.

Associate Professor of New Testament, Fuller Theological Seminary, Northern California Campus, San Francisco, California

What does it mean to be forsaken by God? As Christians we sometimes take a few quick leaps that go something like this: Jesus cried out, "My God, why have you forsaken me?" This, then, is when God the Father turned God's back on the Son while the Son was bearing our sins. And so, being forsaken by God is an experience of spiritual abandonment, when we no longer experience the presence of God with us.

Spiritual abandonment, or a "dark night of the soul," is a real and significant spiritual experience for many. Yesterday we saw how the hiddenness of God worsened Job's experience of rejection. But it begins with the realities of embodied life.

This is the psalm for people who can boldly and rightly cry out to God because God has not done what God has promised. When Israel trusted in God, they were delivered from their enemies—this is the God of Israel living up to the promises God has made!

When God does not protect the people, when outsiders can mock because their prayers remain unanswered, when God's beloved son is conquered by being hung to die on a cross, then God has forsaken.

This is why we must cultivate the radical act of lament within the people of God. To feel forsaken by God is to be in a place where God has not acted as God has promised. The only mechanism for righting this situation is the people of God standing together and demanding of God that God act according to divine character.

By placing such cries within the book of Psalms, the Bible teaches us that we discover part of our corporate identity in siding with the forsaken of the world and crying out to God for rescue. In this, we embody the saving faithfulness of Christ who sided with the forsaken in being himself forsaken on the cross.

God of our salvation, show yourself faithful by saving those who are mocked and even killed for trusting in you. Amen.

Never underestimate the power of the past. In ways that we often are not even aware of, the past shapes our understanding of the present and our hopes and fears about the future. We connect the dots between the past and the present, telling stories that make sense of how our lives (or the world) hold together. But sometimes the stories don't work out as we would expect. Sometimes the hopeful pursuits of our life are derailed; sometimes a life of promise is cut short.

Psalm 22 expresses the expectation that the God known in grace, care, and salvation is the God who will be present in the same way yet again. The God who brought us into this world, the God who saved us from the powers of sin and death in the life of Jesus, is the God to whom we now look for deliverance.

Lament involves more than complaints to God about life's being off kilter. Lament is complaining to God that life is off kilter *because* God has not been as consistent in living up to the standards of loving care that God has set.

In lament we lay bare before our Great Caretaker the places where the people of the earth suffer and die—and therefore need divine intervention. In lament we call to God from the midst of the darkness. We bring God into the suffering and injustice, and we demand an answer.

The strange reality seeping its way through lament is this: We not only have a calling to proclaim God's good news to the world, we also have a calling to proclaim the world's bad news to God. These are perhaps the two greatest tools God has given us to participate in the great project to make all things new.

Father, you have shown us in the life, death, and resurrection of Jesus that there is no length to which you will not go to save and deliver your people. Open your eyes to the pain of the dying, the abused, the trafficked, the lonely, the sick; show yourself to them and the world as the God of all comfort. Amen.

This week, Job and the writer of Psalm 22 have come before God boldly. They have come more boldly than most of us would dare. We are too aware of our own hearts. We are too aware of the ways we have fallen short.

Hebrews provides some vindication of this caution. The word of God is living and active—scripture is personified as an agent that has the power to sort out our fidelity to God from our self-preserving faithlessness. It has the power to summon us to perseverance right at the point where we are ready to quit.

But Hebrews and Job actually proceed from the same starting point. Job knows that if only he can get an audience with God, God will have to vindicate him. Why? Because God knows everything. Hebrews too tells us that God sees everything. We must give an account before God.

One crucial difference exists between these writers, however. While Job cannot get the ear of God to save his life, the writer of Hebrews knows uninterrupted access into the very throne room of God. As the great story of God continues to unfold, there appears the Living Redeemer who sits at God's right hand with one particular task. He intercedes for the saints, for us, according to God's will.

This week we have been called to lament by Job and by the Psalms. We cry out to God in times of distress because we know that God will hear. Moreover, Jesus, who ensures we will be heard, himself has spoken the words of lament that we have read in Psalm 22—and has been answered by God the Father through the resurrection from the dead.

Lament is a great act of faith. It is prayers to a God whom we believe can and will act because this God gives life to the dead.

God who hears, even when we know our shortcomings give us faith to cry out, knowing that you will hear us because of the perfection of your resurrected son, our Lord. Amen.

Job and Psalm 22 reflect the cries of the confident. But sometimes our darkness is more our own doing. The living and active sword of God's word calls us to faithfulness; it calls us to endurance; and it shows us the ways in which we have failed.

At times, the heaviness we experience is less a matter of injustice than the just chastisement of a father who disciplines those whom he loves. Since we will have to give an account to God for what we have done, our experiences of pain and suffering can remind us of our need to cling to God's love and that of our neighbors.

The message of Hebrews paints a magnificent portrait of grace. Immediately after holding up before us the inescapable eye of the God to whom we must give an account, the letter reissues the invitation to approach the throne of God—not as a judgment bench but as a throne of grace and a source of help. Crying out and lamenting before God, seeking help and deliverance and justice—these are not simply the postures of the righteous who demand that God repay in kind; they are also the postures of the sinners who demand that God repay in Christ.

Whether as champions of justice or as petitioners who desire grace, we come before God in time of need. In both cases we require God's intervention to transform this world so that God's kingdom will come, God's will will be done on earth as it is in heaven.

We can be pulled away from our faith in different directions. Whether frustrated with God or frustrated with self, the same, transformative offer of help is extended to us by the crucified and risen Christ who knows our suffering and the triumph over it, who knows our weakness and temptation and also the life without sin.

Father in heaven, draw us to your light whatever the cause of our darkness, and allow us to find in you grace to help in time of need. Amen.

If we ever wish to come face-to-face with where our day-in, day-out lives demonstrate how far we are from the kingdom of God, we can do no better than listening to what Jesus has to say about money. If we were shocked by the particular demand Jesus laid on the rich man to sell his possessions, we will find ourselves even more troubled when Jesus turns the earlier story into a general principle.

In the twenty-first century, we are all embedded in a worldly kingdom whose standard of justice is not equality or democracy or liberty but the acquisition of wealth. From a young age we are formed to be wealth producers or, more importantly, consumers who produce wealth for others. Ours is a world, across numerous cultures, that strives above all else to show signs of wealth (even if what these signs truly signal is crippling debt). We strive for good-paying jobs, for high-paying opportunities out of college. We appoint people to church leadership who have attained these ends that we hold most dear.

Each act of complicity in the belief system of capitalism is a potential denial of the kingdom of God. Defensively we reinterpret Jesus' words. Surely he can't mean us! Surely those of us who live in cities with hundreds of churches can't be the least likely to inherit the kingdom! Surely our success within the system we were born into signals God's great favor!

But Jesus keeps repeating: It is hard for the wealthy to enter. You could more easily cram a camel through a needle's eye than cram one person of wealth through the gates of God's kingdom. Our only hope lies in God overcoming this impossibility through God's own great power of grace.

God, we have worshiped before the gods of wealth that have promised us life. Free us from the chains that bind us, that we will know the true wealth that pours out from your holy presence. Amen.

Following Jesus calls us into what can be a harsh reality. It's a calling to give up all that we have and all that we think we are. It's a calling to rethink how we value the world around us and the things for which we pour out our lives.

When we weigh the cost of discipleship and the insistence that we leave houses and siblings and parents and sources of income for Jesus' sake, we all too easily envision a life alone. Western people have transferred our deeply individualistic way of viewing and interacting with the world to our understanding of Christianity. But Jesus reminds us that our thoughts of "going it alone" are not God's thoughts about the Christian life.

God provides us with a new family—the family of those who, like us, have chosen to forgo the world's way of reckoning family, of accumulating wealth, of attaining long-term security. Church is not simply supposed to be the place to which we head off on a Sunday morning. It is supposed to be the place that makes possible our obedience to the impossible calling of Jesus.

The gospel faces all sorts of challenges today from those who claim to follow Jesus. Some of the most severe, however, are not acts of moral failing but the day-to-day tasks of the church to create a community with an alternative value system that makes itself known in the riches of self-giving love.

Are we the kind of people who can be family for those who have left family for Jesus' sake? Can we be the kind of people who can create an alternative economy so that the pursuit of wealth no longer defines us either as persons or as the people of God?

Father, draw our lives into a new way of being that demonstrates to the world that your kingdom is a greater source of life than the kingdom of cash. Make us agents of self-giving love that will make possible for other people the self-denying obedience that comes with accepting Jesus' call to follow him. Amen.

Bless the Lord!

OCTOBER 12-18, 2015 • MARJORIE HEWITT SUCHOCKI

MONDAY, OCTOBER 12 ~ *Read Job 38:1-7; Psalm 104:1*

What an amazing combination of texts this week! The Voice from the whirlwind touches on the immensity and mystery of creation in words of magnificent poetry. The psalmist adds his own refrain to the song the morning stars sing together, with angels shouting for joy! The New Testament texts take us from these heights, plunging us into history—but not quite, for the Hebrews text intersects time with eternity. Incarnation! The God of all time and eternity breaks into history. How do we respond? Job responded to God's revelation with humility, but in the Gospel text James and John give a quite different response to the revelation of God in Christ. They fret about their "rewards" for being disciples.

Job and the disciples parallel each other in the questions they bring to God, for they are all caught up in their own concerns. Job, beset by so many reversals of fortune, demands, "Why me?!" James and John, far from being overwhelmed by the wonder of Jesus' person and actions, think only of themselves, calling on Jesus to raise them to rule beside him. We may have more sympathies for Job, but Job as well as James and John fails to see beyond himself—until he sees the majesty of God. And where are we in the mix of God's questioners?

How difficult do we find the shift from our own small concerns to the wider concerns of the world? How can contemplating the majesty of the God of the universe move us beyond self-absorption?

Professor Emerita, Claremont School of Theology; author of numerous books and articles

S tay with the text from Job, recalling its wider setting. Job, upright and successful, venerated by his community, begins a vast descent. His property, his family, and finally his health are taken from him, and in the dominant theology of his day, this surely signals egregious sin on his part. Even his wife and friends, who presumably know him best, counsel him to confess his sins. But he knows that he is righteous according to the law and holds on to this despite others' accusations. He appeals to God to exonerate him—or, at least, to explain his horrible losses.

What Job receives in response is the whirlwind and words of awe: "Where were you when I laid the earth's foundation?" (38:4, NIV). The Voice continues with one unrelenting question after another, dwarfing Job and his concerns. Strangely enough, the Voice never does answer Job's questions directly.

Some scholars claim that the final chapter of Job, exonerating Job by giving him twice what he lost, is a late addition to the text—possibly added by those who could not remain content with answering mystery with majesty. In a sense, the final chapter undoes the whole text, for Job's situation radically questions the theology that good deeds merit good fortune. A prosperity gospel gets no support from Job 2–41! We do not live in an "only good things happen to good people; only bad things happen to bad people" world. Indeed, Jeremiah's inquiry as to why the wicked prosper (12:1) undercuts a theology that claims that right living guarantees good fortune. With that understanding, why do we choose to do good?

What is the value of the Voice from the whirlwind? Why is it the "answer" to Job? Why do people so often respond to bad fortune with the question, "Why did this happen to me?" If we echoed the Voice from the whirlwind by answering that question with comments about God's majesty, how would we receive this response?

Iam a theologian whose study of geology for the past year has in many ways been like listening to the Voice from the whirlwind. To learn about this earth, its place within the solar system, the solar system's place in the galaxy, and the galaxy's place in the universe is something like hearing that Voice! I wonder how any Christian can fear what the sciences discover about creation, since each revelation dwarfs our own concerns by placing us in a wider and more magnificent context.

Tracing the finger of God in an early earth with volcanoes spewing life-giving gasses that will create an atmosphere and where water can provide the matrix for chemicals that will yield life—and then to follow that mind-boggling route to more and more complex forms of life is only to grow in joy! Imagine following the finger of God in such ways! Majesty, immensity, and mystery indeed! And we, mindful of God's immensity and our smallness, echo Job's words: "I had heard of you by the hearing of the ear, but now my eye sees you" (42:5). What does knowledge of God's majesty do to our concerns?

Perhaps it both relativizes us and lifts us up. What we learn through the sciences is "the other side of God," whose mystery we will never plumb. But this ever-creating God is also the omnipresent God we know through Christ; it is God who is with us! We can dare to bring our questions, concerns, joys, thanksgiving and allow the mystery to hover over the revelation. Like Job, we can bow in humility, and like the psalmist, say, "Bless the LORD, O my soul. Praise the LORD!" (Ps. 104:35).

How can we come to accept the poetry of scripture and the musings of the ancients as their response to an immensity that was more than they could fathom? How can faith, informed by discoveries of science, rejoice in knowledge?

This text from Hebrews reorients us after the heights of Job and their echo in Psalm 104. What a way to come back to earth! The text is especially marvelous for pastors and those in church leadership, beginning with a description of the tasks belonging to them. Read: "[Ministers] chosen from among [believers are] put in charge of things pertaining to God on their behalf, to offer gifts and [the sacraments] for sins. [They are] able to deal gently with the ignorant and wayward, since [they are also] subject to weakness, and because of this, [they] must offer [sacraments] for [their] own sins as well as for those of the people. And one does not presume to take this honor, but takes it only when called by God, just as Aaron was." Those ministering to the people of God are called by God, and God empowers them for that calling.

Sometimes this call seems more than one person can do. But the text reassures us by putting Christ beside us: Christ is also appointed to minister, ministering alongside! If this holds comfort for clergy and those in church leadership, verses 7 and 8 bring laity into the equation—for who among us has not experienced suffering and tears, along with the supplications that arise from grief and pain? Jesus stands beside us, having gone through the same; he is the comforter who understands because he has been there.

Eternity intersects time in the Incarnation; God in Christ is beside us. Our small times—times like Job's, like those of James and John, like those of ordinary and extraordinary ministry—are embraced by God's time. Sometimes I think that given this fact, we can endure anything.

Why in times of sorrow do we take comfort from someone who has experienced similar grief? How have you experienced the magnificent and magisterial Voice from Job as the "still small voice" of the One who knows all our sorrows?

The conclusion of the text speaks of Christ as Savior: "Having been made perfect [through suffering!], he became the source of eternal salvation for all who obey him."

The church through its two thousand years has found divergent ways to say how Christ saves us. Augustine argued that God saved us by tricking Satan. Satan could only lawfully take into death those who had sinned. But Jesus never sinned. God dangles Jesus before Satan, like a worm on a hook (Augustine's metaphor!) daring Satan to take him. When Satan takes the bait, he must not only release Jesus, but all those who by faith cling to Jesus: We are "ransomed from Satan."

Anselm of Canterbury lived in feudal times. If a serf offended his "liege lord," the serf had to make "satisfaction" equal to the offense. God is our infinite "liege lord." By sin we offend God and must pay an infinite satisfaction. But we can't! Through Incarnation, the infinite God becomes finite and makes satisfaction for us.

Twelfth-century Abelard argued that Jesus saves us weak and ignorant sinners by showing us how to live and by everlastingly interceding for us in heaven. All these theories are Christian, but they subtly contradict one another.

What if we learn from the mysteries of Job? The humility Job feels should belong to us all. This we know: However it "works," God saves us, teaches us, comforts us, sustains us in and through Christ, "the source of eternal salvation."

How do you understand that Jesus saves us? How do you respond to the Hebrews suggestion that our salvation comes "through obedience"? What is your theory of the Atonement? How would you articulate it to another?

Bless the Lord!

This text contains an amazing reversal; its implications have echoed through the ages. When James and John ask to be on the right and left hand of Jesus, they seem to have positions of power and glory in mind. They will be "high and lifted up," presumably pleased at such exaltation. The other disciples who overhear them and Jesus' response, are irritated: Who are James and John to be promoted over and above their colleagues?

The reversal is dumbfounding. We are so used to the phrase *servant leader* that we hardly notice that Jesus has redefined rulership. All four Gospels repeat the theme—we have only to remember the foot-washing scene in John. Jesus explicitly states that "whoever wishes to become great among you must be your servant, and whoever wishes to be first among you must be slave of all." Imagine James's and John's thoughts upon hearing this! They have asked for positions of glory, but Jesus interprets the positions as ones of slavery. They imagine that they will receive great fortune; they find that being on Jesus' right and left hand risks death!

We remember that the Gospel of John consistently equates Jesus' glory with crucifixion, when he is "high and lifted up." There are indeed two with him, one on the right and one on the left. Do James and John remember their request when they witness Jesus' death? According to tradition, James was eventually beheaded for Christ; John lived in exile on the island of Patmos. They finally understood and knew what it was to live, serve, and die in the glory of Christ. Do we?

What other great reversals happen in Jesus' ministry? Read through a Gospel, and count the reversals. Is this reversal the greatest of all? Why, or why not?

Muse a while longer on the reversal entailed in "servant leadership." We have lost the shock value of Jesus' words and actions by specifying that true leadership is serving others, not ruling them. In many ways we have reversed Jesus' reversal, accepting the term *servant leader* but reinvesting it with the trappings of power and privilege. We are all familiar with the title of the supreme pontiff of Rome, "servant of the servants of God." While we rightly praise humble pontiffs, in actual fact the position is vested with authority and power not much different from the authority and power of any political leader.

Protestants can easily become self-righteous, noting with disapproval the pomp, power, and privilege accorded the "servant of the servants of God." But haven't we done the same? We have avoided the term "servant of the servants of God," but don't we give greater authority and veneration to supervisory leaders than to pastors? In United Methodist circles, bishops are no longer called by name but by title. And don't we value serving affluent churches more than poor churches? Why are our best pastors sent to big churches as their reward for doing well, rather than to our poorest churches where they might help the church grow? If we truly valued servant leadership, wouldn't pastors vie for appointments to rural or inner city or poor churches, where leadership would indeed be sacrificial? In Mark 10 Jesus explicitly reverses the social position of leader from a place of power to a place of sacrificial service, even to a place he calls slavery. His crucifixion sealed this reversal, where the Highest suffered with the most lowly for the sake of saving the lowly. We are followers of Christ.

How do we guard against the dangers of pride of place when we choose where we want to serve? Does this keep Christ's great reversal intact? In what ways are we servant leaders?

God's Good Intentions

OCTOBER 19-25, 2015 • LYNNE M. DEMING

MONDAY, OCTOBER 19 ~ *Read Mark 10:46-52*

This week's scripture passages help us take in the amazing and powerful message that God has good intentions for us all. That theme is nowhere more evident than in the Gospel story of Bartimaeus, the blind man. This brief story leaves a number of unanswered questions. For instance, does Bartimaeus know of Jesus and his ability to heal? Does he position himself where he will certainly encounter Jesus? Does he know Jesus will be there that day? Although we lack many details, we can nevertheless appreciate the story and its message.

Bartimaeus asks for help and receives it. We don't know whether Bartimaeus has been blind since birth or whether he sustained an injury or an illness that caused him to become blind later in life. Either way, he desperately desires healing for his blindness and will employ any measure to bring that about, including shouting loudly to get Jesus' attention. He causes such a scene that others around him attempt to quiet him. Ignoring the outrage of the crowd, Jesus stops and asks Bartimaeus to come to him. Then Jesus asks, "What do you want me to do for you?" The answer is simple: "Let me see again."

This story's good news is that the scene Bartimaeus creates does indeed get Jesus' attention, and he heals him immediately. This is a story about persistence in the face of adversity and about faith that results in healing. The story also offers a call to discipleship. After Jesus heals him, Bartimaeus becomes a follower "on the way."

Jesus the healer, help us to be persistent in our faith so that you bid us come to you. Amen.

Former World Editor, *The Upper Room* daily devotional guide, Nashville, Tennessee

TUESDAY, OCTOBER 20 ～ *Read Mark 10:46-52*

Imagine the scene. A large crowd of people walks along the road with Jesus and his disciples. Suddenly a man begins to shout loudly, "Jesus, . . . have mercy on me!" When the crowd tries to stifle him he continues to shout, and his voice grows louder. How embarrassing for him! What would you do if you were there? How would you respond? Few of us would intervene—we would more likely look the other way. Jesus, on the other hand, intervenes and changes Bartimaeus's life forever.

Many years ago a New Testament scholar and storyteller conducted a workshop at my workplace. The day's purpose involved helping us (we were curriculum editors) learn how to treat stories in scripture in creative ways. Part of the workshop also focused on learning to memorize scripture and retelling it in response to a voiced need. The workshop leader chose the story of the woman with the hemorrhage (Mark 5:25-34)—a passage quite similar to the story of Bartimaeus.

The story in Mark 5 concludes with Jesus' declaration to the woman: "Daughter, your faith has made you well; go in peace, and be healed of your disease" (v. 34). Reading today's passage in Mark 10 brought back memories for me, since it concludes in a similar way: "Go; your faith has made you well." The Greek word that the New Revised Standard Version translates as "made you well" has a variety of translations: saved from danger, from disease, or from death—among other possibilities. In these two healing miracles in Mark's Gospel, Jesus proclaims to these persons that their faith has brought about their salvation from disease, or their healing.

Because of his persistent faith, Bartimaeus receives his sight and becomes a follower of Jesus. Healing encompasses the spiritual as well as the physical. Empowered by Jesus' response to his cries, Bartimaeus becomes a new person.

Loving God, we need to be saved. Give us the persistent faith that can make us well. Amen.

This passage summarizes a rather long discussion of the priesthood of Jesus, which begins at 4:14. The section opens with the assertion that Jesus, the "great high priest who has passed through the heavens," is the high priest par excellence, the one who can sympathize with our human weaknesses while remaining free from sin. The theme of confidence in God's mercy and grace appears in the introductory statement (4:16). God has good intentions for us!

At the conclusion of today's passage, we read that the law appoints high priests who are vulnerable to human weakness, as opposed to Jesus, the high priest "who has been made perfect forever." As I write this meditation, the media is reporting that in the years 2011 and 2012, as many as four hundred priests were defrocked due to allegations of sexual abuse of children. In a negative way, these priests exemplify the kind of priest Jesus is in comparison to them: innocent, incorrupt, and sinless.

The writer boldly states that the priesthood of Jesus means there is no longer any need for human priests. How can that be? First, Jesus the high priest will live and serve forever, in contrast to the temporary nature of human priests (death prevents them from continuing to serve). Also, like earthly priests, Jesus provides access to God through his role as high priest. However, Jesus is the only priest who can bring about our salvation when he intercedes for us. Finally, human priests are no longer needed because Jesus' high priesthood is a model of perfection. In that role, Jesus can save humanity on God's behalf. We can be confident of that!

Gracious God, we are grateful for your good intentions for us. Forgive us for our weaknesses, and help us remain confident of your mercy and grace. Amen.

In this psalm of thanksgiving, the writer expresses gratitude to God for deliverance from some kind of trouble. The psalm as a whole moves from specific experiences and concerns to a general application of God's protection and care for all of humanity. We read evidence of the weekly theme of God's good intentions for us in this passage: The psalmist humbly asks God to deliver him from all his fears, and God responds positively.

The opening of this psalm credits King David as its author and connects the psalm to an altercation between David and Abimelech. Some scholars believe that this psalm refers to an experience in David's life described in 1 Samuel 21:10-15. However, many psalms are attributed to David because he was such a highly revered historical figure.

In verses 1-3 the writer describes God using language reminiscent of a hymn of praise. This type of hymnic language is prevalent in the Psalms and much of the prophetic literature. In verses 4-6 the psalmist switches to a more narrative style in which he alludes to his fears as well as God's deliverance. Interestingly enough, both Bartimaeus and the psalmist cry out for help. Their cries attract the attention of the Lord. Their cries mobilize the Divine into saving action on their behalf. The Lord responds decisively in both instances. When have you cried out to God? When have you experienced God's saving action on your behalf?

Verses 4-7 are antiphonal, alternating between praise (verses 4 and 6) and testimony (verses 5 and 7). Verse 8 summarizes this section by advising us to "taste and see" God's goodness. Those who take refuge in God are happy.

Gracious God, we offer our own psalm of thanksgiving for your good intentions for us. Amen.

These verses summarize the main theme of the psalm: We can have faith in God's constant presence in our lives. God has good intentions for us! In the first part of the psalm (verses 1-8), the psalmist offered praise to God and alluded to his personal experience of God's deliverance from a fearful situation. Now in these final verses, the psalmist generalizes that affirmation and applies it to the rest of us.

These verses assert that we can trust God to deliver the righteous from every kind of trouble and to protect them physically. Verse 20 is alluded to in John 19:36: "These things occurred so that the scripture might be fulfilled, 'None of his bones shall be broken.'" The Gospel writer is explaining why the Roman soldiers did not break Jesus' legs (as they did to the other bodies left on the crosses).

Yes, God will deliver the righteous. But evildoers will not fare so well, according to the psalmist. They will die because of their sinful ways.

As we will see when we read the Job passages, both Job and the psalmist write as they look back on their dire circumstances. Both have experienced restoration; they impart their wisdom to us from that perspective, which seems to be a wise strategy!

Some years ago I received a cancer diagnosis and endured a six-month chemotherapy regimen. During those months, I resolved to determine what good could possibly come from my experience (in addition to my remission!). One positive result is that I am able to advise, listen to, commiserate with, and pray for others I know or encounter who find themselves in a similar situation. In the same way, we can perceive this psalm as one of hope that can inspire persons in similar situations.

Gracious and loving God, help us find ways to bring about positive results from negative circumstances. Amen.

Verses 1-6 contain Job's final response to God. Read these verses, and then read Job's first response to God in 40:3-5. Comparing these two passages provides a glimpse of Job's emotional journey over the course of the book. How would you characterize Job's attitude in the first response? Is he humble? stubborn? defiant? obnoxious? self-absorbed? Perhaps all the above? And how would you characterize Job in today's passage? Is he realistic? humble? chastened? courageous? truthful? obsequious? Again, perhaps he embodies all these qualities.

Job's first few words praise God, the all-powerful and all-knowing. In verse 3, Job raises the rhetorical question he heard God ask earlier: "Who could possibly misunderstand what I am trying to say?" (AP). Here in response, Job seems to be saying, "I did that out of my confusion and ignorance." Job has come a long way in his thought and approach from where he first started!

In verse 4, Job repeats word-for-word what God told him earlier (see 38:3). This repetition could well signal Job's respect for God and the truth of God's earlier statement. According to verse 5, everything that Job has heard and experienced until this point was speculative. But now it is reality. Again, we can get a glimpse of Job's emotional journey if we compare verse 5 with what he said about God much earlier: "He passes by me, and I do not see him" (9:11).

Plenty of commentary has been written about the meaning of verse 6. What is Job saying exactly? The Hebrew word that the New Revised Standard Version translates "repent" can also mean "regret" and "be consoled or comforted." We may not fully understand Job's meaning, but we see that he is a changed man as a result of this experience.

Gracious God, be with us in our emotional journeys as we come closer and closer to you. Amen.

Today's verses constitute the epilogue to the book of Job. The style and content of this passage resembles that of the prologue (chapters 1–2)—it is more narrative and less conversational than the remainder of the book. This section of Job is often called the book's "happy ending." However, the message is more complicated than a simple "all's well that ends well."

The friends of Job—Eliphaz, Bildad, and Zophar—who were introduced in the prologue (vv. 7-9) are brought back into the story in this epilogue, beginning in verse 7. Clearly God's consideration is for Job and not for his friends, since God asks Job to pray for them after they make a sacrifice. We learn in verse 9 that God accepts Job's prayer on their behalf. Verse 10 states that Job's situation is "restored" *when* (not *because*, as is often assumed) he prays for his friends as God has requested.

Verses 11-15 describe a glorious celebration and complete restoration of Job's former life. In fact, we read that his new life is even better than his former life: "The LORD blessed the latter days of Job more than his beginning." We may find verse 15 rather astonishing, considering the social mores of the time: Job gives his daughters an inheritance in addition to giving one to their brothers.

This epilogue does not neatly resolve the issues raised by Job's experience. Rather, it leaves many questions unanswered. How does Job come to understand what really happened to him and why? And how can we understand why Job endured what he did? What we can learn from the resolution of the story is this: Job's suffering did not result from some sin(s) he committed, and his restoration does not occur because he suddenly becomes righteous. God's ways are indeed mysterious, and God's intentions are indeed for good.

Ever-present God, guide us as we struggle to understand life's mysteries. Amen.

Seed or Stone?

MONDAY, OCTOBER 26 ~ *Read Ruth 1:1-5*

Within the space of the first five verses of the book of Ruth we hear a story of devastating pain and loss suffered by a woman called Naomi. A severe famine forces her and her husband, with their two sons, to leave their homeland and move to a foreign country. Starting over as refugees in an unfamiliar place is tough enough, but then further disaster strikes—Naomi's husband dies! Thankfully she still has her two boys, who marry Moabite wives—surely not the future she has dreamed of for them. But under the circumstances, she will not complain. At least she can now hope for the gift of a grandchild or two, and the pattering of little feet will help ease her grief over the death of her husband. So when her two sons also die, it feels like it is all too much. How much can one woman be expected to endure?

Few of us have a story as dramatic as that of Naomi, but all of us have our own stories of pain and loss. Some years ago I emerged from a dark season of my life. I remember a letter sent to me by my parents that contained one line of verse: "O memory of a painful time, are you seed or stone?" My parents went on to write, "We pray that you will find every day of that painful time to be seed that produces the harvest of the Spirit!"

What a hopeful thought that our experiences of pain and loss can be seed in our lives that produces the harvest of the Spirit. This is what happened for Naomi. Her experience of pain and loss was not the end of her story but the beginning.

Gracious God, thank you for taking my experiences of pain and loss and transforming them from stones of bitterness to seeds of hope. Amen.

Ordained minister, the Methodist Church of Southern Africa

Following the tragic deaths of her husband and two sons in Moab, Naomi decides to return to her homeland of Judah. This theme of returning becomes an important one in the passage that follows. No fewer than nine times in the ensuing verses does the Hebrew word for "returning" or "turning back" appear. On the one hand, Naomi remains determined to return home. On the other hand, she urges her Moabite daughters-in-law to leave her and return to their own people. In the end one of them, Orpah, whose name tellingly means "back-of-the-neck," turns back. But Ruth refuses to turn her back on Naomi. In one of the most beautiful and beloved passages in the Bible she says, "Do not press me to leave you or to turn back from following you! Where you go, I will go. Where you lodge, I will lodge; your people shall be my people, and your God my God."

Their story raises for us the question: When should we turn back, and when should we press on? On one level it seems like a straightforward question with an obvious answer. We should turn back when we have wandered off the path and lost our way, like the prodigal son in Jesus' parable who finally returns to his father's house. On the other hand, we should press on when we're following God's call for our lives, no matter how tough it may be.

However, sometimes it's hard to know which is which. For this reason we need companions along the way. That's what Naomi and Ruth provide for each other. In Naomi's returning and Ruth's persistent pressing on, they become a support and encouragement to each other; each stays true to what she has resolved to do.

Thank you, Lord, for the gift of faithful companions who help me to know and follow the path that is mine. By your grace, may I be a faithful companion to others. Amen.

Psalm 146 is the first of five concluding psalms that bring the book of Psalms to a rousing climax with a glorious burst of praise. They are known as the "Hallelujah" psalms, which literally means "Praise the LORD!" That is how each of these five psalms begins and ends.

Imagine for a moment what your life would be like if it were a Hallelujah psalm. If every day began and ended for you in the praise of God. If the departure point of everything you did and the goal of every activity were to bring praise to God. Imagine what would happen to your work, your relationships, your home, your leisure time if all these things were enfolded in the praise of God and if you recognized in these things a beautiful opportunity to proclaim God's praise. What would our world be like if all of us made praise of God our highest priority?

All of us with the breath of life within us have been shaped to be an instrument of praise to the glory of God. And not just for an hour in church on Sunday. The entirety of our lives is intended to fulfill this purpose. As the psalmist puts it, "I will praise the LORD as long as I live; I will sing praises to my God all my life long."

How do we begin to live in such a way? Well, according to Psalm 146 it starts with a basic and fundamental choice about where we will place our trust. The psalmist urges us not to trust in fleeting human agency but rather in the eternal God, our Creator, Liberator, Provider, Healer, and Protector. Our trust in God releases us to pour out our lives in praise.

Creating, redeeming, and sustaining God, help me place my complete trust in you, that my life may become more and more a beautiful psalm that proclaims your praise. Amen.

I have largely neglected the letter to the Hebrews. The subject matter of high priests and sanctuaries and blood sacrifices and the holy of holies seems archaic, obscure, and far removed from the realities of our contemporary experience of faith. It's a letter that remains unopened by many.

Which is a great shame. For if we dig beneath the seemingly irrelevant references to ancient Jewish religious practices we discover that the letter to the Hebrews addresses a very contemporary concern—religion that is either dead or alive. The central thrust of the letter is that Jesus Christ ushers in a whole new deal that is far superior to the old order of things. The inadequacies of the old covenant that led to "dead works" have been supplanted by what Christ has done, enabling us to truly worship the living God!

This is indeed good news, for it reminds us that at the core of Christ's purpose is the desire to see us come alive in our faith and for our faith to be life-giving to others. Sadly, we are all too familiar with expressions of faith that seek to legislate rather than liberate—convictions become calcified, practices become rigid, habits become entrenched, requirements become laws unto themselves. We forget that Christ's self-offering, as today's passage reminds us, comes to us through the Spirit who blows and moves in surprising and unexpected ways.

How might you open yourself today to the refreshing and renewing work of Christ who longs for you to be fully alive?

Come, Spirit of Christ, blow through me today with your reviving grace, and take from me any sense of musty familiarity with the things of God. Amen.

Some years ago I had the privilege of interviewing Nelson Mandela. I went into the interview not knowing how long it would last, so I agonized over which question I should put to him first. What would be my one question above all others that I wanted him to address? I can't recall my final decision, but I do remember that the ensuing conversation was one of the most remarkable of my entire life. (There was also, thankfully, time for more than just one question.)

If you had the opportunity to ask Jesus just one question, what would it be? That is the situation presented to one of the scribes in today's Gospel reading. In our devotions tomorrow we'll explore the question he asked and Jesus' response, but for today I would like you to think about the question you would ask if you had the same opportunity. Really think about that. What question would you want to put to Jesus?

The questions that arise from deep within us can reveal a great deal about what is going on in our lives. As such, the questions we ask are every bit as important as the answers that we seek, sometimes even more so. Questions alert us to that which is unsettled within us. They are like flag posts over the longings of our hearts. They highlight the hunger of our souls.

So cherish the questions that well up inside of you. Do not be afraid of them. Let them open you up to new possibilities and fresh perspectives. As you bring them before Jesus, may the ensuing conversations that unfold between him and you thrust you deeper into the mystery of his goodness and grace.

Forgive me, Lord, for the foolish assumption that I need everything neatly figured out. Thank you for the unanswered questions that arise within me that remind me that I always have more to discover about you. Amen.

Like beautifully wrapped presents, the questions that arise within us can surprise us when we open them up and discover the treasure they contain. In today's reading a scribe poses a question. To understand this story we must remember that the scribes, as a group, opposed Jesus and consistently challenged his authority. The antagonism seems to have been mutual, for just a little later Jesus says, "Beware of the scribes. . . . They devour widows' houses" (Mark 12:38, 40). When this particular scribe steps forward, we expect a conflict story, yet the question he asks seems genuine. Certainly, Jesus answers him sincerely and directly but in a way that draws him out to a new place of understanding and challenge.

The first part of Jesus' answer is quite orthodox and even predictable. He quotes from Deuteronomy 6:4-5 (which is part of the scripture known as the Shema) about the importance of loving God. But then he adds another quote (from Leviticus 19:18) about our obligations to our neighbor and concludes that "there is no other commandment greater than these." The Leviticus quote sums up a section that defines love of neighbor in terms of nonexploitation.

In other words, Jesus says that there is no love of God apart from a love for one's neighbor, which shows itself in the refusal to exploit one's neighbor. This practice is precisely what the scribes have been guilty of. In reflecting on the connection between these two commandments, the scribe who asked the question recognizes the validity of Jesus' reply. Jesus tells him that he is "not far from the kingdom of God"; it depends on whether he will actually live this way. This truth strikes like a punch in the solar plexus for all the scribes present, and they no longer dare to ask Jesus any more questions.

Lord God, may my love for you be seen today in the ways in which I treat others. Amen.

ALL SAINTS DAY

When a young friend of mine died suddenly and tragically, I wished for all the world that I could do something to bring him back. In the anger that was a natural part of my grief, I thought that it was monstrously unfair that Jesus would bring his own friend back to life but not mine. But in time, as my anger shifted, the story of the raising of Lazarus became a source of great strength and hope for me. Today I would ask you to notice two aspects of it.

First, notice the depth of emotion that Jesus evidences. In response to the situation we read that Jesus was "greatly disturbed in spirit and deeply moved," that he "began to weep" and was once again "greatly disturbed." In the face of the painful and sobering reality of death Jesus does not remain unaffected. He feels the anguish of bitter loss. I realized that in my anguish over the tragic death of my young friend, I was not alone.

Second, notice that Jesus exercises an authority over the power of death that dares to proclaim that death does not have the final word. Unintimidated by the stench and decay of the tomb, he orders the stone to be taken away and then cries out to the dead man in a loud voice to "come out!" Remarkably, that's exactly what Lazarus does. Jesus then says, "Unbind him, and let him go."

In my grief this story reminds me that death is an undeniable reality, but it is not the ultimate authority. It does not have the final word, and its power to bind is limited. We affirm this hope on this All Saints' Day—a day to remember those who have died; those who have lived lives of extraordinary beauty, devotion, and grace; those whose unbound witness, ministry, and influence continue beyond the grave.

Thank you, Lord, that even though we all will die one day, because of you not even death is the end. Amen.

Heeding God's Direction

NOVEMBER 2–8, 2015 • TREVOR A. HUDSON

MONDAY, NOVEMBER 2 ~ *Read Ruth 3:1-5*

One sign of genuine self-giving love is other-centeredness. By this I mean true commitment to the other, an interest in his or her well-being, even a willingness to suffer on the other's behalf. God relates to us in this way. Sometimes we glimpse this kind of love in the lives of God's people. We certainly see it expressed in Naomi's life in these opening verses of chapter 3.

Naomi has returned to Bethlehem from the land of Moab with her daughter-in-law Ruth who remains determined to support her mother-in-law, Naomi, through a devastatingly painful time. Naomi's husband, Elimelech, and her two sons Mahlon and Chilion have died. Her return to Judah is one of heartache and sorrow: "I went away full, but the LORD has brought me back empty" (1:21).

Yet the opening verses of chapter 3 bear witness to the shift taking place in Naomi's heart. No longer does she lament the emptiness of her life. Now she thinks of others, especially Ruth, who had abandoned any hope of a future for herself when she left Moab. Ruth now finds herself supported by Naomi: "My daughter, I need to seek some security for you, so that it may be well with you." The next four verses reveal Naomi's bold plan to secure Ruth's future—a future of safety, rest, and care. Naomi's involvement indicates that she now focuses on the future and security of her daughter-in-law rather than herself. She is gradually becoming other-centered, a person of self-giving love.

Lord, show me what shift needs to take place in my heart to reflect more of your self-giving love. Amen.

Member of the pastoral team, Northfield Methodist Church, Benoni, South Africa; author and speaker

Faithful commitment is the hallmark of self-giving love. We witness this in the way God relates to the world and each person within it. Naomi utters a powerful statement upon hearing of Boaz's thoughtful care for Ruth in the gleaning fields. She speaks of the "LORD, whose kindness has not forsaken the living or the dead!" (2:20).

We clearly see this quality of faithfulness in Boaz's commitment to Ruth. He takes Ruth as his wife; she conceives and gives birth to a son. The journey up to this moment has been neither easy nor uneventful. The earlier verses of chapter 4 relay the complicated traditional legal procedure that Boaz negotiates with an anonymous kinsman-redeemer in order to marry Ruth. He will show kindness to her, be her protector and guardian—whatever it takes. Little wonder that the women of Bethlehem speak so affirmatively of him. They tell Naomi, "Blessed be the LORD, who has not left you this day without next-of-kin; and may his name be renowned in Israel!"

Boaz's faithful commitment to Ruth restores and rebuilds the lives of both Naomi and Ruth. His life becomes for us a striking parable of God as our "next-of-kin," our redeemer. This is what God's self-giving love looks like. God never gives up on us, no matter what mess we find ourselves in. God negotiates on our behalf to restore and rebuild our lives. And as we see in this story, the redemption and restoration go far beyond these two women. Ruth's child Obed becomes the father of Jesse and the grandfather of David. From this family tree the Messiah will come.

Lord, I thank you that through my faithful commitments you continue to restore and rebuild human lives. Amen.

The book of Ruth reveals how God weaves little actions of ordinary people into God's big story of healing and redeeming this world. This proves to be particularly true when the actions show self-giving love.

The key figures in these two passages are ordinary people: Naomi from Judah, Ruth the Moabite, Boaz the farmer, Obed the newborn child, and the women of Bethlehem. We read of no prominent kings or queens, no well-known prophets or priests, no outstanding preachers or judges. This simple story involves the faithful and loving efforts of two widows, a farmer, and some anonymous women—plain people living everyday lives.

Notice also that these people become part of God's story through small actions of self-giving love: Naomi's shift toward other-centeredness and encouragement of her daughter-in-law, Ruth's risking herself in relationship with the farmer, Boaz's willingness to travel the path of faithful commitment. However, these seemingly insignificant efforts are powerfully woven into the fabric of God's redemptive narrative. Ponder again the closing lines of the book, "They named him Obed; he became the father of Jesse, the father of David." Ruth becomes the great-grandmother of King David!

Sometimes our lives and actions in this world seem nothing but ordinary. They do not make the headlines of the daily newspaper or merit mention on television or have books written about them. However, when we willingly give ourselves to others in sacrificial love and faithful commitment, God can take these small efforts at loving and make them part of the divine salvation epic.

Lord, please weave my small actions of caring into your epic story of salvation. Amen.

Accrding to the psalmist, there is a right and a wrong way to go about our work. He makes this clear in the opening lines of Psalm 127: Work can be done badly. We can build a house in vain, stand guard in vain, rise early and toil in vain. What sense do we make of this warning for our lives today?

These words do not denote that work itself is a bad thing. We are not told to do *no* work. Indeed, the strong reminder that surfaces in these verses is that work is God's idea. This psalm reinforces what we learn about God in the book of Genesis: "Unless the LORD builds . . . " continues the theme announced in the first lines of the Bible, "In the beginning . . . God created. . . . " Putting it bluntly, God creates. God works. God labors. Our creation in God's image implies that we have been made for good and creative work. In Genesis 2:15 we read, "The LORD God took the man and put him in the garden of Eden to till it and keep it."

So how does our creation in the image of a God who creates and gives us the task of tilling and keeping (working) go wrong? Work becomes vain when we labor apart from God. When we pursue our tasks and responsibilities separate from God, we work for our own gain. Often people work addictively and compulsively or lazily and resentfully. However, when we align our work with God's purposes, we approach it in a different fashion. Then we work to provide for ourselves and our loved ones, as well as to bless those around us. We no longer work in vain. It becomes the means through which God's self-giving love becomes tangible.

Think for a moment about your daily work. How do you work? Do you work for yourself alone? In what ways do you see your work as a way of making God's love visible?

Lord, may my work make your love real for others. Amen.

Children serve as a constant reminder of how we best work together with God. On the one hand, they are God's gracious gift to us, born through the miraculous capacities of conception and birth. To borrow an image from the psalmist: They are a legacy, "a heritage from the LORD." In the psalmist's patriarchal society, sons, in particular, embody the generative aspect of a family. Both sons and daughters remind us that every day we waken to a world that we did not create but is freely given, that we enjoy a salvation that we have not earned.

Yet children are not born without our participation. We play a vital role in the process of bringing a child into the world. Without our efforts there would be no children. Nevertheless, our participation in the birth of children is always collaborative, cooperative, and co-creative. Ultimately God remains the Lord and giver of life. Without the work of God, all attempts at new life would be in vain.

The psalmist's conviction is clear: We work best when we participate in God's activity, consciously acknowledging the Giver. As we perform our assigned jobs and tasks, we learn to give patient attention to God's activity in our workplaces. How is God calling us to help and to heal, to serve and to save, to bless and to build? Recognizing and responding to God's activity enables us to enact God's self-giving love with our colleagues and work friends.

Psalm 127 challenges us to keep God at the center of all our efforts. Work becomes vain when we exclude God. But when we regard work as a way of partnering with God to make divine love real in the world, our work produces lasting good.

Lord, help me to recognize and respond to what you are doing in my work setting. Bless my efforts. Amen.

Sacrificial self-giving love lies at the heart of God. This becomes clear to us when we gaze on the Crucified One. The writer to the Hebrews proclaims this good news in what may seem a rather puzzling passage. In his "once-for-all" death on the cross, Jesus' sacrificial love goes far beyond the "again and again" sacrifices of the Temple. One powerful consequence flows from this vivid contrast between Jesus' unrepeatable sacrifice and all other repeatable sacrificial actions by human beings. It is mind-stretching, liberating, and very good news. Here it is: The crucified Jesus, now living beyond crucifixion in God's holy presence, fills the heavenly space with his self-giving love *on our behalf*. Christ's sacrifice is not for self-glory but to meet the need of humanity.

Biblical revelation suggests that the primary word to describe God is *holy*. Attending a Communion service recently, I was struck again by the words of the eucharistic chant: "Holy, holy, holy Lord; God of power and might, heaven and earth are full of your glory." Sometimes we choose to pit God's holiness against God's love. But the crucified Jesus in God's presence reminds us that the fire of God's holiness is the fire of self-giving love. God is set apart from us by self-giving, sacrificial love. The Wholly Other is wholly for us!

Hence, we live now with the wonderful assurance that Christ has readied heaven for the arrival of people like you and me. We may wonder how sinful human beings can have the audacity to enter the presence of the holy God. On our own, we simply could not. But Christ, who is in God's presence, has given himself utterly and completely on our behalf. We can enter the heavenly sanctuary without fear or shame. Human sin has been forgiven once and for all.

Jesus, I realize that only your self-giving love has removed my sin. I eagerly await your coming. Amen.

How often do we hear this thought: "If only I had more, I would be able to give so much more to God and to others." Perhaps we have even thought this ourselves.

The incident recorded in today's Gospel reading challenges this way of thinking. It comes immediately after Jesus strongly warns his hearers against the teachers the law. They had turned their religious activities into a show for the sake of gaining certain privileges. Then the Gospel describes Jesus sitting in the Temple, watching people putting coins into the Temple's treasury. Afterward Jesus draws for his disciples a vivid contrast between those who are able to give from plentiful resources and the widow's self-giving of "two small copper coins."

Consider why Jesus highlights this contrast. Does he want the disciples to realize that if the widow had thought she could only contribute if she had more money, she may never have given at all? that she would have missed out on the joy and dignity that sacrificial giving can bring? Maybe he wants them to realize that even though they do not have much, they can still experience the joy that comes with sacrificial self-giving. More than this, does he want them to see that her act of generosity symbolizes her total surrender to God and God's reign? that it is difficult for those who have much to abandon themselves in trust to a self-giving God?

At first glance the story may seem to be an idyllic end to a stormy chapter. But we must not be misled. Jesus focuses on giving all in radical trust and full commitment to God—then and now.

Lord, help me to give of myself to you and to others. Amen.

Praise for the Only One

NOVEMBER 9–15, 2015 • JAMES C. HOWELL

MONDAY, NOVEMBER 9 ~ *Read 1 Samuel 1:4-8*

Sorrow and unfulfilled dreams can create an ache within us, especially when we compare ourselves to others who seem to be doing very well. Hannah not only grieves her infertility but has to deal with the cruel taunts of her husband's other wife. Elkanah, the dutiful husband, attempts to juggle the emotions of a depressed wife and a haughty one. He offers comfort to Hannah, "Am I not more to you than ten sons?" Nice try—but even the noblest human love cannot satisfy the emptiness that accompanies crushed dreams.

Hannah's story ends happily. Hannah finally gives birth to the child she has desired. But for many, their prayers never "work." These women have no sons and are left with nothing. That's the darkest dread, isn't it? Not only to bear unfulfilled dreams but to drift into oblivion.

Here's where the good news of the gospel helps. Elkanah, though a devoted, compassionate husband, isn't worth more to Hannah than ten sons. But the God Hannah prays to is worth more than dozens of sons—although we come to that way of believing only by faith, and the ache may linger for a lifetime.

God came to us as the child everyone has always wanted. "For unto us a child is born." To the infertile, to the jobless, to those whose marriage is wrecked, to the one just told, "It's malignant," to all who bear sorrow—God comes as this child, and we are not alone. This God, and only this God, fills the gaping hole and brings the new life we'd dreamed of. We may not understand this gift this side of eternity, but the promise is sure.

Lord, help me trust that you are, and will be, enough. Amen.

Senior pastor, Myers Park United Methodist Church; Adjunct Professor of Preaching, Duke Divinity School; author of fifteen books

The disciples came to Jesus and said, "Lord, teach us to pray." We may assume they did so because Jesus exhibited an enviable intimacy with God. Jesus responded by giving them the Lord's Prayer. But he could just as easily have said, "You want to learn to pray? Consider the prayer of Hannah."

In her distress Hannah prays. But you get the sense she isn't speaking to a stranger. She is on close terms with this God who remains seemingly apart from her distress. The priest Eli certainly saw many people at prayer—but Hannah stood out. How moving is scripture's portrayal of her supplication. Hannah "wept bitterly. . . . [She] was praying silently; only her lips moved, but her voice was not heard." An inaudible—even incoherent—praying; nothing more than groans, "sighs too deep for words" (Rom. 8:26). True prayer need not issue in rational sentences. Hannah pours out her soul.

Eli presumes Hannah is drunk! Have you ever prayed in such a way that someone would suspect you'd been hitting the bottle? Unsteady on your feet, a bit too loud, not under control? And what was it like on the Day of Pentecost? The little band of Jesus' followers were praying in a room, and when they spilled out onto the streets onlookers mocked, "They are filled with new wine" (Acts 2:13). Indeed.

Our society looks to alcohol to do what only the Spirit can do for us: bring us joy, create good fellowship, cope with a bad day, steel us for bad news, celebrate goodness, and get to sleep at night.

Hannah is intoxicated by her own prayers or by the communion she shares with the God who has not granted her wishes, but who has never left her aching heart for a moment.

Ever-present God, may I pray like someone intoxicated with your Spirit. Amen.

Hannah, having battled infertility for so long, finally gives birth. Chapter 1 closes with her having weaned the child and then taken him to Eli with an offering. Hannah leaves Samuel with Eli for the Lord. This child for whom she has yearned now falls to Eli's care. What does Hannah do next? Lifting her gaze to heaven, she voices a hymn of praise. We expect praise such as "Thank you for getting me through this alive," or "Thank you for fulfilling my lifelong desire for a child!" Instead, she seems almost to forget her child—or maybe we would say she remembers what the birth of her child and every child is all about. She extols God's greatness. Lost in wonder, she adores God simply for who God is.

Then Hannah's surprising, instructive prayer turns to God's wonderful action—but not for her, as if God existed for her exclusive benefit. She marvels at God's flinty opposition to the proud and arrogant. This God of knowledge weighs actions and breaks bows. This God lifts the lowly and empowers the needy.

Hannah's hymn of praise sounds downright political! The mighty will be brought down. In this divine realm, the poor sit on thrones and in places of honor. In ancient Israel, average citizens would delight in Hannah's song, for persons prevail not by might but by faithfulness.

Such is the truth of God's kingdom. Another child, God's own, forsook the riches of heaven to become poor and to implement God's great reversal of fortune—the joke being on our social status, the punch line nothing less than God's extravagant grace that cannot be earned or bought. "For this child I prayed; . . . as long as he lives, he is given to the LORD" (1 Sam. 1:27-28).

God of grace, we praise you for who you are and for your grace, the reversal of all fortunes. Amen.

The climax of *The Wizard of Oz* comes when Toto pulls back the curtain and exposes a mere mortal, "a very good man . . . but a very bad wizard." Theologically speaking, it's a sad anticlimax. Many people in our modern culture believe the curtain is pulled back to reveal no God, just a very good man, and it's up to us humans to have brains, courage, and love.

How fascinating: Jesus never entered the holiest precinct of the Temple. He wasn't a priest, and he certainly wasn't the high priest who penetrated the inner sanctum to the place where a curtain hung before the epicenter of God's presence. What did Jesus do for us? He opened for us a "new and living way . . . through the curtain," so we could draw near to God. Jesus gives us direct access to God.

Jesus wasn't an ordained priest, and his executioners didn't envision his crucifixion as sacred. But now we see Jesus as the ultimate priest and as the one perfect sacrifice. Jesus offered himself. Our greatest privilege, our most profound craving, is for the curtain to be opened—and the opening is Jesus' own crucified flesh.

The book of Hebrews promises that we may draw near: just near, never fully there, but not far away either. We never fully possess God, and we do not become God. But we can get close.

The Wizard of Oz got it wrong. No one of us is good enough to muster heart, courage, and brains on our own. We are happily dependent on God. Jesus did for us what we could never do for ourselves. And his work was total and finished; Hebrews says "he sat down." He rested, so we can rest in him. We're the recipients of the most marvelous gift conceivable: the direct presence of God.

Lord Jesus, draw me near to you. Amen.

Several trends in modern society have left us as lonely spiritual people. The first is the anti-institutional mood that says we are spiritual beings who do not need the church. Many think they might be *more spiritual* without church, without the encumbrances of difficult people, the politics, budgets, and buildings.

The second shift comes in the way we now think of friendship. We consider a friend to be a person we choose by preference, someone who shares our interests and our notions of fun. When with our friends, we talk about sailing or cooking or golf—nothing of life-transforming substance; when we turn our attention to God, we are alone.

What is Hebrews' brilliant counsel? "Let us consider how to provoke one another to love and good deeds, not neglecting to meet together, as is the habit of some, but encouraging one another." Having encouraged true hearts of the assurance of faith and holding fast to hope, the writer goes on to remind his readers of the importance of gathering as a committed body. These verses imply that some in the faith community were choosing not to attend worship, thereby missing out on a crucial aspect of instruction: the example without words.

Our best chance for a meaningful experience of God comes when we hear and see God's activity demonstrated in the lives of others. We receive a special blessing when we gather with those who are different or difficult. Friction seems like a problem until we realize friction creates warmth. And friction polishes so that we can become clear mirrors of God to others.

Jesus saved us to be part of the body rather than independent practitioners. The body has various members; its differences prove to be the beauty and the hope of the faithful.

Lord Jesus, move me to join with others so we can encourage and rouse one another to good works. Amen.

The Bible rightly vilifies King Herod, but he was the greatest builder in the ancient world. His showpiece was a holy place, the rebuilt temple of Jerusalem. Tourists today are awestruck, as were the disciples of Jesus, who said, "Look, Teacher, what large stones!"

Herod's stone masons exhibited great skill. The largest excavated smoothly cut stone measures 44 by 16 by 100 feet and weighs 570 tons! The massive stone foundations, walls, and gleaming Temple that Herod built were presumed to be utterly indestructible.

Yet Jesus foretells a day when "not one stone will be left here upon another." Shocking! In a mere forty years, the Romans—after quelling the Jewish revolt—would dismantle the Temple and throw the gigantic stones into a heap.

The mock religiosity of an impressive religious structure that had lost its heart distressed Jesus. The fate of the Temple will eventually prove to be the fate of all grand buildings, all institutions—even the most noble and respected, even the holy church, consecrated as it may be to God.

We need our buildings, institutions, governments, denominations, churches. But they are not absolutes. They are not our reason for being; we do not exist to keep the church intact. Some theologians have conceived the church as an ark or perhaps a manger in which the Christ child is laid, displayed, worshiped, and adored. The buildings, budgets, committee meetings, votes, and policies have one and only one reason for being: the worship of God. Frederick Buechner suggested that a refreshing change for the body of Christ would involve the sweeping away of buildings, bulletins, and budgets. All that would remain for church members would be Jesus and one another. We need the big stones, places to meet, work to do. But let us remember whose church it was in the first place.

Lord Jesus, we admire the stones; we love you. Amen.

Jesus makes the following statement shortly before he dies, "Many will come in my name and say, 'I am he!'" The biggest mistake we ever make—in religious life and also in romantic life or investing or politics—is to vest any human being with our ultimate trust and passion. Leaders disappoint as do lovers and charismatic leaders. They are all mere mortals with feet of clay.

Only one can be the One. I find the most compelling proof of the truth of Christianity in this fact. Many in Jesus' epoch claimed to be the Messiah—and plenty of other heroes and mighty men such as Julius Caesar, Alexander the Great, Augustus, even Spartacus the slave rebel existed. When each one of these died, their followers hung their heads and trudged home. When Jesus died, his followers hid out. But after receiving the Spirit they came out of hiding. Rippling with joy, unable to keep their mouths shut, they plunged out into the known world and told everyone that Jesus is the one. They risked life and limb to tell everybody that he has risen and that to worship and follow him is good, noble, sheer delight, the way to heaven.

But this Jesus wasn't a purveyor of success. He spoke of suffering—and endured plenty. Many think God and suffering are alien to each other, but we know better. When we suffer, God is there. And the suffering has a purpose, a stunning end game. Jesus anticipated agonies but added that the pains would be birth pangs. For the child in the womb, the contractions must be uncomfortable. There is no light, no awareness of life outside the womb. But the pangs prepare the way for birth, new life, the day when the one who's been carried in the dark finally emerges on the other side, sees mother and father, and cries for joy.

Lord Jesus, you are the one—the only one—for me. Amen.

Belonging to the Truth

NOVEMBER 16–22, 2015 • L. ROGER OWENS

MONDAY, NOVEMBER 16 ~ *Read 2 Samuel 23:1-7*

These verses offer us an image for just, faithful leadership: "One who rules over people justly, ruling in the fear of God, is like the light of morning, like the sun rising on a cloudless morning, gleaming from the rain on the grassy land." The night may be dark, cloudy, and rainy, but when morning comes the darkness disappears. How refreshing and enlivening is the clarity of such a morning!

You need only to think of a world leader like Nelson Mandela to understand this image. After the long, stormy night of apartheid in South Africa, Mandela's leadership, marked by a commitment to justice and reconciliation, was like the light of a new day. However, political leaders are not the only ones called to this ideal of just leadership. These verses speak to parents, pastors, and principals as well—all who hold positions of authority and leadership. How can each of us exercise authority in ways that are just, so that clarity like that of a new dawn will be their hallmark?

King David in these verses speaks of his own reign, which had its dark, stormy periods. When we remember that aspect, we can hear his words as ones of hope. When we fall short of this type of leadership, we know that with God, renewal is possible.

When we lead with justice, in the "fear of God," we become signs of the reign of Jesus himself, the heir to David's throne, who, as the book of Revelation says, is himself the light of the city of God.

Lord, help me see where you are calling me to leadership today, and give me the wisdom to lead with equity and justice. Amen.

Associate Professor of Leadership and Ministry, Pittsburgh Theological Seminary; author of *Abba, Give Me a Word: The Path of Spiritual Direction*

This psalm begins with the celebration of King David's oath: "I will not give sleep to my eyes . . . until I find a place for the LORD." A few verses later the writer calls on God, "Rise up, O LORD, and go to your resting place." What is the relationship between David's promise to find a place for the Lord and the psalmist's cry for the Lord to come to a resting place?

After my lecture on Christian spirituality, a student asked me, "Where is the place for God in my life?" I replied, "There is no place for God in your life." Even though David finds a "place for the LORD," God's presence is never under our control. A better question might be this: "Where is my place in God's life?" God is present not because David found a place for God but because of God's promise to be with the people.

The divine decision to be with people finds its fulfillment in Jesus, in whom God rests. In freedom God chooses to live among us. And God's place continues to be among us in the Spirit of Christ, who makes the church Christ's body, the ongoing incarnation of God in the world. We need not find a place for God in our lives but, instead, perceive the shape of God's sovereign presence and activity already at work in our lives.

The spiritual life entails discerning God's activity in our lives. Sometimes we imagine that our prayer practices *are* our work of making a place for God. But we should consider them ways we glimpse God's sovereign presence and redemptive activity in our lives, remembering that God has chosen us as God's resting place.

Lord, help me remember that it's not my job to find a place for you. Instead, may I find the places where you are already at work in my life. Amen.

The sixteenth-century reformer Martin Luther said that the gospel comes to us in the form of promise: God has acted and will act to save us. The God of the Bible is a promise-making, promise-keeping God.

This psalm celebrates the promise God made to continue the line of David's rule and to make Zion God's ongoing home, a freely given promise based on gracious desire: "For the LORD has chosen Zion; he has desired it for his habitation."

When we forget that God relates to us on the basis of gracious promise, we may be tempted to turn our relationship to God into an if-then relationship. *If* I am good, *then* God will love me; *if* I study my Bible, *then* God will listen to me; *if* I tithe, *then* God will bless me; *if* I serve the poor, *then* God will reward me.

Whenever we take this approach, we are reshaping the gospel. Gospel comes as God's promise, expressed in this psalm by the word *chosen*. The promise to David is not a response to David. God's promise of salvation never comes as a response but as a free, unconditional gift.

Christians see God's promises fulfilled in Jesus Christ, the Son of David and the new Zion, the one whom God has chosen to embody divine saving presence in the world.

When you feel tempted to believe that you have to pressure God to keep the promise or coax God to be present with you, reconsider that temptation. In Jesus, God offers an unconditional promise: I am with you always, even to the end of the age.

Gracious God, give me the faith to receive your promised gift of love, and free me from the belief that I have to earn that love. Amen.

Some of us attend faith communities where we call the pastor a priest, and it's his or her role to celebrate the sacraments and pronounce God's forgiveness. Others of us go to churches where we call the minister "pastor" or "preacher," but it's still easy for us to imagine that he or she has a privileged relationship with God—a relationship we think we could never have.

During the sixteenth-century Reformation, a renewed understanding emerged of a concept called the "priesthood of all believers." That phrase doesn't mean that we don't need human pastors and priests to lead, teach, and guide the people of God. It means that the whole people of God—the church itself—is a priestly community. Clergy and laypeople together make up this priestly community. This community serves God by serving as a priest to its neighbors, offering a sign of God's presence to them.

Some people believe that the term "priesthood of all believers" means that each one of us is our own priest, that we don't need others to help us in our relationship with God. Rather, it means that in baptism we become priests for one another precisely because we *do need* to help one another relate to God. We need to announce God's forgiveness to one another. We want to intercede in prayer for one another. We desire to allow our voices to carry words of praise on behalf of others when their own voices can't. We need to be the kingdom of priests God has made us.

And in our priestly praying, we will thank God for those pastors and priests whom God has given to guide us and equip us as we grow into our own priestly role as bearers of God's love, forgiveness, and presence in the world.

Almighty God, as a member of your priestly people, help me see how I can make your presence and grace known to my friends and neighbors. Amen.

Dietrich Bonhoeffer, the German theologian and martyr during World War II, once said that the most difficult thing for human beings to come to terms with is the reality that we were not in the beginning. We struggle with being in the middle, with being creatures.

Today's passage clearly states that God alone is the beginning and the end, the Alpha and the Omega. God is the one "who is and who was and who is to come"—not us. We are in the middle.

Often we think of sin as actions and behaviors prohibited by God. But a broader concept of sin involves the human tendency to chafe against our creaturely place in the middle, to be beset by dreams and aspirations of being more than creatures and then trying to live them out those dreams.

I prefer to think of the Christian spiritual journey as the journey of learning to be creatures with limits. Creaturely limits don't constrict us except when we rebel against them. Within our limits as creatures we find our truest freedom. Saint Irenaeus noted, "The glory of God is the human being fully alive." Being fully alive implies embracing the reality that we are human beings, not God.

In Jesus, God entered the middle to show us the beauty of creaturely life, to restore us as the image of God in creation, and to show us what "fully alive" means for being human. Salvation from sin does not mean that we are no longer creatures. It means that we will embrace being creatures in the appropriate way and flourish within our human limits.

God of our Lord Jesus Christ, help us embrace ourselves the way you created us—limits and all. Give us patience when we get frustrated with our creaturely limits. Amen.

Earlier in John's Gospel the crowds try to make Jesus king, but he slips away. In truth, Jesus is already king—just not the kind of king the people desire. And so Jesus tells Pilate, "My kingdom is not from this world."

We often interpret Jesus' words to mean that his kingdom is otherworldly, merely spiritual, which is why we often hear people say that the church should stay out of politics. Saying God's kingdom is spiritual gets us off the hook. Then we don't have to be held accountable for how we engage in what the world calls politics.

When Jesus says this to Pilate, he's not referring to a spiritual kingdom. He means that the realm that acknowledges his rule is not governed by the coercive social conditions of worldly kingdoms. If his kingdom were from *this world*, he states, his followers would resort to violence to protect him.

We take it for granted that violence and coercion are a necessary part of life, but Jesus doesn't think so. He came to introduce a new social reality that we call church—real people in real relationships who have discovered that because Jesus chose to die rather than fight, we can live together without coercion or violence. Thus, we can signal to the kingdoms of this world— whether local communities or national governments—that alternatives to violence exist.

Jesus does not rule a merely spiritual kingdom. He rules over a kingdom *in* but not *of* the world. In Jesus' kingdom, the practices of forgiveness and reconciliation have overcome the practices of threat and coercion. God invites us to enter this reign and let it shape our lives and the communities in which we live.

King Jesus, help me to live today in a way that witnesses to your kingdom of love and peace. Amen.

REIGN OF CHRIST SUNDAY

Everyone who belongs to the truth listens to my voice." We send our children to school hoping they will learn things that are true. We go to Sunday school and study our Bibles believing they offer us truth. Some people believe that to be a Christian you have to assent to a certain set of propositions about God, that you have to believe these principles are true. In each case, we believe that the truth of what we read, learn, or believe corresponds to "the way things really are."

When Pilate interrogates Jesus, Jesus makes a statement that upsets our conventional notions of truth: "Everyone who belongs to the truth listens to my voice." What does it mean to belong to the truth?

Maybe Jesus is saying that truth involves more than believing certain propositions are correct, something we do with our minds. Truth involves a relationship. In this case, truth is the relationship of learning to belong to Jesus. So truth isn't just in our minds—what we believe; it's in our lives as they become conformed to Jesus' image. And this process occurs as we listen to him.

We let Christ the king reign in our lives when we let our lives be conformed to the life of him who is the Truth. Spiritual disciplines help us do this. They help us listen to Jesus and thus belong to him as we learn to obey what we hear. Through the spiritual disciplines we learn to listen to Jesus, receive him, and respond with our lives. The more we do this, the more we will find ourselves belonging to the truth. And this belonging might actually change what we believe.

Lord, help me grow in my relationship with the truth—with you—as I seek to listen to your voice this day. Amen.

Hopeful Waiting

NOVEMBER 23–29, 2015 • SALLY O. LANGFORD

MONDAY, NOVEMBER 23 ~ *Read Luke 21:25-36*

At dawn this Monday, I am frantically cleaning house, washing dishes, and making a grocery list in preparation for Thanksgiving dinner. Jesus warns us that the Son of Man will return one day with power and glory. We must pray and stay alert if we want to be ready for God's coming judgment and redemption. But for me, there's no time this week to get ready for anything other than the perfect family feast on Thursday.

I do believe in the Second Coming of Christ. However, Jesus appearing suddenly on a cloud in the sky is not central to my Christian faith. Pulling the house together for company is a far easier task for me than preparing for Christ.

And yet, in admitting that I would rather not prepare for the coming of Christ, I find myself hoping to do just that. Too often I get caught up in the busyness of Christmas shopping, party planning, and house decorating. What if I took seriously the invitation of Advent to watch and wait for the coming of Christ? Instead of letting the anxieties of day-to-day life weigh me down, what if I carved out quiet moments for meditation and prayer each morning?

This Advent we can prepare for the birth of the baby Jesus and the return of Christ in final victory. We can live in the tension between God's promise of a restored world and the pain that comes with transformation. By doing so, we will discover that getting ready for Christ is more meaningful than getting ready for Thanksgiving and Christmas.

Stir up in me, O God, the desire to watch and wait for the coming Christ. Come, Lord Jesus, come! Amen.

Elder, Western North Carolina Conference of The United Methodist Church, currently serving as assistant to the bishop

As I write today's devotional, the United States weighs its options for military intervention in Syria. So at the beginning of Advent, I pray for peace and justice, even as I realize that peace and justice are difficult to achieve.

In the time of the prophet Jeremiah, Judah's King Zedekiah desperately aligned with Egypt. Zedekiah hoped against hope that Judah would yet withstand the power and might of Babylon. But Zedekiah's revolt to free Judah led to the Babylonian invasion of Jerusalem and the destruction of the city and the Temple in 586 BCE.

Jeremiah had warned of God's coming judgment that would be exacted through the Babylonian forces. Jeremiah also promised that judgment would lead to healing and forgiveness. After the people lived in exile in Babylon and were feeling as dead as old stumps, God would raise up a new branch. This new Davidic king would rule justly and would be called "The LORD is our righteousness" (Jer. 23:16). Today's reading identifies a city by this same name. Both the ruler and the city, by their very name, give expression to characteristics of those who dwell in such a place, those who believe themselves delivered, redeemed, and cared for by the Lord.

This Advent, we prayerfully wait for the coming of Jesus Christ who is in truth "The LORD is our righteousness." What experiences of delivery and redemption can you recount? How do you see the Lord's care in your life?

On our own, we cannot overturn the powers of evil and injustice, not in countries far away or in our own home communities. But we can trust Jesus Christ to bring lasting peace and justice. And God can use us as faithful witnesses to the coming Christ.

Forgive me, Lord, for my own participation in war and injustice. I pray for peace. Make me a witness of your never-failing righteousness. Amen.

When I was a child, each Advent my mother placed an Advent calendar on the piano in our living room. My sister, brother, and I took turns opening each day's "window." We could hardly wait to see if that day's picture revealed a toy or an animal or a character in the Christmas story. On Christmas Eve, we eagerly opened the last "window," and always we would see Mary, Joseph, and the baby Jesus. Christmas had finally arrived.

As a child, I excitedly waited during Advent for the arrival of Christmas. Christmas brought the birth of the baby Jesus and also school vacation, family get-togethers, and presents from Santa Claus.

As an adult, I now know that awaiting the arrival of Christmas is anything but exciting for many people. For individuals who have experienced the death of a loved one, a serious illness, financial difficulties, family conflict, or divorce, Christmas can be a holiday to endure, not a season to enjoy and savor.

Jeremiah understood the struggle of watching and waiting in the midst of a seemingly hopeless situation. While confined to prison quarters, Jeremiah heard God's message of judgment. The invading Babylonians would destroy Judah; there was no escape. But Jeremiah also heard God's word of hope: "The time is coming, . . . when I will fulfill my gracious promise with the people of Israel and Judah. In those days and at that time, I will raise up a righteous branch from David's line, who will do what is just and right in the land" (CEB).

During these days of Advent, when we confront our failures, limitations, and feelings of sorrow and grief, may we find hope in God's promise of Jesus Christ. While we wait for Christmas, we are not alone. God is with us.

Thank you, God, for staying with us while we watch and wait for your coming reign in Jesus Christ. Help us to trust in you, even in the midst of our seemingly hopeless situations. Amen.

THANKSGIVING DAY, USA

One Thanksgiving, when my husband, our daughters, and I could not travel home to be with extended family, we gathered for Thanksgiving dinner with church friends in the church's fellowship hall. People gathered from North Carolina, Georgia, Oklahoma, and New York—and also from Mexico, Zimbabwe, India, and Korea. Our individual dishes became a wonderful smorgasbord of turkey, cranberry sauce, fried rice, noodles, beans, chicken curry, papaya, biscuits, and tortillas.

Before eating, those of us who had assembled for the meal joined hands for prayer. Children, teenagers, singles, young couples, middle-aged adults, and older adults prayed. All of us missed family back home, but we were grateful for the opportunity to gather with new friends. The psalmist's words could well have been our grateful prayer that day: "I offer my life to you, LORD. My God, I trust you. . . . I put my hope in you all day long" (Ps. 25:1-2, 5, CEB).

This Thanksgiving, my extended family will gather at our house for dinner. Our grown daughters and their families will be there, as will my mother and my sister and brother and their families. Four generations will gather around the table for our traditional turkey dinner. This Thanksgiving, like that Thanksgiving many years ago, I am grateful for God's blessings. This Thanksgiving, when we bow in prayer to say thank you, I will remember the words of the psalmist: "The LORD is good and does the right thing; he teaches sinners which way they should go. God guides the weak to justice, teaching them his way. All the LORD's paths are loving and faithful for those who keep his covenant and laws" (25:8-10, CEB).

Thank you, Lord, for our blessings. May we be a blessing to others. Amen.

In the United States, Black Friday, the day after Thanksgiving Day, is one of the busiest shopping days of the year. The name comes from an old way of keeping business accounts, in which losses were recorded in red and profits in black. On Black Friday, retail stores have extended hours, huge sales, and special offers, all in hopes of bringing in record numbers of shoppers for profit-making sales.

Like so many others, I have shown up at stores before dawn on Friday, eager to find sought-after Christmas gifts. Black Friday shoppers can be rude and aggressive; sometimes, shoppers even trample other shoppers in frantic attempts to get the best deals on products before the supplies run out.

The anxious spirit of Black Friday contrasts strongly with the loving spirit of Christ, which the apostle Paul holds up as an example for the Christians of Thessalonica. Paul prays that God might increase and enrich the Thessalonians' love for "one another and all," in order that they might become pure and holy for the coming of Jesus Christ.

This Advent, through God's grace, will our spirits become more loving and less anxious? We, like the Thessalonians, can focus more on sharing God's love with others. Then, amazingly, the more love we share, the more we receive.

I have witnessed such love. One church hosts a spa day during Advent for women who are homeless. In the midst of manicures, pedicures, and massages, women accustomed to the extras in life find joy in sharing simple pleasures with others. Another church partners with hospice and holds a Blue Christmas worship service. While worshipers quietly pray and light candles in memory of loved ones, church members understand more fully that the coming Christ is Emmanuel, God with us.

God, take away my anxious spirit. Fill me with your love. Move me to share your love with others. Amen.

Today's passage lifts up two recurring themes in Paul's letter: love and holiness. Paul knew the importance of Christians depending upon one another. He sent Timothy to Thessalonica to encourage and support church members in their Christian life.

In order to become the loving and faithful people God calls us to be, Christians need the support of both the Holy Spirit and other people. Without an intentional focus on growing together in Christ, the Thessalonians could well drift back to life apart from God. The same is true for us. During Advent, we easily get caught up in the commercialism of the holidays and can lose our distinctiveness as the people of God. But there is another way.

During Advent, we can partner with brothers and sisters in Christ to strengthen one another's faith. Instead of trying to resist the excess and busyness of the holidays on our own, we can find ways to make the season holy together. A small group can gather to unpack the Chrismons and reflect on the meaning of each Christian symbol as they decorate the sanctuary tree. Youth can meet for breakfast before school to talk about the meaning of the Advent scriptures. Children and adults can decorate cookies in the fellowship hall and deliver them to homebound members. Families can light an Advent wreath and share joys and concerns over dinner.

We, like the Christians of Thessalonica, live between the "already" of what God has done for us through Jesus' life, death, and resurrection and the "not yet" of Jesus' Second Coming. Through Christ, we are a new creation. And yet, the old age intrudes, even in the midst of our holy Advent season. We will keep our focus on the coming Christ by joining together in worship, prayer, Bible study, and service.

Lord, help me never to go it alone. May I rely on your help and that of Christian friends. Amen.

FIRST SUNDAY OF ADVENT

The Gospel of Luke does not sound the Advent message that the world is falling apart. It communicates the message that when the sun, the moon, and the stars spin out of control and the oceans and rivers flood the land, our redemption is coming near.

Despair would overwhelm us if we focused only on the sins and failures that corrupt our world. Hopelessness would overcome us if we saw only our limited skills and resources as sources of change. But we believe that God is faithful. Just as God once became flesh and lived among us as Jesus, so too will Christ come again to fulfill the promise of his resurrection.

In Jerusalem, Jews, Christians, and Muslims have cemeteries on the hillside below the Mount of Olives. According to some traditions, at the end of time the Messiah will appear here first and will march with his saints down the Kidron Valley and up to the Temple Mount. While Jesus may return first to Jerusalem, it will not matter where we or our graves are on that day. We can boldly follow Jesus in any time or place. And although we bear witness all year to our faith, the light of Christ must shine brightly in our lives during Advent. To those who assume that the church has nothing more to offer than our culture's sentimental and materialistic presentation of Christmas, we share the joyful story of God's gift of love and life through Jesus Christ.

During Advent we keep our eyes and our hearts open for the coming Christ. Fearful and hopeless people might huddle in the dark with eyes closed against coming destruction. But we as people of hope excitedly await the dawn of Christmas morning. We stand on tiptoe, peering through the darkness to glimpse the gifts of God. Indeed, we stand up tall and raise our heads, for our redemption is coming near.

God, may we watch and wait in joy for the coming of our redemption. Eagerly we pray: Come, Lord Jesus, come. Amen.

God's Messengers

NOVEMBER 30–DECEMBER 6, 2015 • LUTHER E. SMITH JR.

MONDAY, NOVEMBER 30 ~ *Read Malachi 3:1-4*

God announces that a messenger is being sent to prepare the way for God's coming. This announcement is a response to prayers that God be made manifest and specifically to the question, "Where is the God of justice?" (Mal. 2:17). This text does not identify the messenger, nor does it state the specific time of arrival. Even the message itself is not delineated. Yet, it conveys the certainty that a messenger is being sent and God will follow.

This certainty is both reassuring and frightening. The people demand God's justice to overcome suffering, oppression, and injustice. God's presence promises the advent of hope, love, and joy—all causes for rejoicing. Still, the troubling question arises: "Who can endure the day of his coming, and who can stand when he appears?" The question challenges each of us to consider our honest response to the announcement of God's messenger and God's coming.

How sure is our commitment to anticipate and prepare for such a time? What would being subjected to a "refiner's fire" mean in our lives? What would the advent of God's righteousness in society and our lives look like? How are you *preparing* for God's coming and not just *waiting* for it? We answer these questions day by day, decision by decision, and action by action. The messenger and the message implore us to make a faithful offering of our lives that is "pleasing to the LORD." It has been written and proclaimed. God's coming is certain.

O God, with trusting and eager hearts may we come to know the joy of anticipating you and of giving ourselves to your surprising future. Amen.

Professor Emeritus of Church and Community, Candler School of Theology, Atlanta, Georgia; ordained clergy, Christian Methodist Episcopal Church

Zechariah is no longer mute. His season of enforced silence provided a time of spiritual deepening in which he became aware of God's activity in his midst. "Filled with the Holy Spirit," he speaks aloud a prophecy about his son, John. The prophecy begins by proclaiming God as the source of all that has made the present moment of joy possible and who secures the people's future with "knowledge of salvation." The message of hope for the future begins by recounting sacred history. Zechariah remembers God's mighty acts: God redeemed the people, raised up a mighty savior, spoke through the holy prophets, saved the people from their enemies and from any harm. He attributes these mighty acts to God as he remembers the divine covenant with his ancestors. Remembering the past is a spiritual act that establishes the meaning of the current relationship with God. Remembering the past brings forth the basis of future hope.

Zechariah, as God's messenger, is a time traveler. To guide and reassure his generation, he enters the past through remembering and the future through prophetic envisioning. In hearing his message, we travel into sacred history, and we travel forward to a future that is intended for us. In this future we serve God freely, without intimidation and oppression—a future in which we are fully capable of living "in holiness and righteousness."

How can you prepare to discern and embrace this future? Perhaps contemplative listening to God's messengers in your own season of silence is a means that will give depth to your spiritual vision and guide your feet "into the way of peace."

O God, you know the longing of our hearts to experience the present and future you intend for us. Help us to remember who you have been with our ancestors and with us. May we discern your messages and be reassured of your companionship in all times and for all times. Amen.

Zechariah speaks to his child and announces that he, John, will be a prophet whose role is vital to God's saving activity. This title and role are not grandiose directives from an overbearing parent. Zechariah, "filled with the Holy Spirit," merely serves as the messenger about his son, John—who is also a messenger.

As in Monday's reading, a messenger goes before the Lord to prepare the way. Zechariah's message, unlike the pronouncement in Malachi that asks "who can endure the day of his coming, and who can stand when he appears?" is characterized by comforting and hopeful transformations: the knowledge of salvation, forgiveness of sins, light to those who sit in darkness and in the shadow of death, guidance into the way of peace. However, we know that John's future is far more traumatic than the picture created by Zechariah's words. This child will be ridiculed, rejected, jailed, and executed.

The absence of these details of the child's prophetic life does not diminish the truth and power of Zechariah's vision. The message of this vision is the foremost message of the Gospel story: God is about to undertake saving acts for God's people, and John will serve as God's messenger who prepares the way.

This announcement prepares us to hear and understand the Gospel story as God's action for salvation. While confrontations, loving interactions, conflicts, rejections, healing, teaching, and death form elements of the story, at its outset comes the assurance that God's people will be shown the way to live in God's presence. This fact is important to remember before the story begins, as the story is being told, and as we discern the meaning of the story for our lives. How does remembering Zechariah's message inform your reading of Luke?

May we live each day with a guiding vision of God's saving activity in us and for us.

The Gospel of Luke frames the time period of John's prophetic work by naming the political rulers and religious authorities who occupy seats of power. During Luke's time, this approach served as a traditional way to date a particular period in history.

Knowing the time is important, but these two verses tell us more. This is not a period of political and religious anarchy. The positions of power are occupied and authorities are known. John will enact his ministry in a land ruled by an occupying force (Rome) along with its approved local leadership. Priestly authority governs the religious institution. Into this environment John is called.

The verses tell us even more. With all these official authorities—whose influence determined matters of life and death and who were surrounded by rituals and grandeur that signified their power—"the word of God came to John son of Zechariah in the wilderness." What a contrast in status and location. God's message comes to seemingly the unlikeliest of persons who dwell in the unlikeliest of places. God's choice of messengers is often surprising. We can easily ignore or condemn messengers who do not conform to our expectations; then we can ignore or condemn messages that God intends for our salvation (becoming whole).

What criteria and assumptions form the basis for your openness to see and hear someone with a transforming message? When have you been surprised by the source of a transforming message in your life? How do you remain alert to God's unconventional ways of preparing you for God's coming anew into our midst? These questions allow us to identify our response to challenging messengers. These questions also prepare us to hear, see, and experience the future into which God calls us.

God, may we be receptive to the transforming messengers and messages that you have for us. Amen.

John actively proclaims God's message with its overarching theme of "proclaiming a baptism of repentance for the forgiveness of sins." Specifics of his message begin in verse 7 and continue throughout the chapter. Today's reading emphasizes John's identity and the magnitude of his prophetic action. Whatever we are about to hear *from* John and *about* John must be heard as the fulfillment of Isaiah's prophecy for salvation.

In preparing "the way of the Lord," John's ministry will require dramatic transformations. The changes are tantamount to valleys being filled, mountains and hills leveled to the ground, crooked paths straightened, and rough paths made smooth. These images of a radical remaking of the landscape communicate how anything that delays God's arrival must be transformed. The people's need for God is so urgent that seemingly impossible tasks must and will take place to prepare for God's coming.

Just as these verses use words from Isaiah to characterize John's ministry, Martin Luther King Jr. quoted it in his "I Have a Dream" speech to declare his hope for the elimination of all barriers to social justice, mutual respect, and compassion. God's messengers over the centuries have been inspired to speak Isaiah's prophecy as an instructive and relevant message of transformation so that "all flesh shall see the salvation of God."

God's messengers instruct and inspire us to anticipate a time when all persons experience God's salvation. In this Advent season, to what transformations are we committed to prepare the way of the Lord? Name the barriers that we need to eliminate. What makes our time urgent for God's coming? May we embrace our roles in enacting the transformations for such a time as this.

Lord, we anticipate your coming. Empower us to do whatever hastens our awareness of your presence and joy. Guide us in giving ourselves to this mission. Amen.

God's Messengers

It is hard to imagine a more profound expression of love and gratitude than what Paul writes in verses 3-4. Say them aloud repeatedly. Consider how you would feel if these words were spoken about you and to you. These words and the feelings they evoke are essential to understanding the relationship between Paul (the messenger) and the Philippian Christian community.

The connection between the messenger and the community in today's reading differs greatly from the readings from Malachi and Luke. In those scriptures, the messengers come to their communities with a confronting proclamation for change. Even though the messengers live among the people being addressed, their challenges seem fierce and disruptive. We know that Paul can also be harsh when calling people to transformation; in today's scripture, however, he expresses a greeting most tender and intimate. Paul and the Philippian community have been partners in the work for "the day of Jesus Christ." The community has cared for Paul in some of his most precarious times. The relationship is so intense that Paul and the community have become coworkers as messengers of "the gospel."

It would be a mistake to interpret the messengers in Malachi and Luke as detesting the people. The prophetic tradition of rebuke and calls for transformation have at their root profound love for God's people. We can read Paul's letter as stressing another dimension of prophetic love that prepares the way for God: entering into intimate and working relationship with a community. Communities sustain God's messengers and communities become God's messengers. Where do you experience a community that sustains you in your commitment to fulfill a holy purpose? How do you express gratitude for that relationship?

During this Advent season, may we be community minded in the formation of our Christian identity and in the transforming work to which God calls us.

SECOND SUNDAY OF ADVENT

This public prayer speaks to God and to its hearers. The prayer appeals to God on behalf of the community's holy formation in love and divine guidance in discerning how to be "pure and blameless." The prayer encourages the community to increase the love already evident and to pursue righteousness that "comes through Jesus Christ." When the Philippian community heard this letter, it must have felt blessed by Paul's words of appreciation and aspiration for the community. Paul's prayer of preparation for "the day of Christ" is characterized by tones of affirmation, compassion, and hope.

Love is the primary virtue for the right formation of the community. Paul's understanding for the needed manifestation of love goes beyond mere affection for one another. This love must engage complicated and difficult issues "with knowledge and full insight to help you to determine what is best." Times will come when communal covenants are ignored and violated, misunderstandings abound, relationships need healing, and fear of oppressive authorities will present challenging decisions of faith. Only when the community has fully enacted its love "through Jesus Christ" can it attain outcomes "for the glory and praise of God."

Read this prayer with your Christian community in mind. What thoughts emerge about the significance of this prayer to the mission and fellowship of your faith community? What are the opportunities and challenges for love flourishing in ways that glorify and praise God? How does this prayer inspire your commitment to prepare yourself as a messenger for God's coming anew into the world?

O God, help us listen intently to your heart as it longs for all your people. And guide our lives in being a faithful response to what we hear. Amen.

Don't Worry . . .

DECEMBER 7–13, 2015 • MARTHA C. HIGHSMITH

MONDAY, DECEMBER 7 ~ *Read Philippians 4:4-7*

As the song says, "Don't worry, be happy." As Americans, we consider the pursuit of happiness one of our "inalienable rights." We think that having money or being successful or owning the latest gadgets will make us happy, only to discover that having it all is never enough. We become like the rich man who, when asked how much money was enough, replied "just a little more." Rather than freeing us from worry, constantly pursuing happiness can give us even more to worry about!

So the scripture offers a different message: Don't worry, be joyful! Happiness and joy are not the same. Happiness floats on the surface of our lives and is easily disturbed by the storms of life, disrupted by external events. Happiness is situational. Joy, on the other hand, lies so deep within our souls that nothing can disturb it. True joy endures through disaster, disappointment, and loss. Happiness centers on self; joy finds expression in relationships, in serving others. Happiness is often achieved by addressing some perceived scarcity, but joy grows out of a celebration of abundance. Happiness can be fleeting; joy is eternal.

The place of joy is the place of God. To live from that place of deep joy frees us from worry. To live as though "the Lord is near," even when all evidence suggests the contrary, is to practice faith. A line from a Wendell Berry poem puts it this way: "Be joyful though you have considered all the facts" ("Manifesto: The Mad Farmer Liberation Front" from *Collected Poems 1957–1982*). Or as Paul says and then says again: "Rejoice!"

What brings you joy? How can you hold fast to that joy even in the face of difficulty?

Associate Vice President and Lecturer in Divinity, Yale University; copastor, First Presbyterian Church, Hartford, Connecticut

Paul's instructions to the Philippians are so absolute: Rejoice in the Lord always; let your gentleness be known to everyone; do not worry about anything. There is no wiggle room here —it is all or nothing. And I fail on almost every count, especially when it comes to the commandment not to worry. I am a worrier by nature. In fact, for a good part of my career I have been paid to worry, to imagine all the things that could go wrong and develop plans to address those possibilities.

Whether it is part of a job or not, worry seems to be a way of life. Our world is a worrisome place. Terrorism is an ever-present threat, as anyone who has been through an airport surely knows. Closer to home, we worry about keeping our jobs or finding work; we worry about our finances. We worry about our children and whether they will turn out all right. We worry about our health and the health of those closest to us. In short, we worry about almost everything.

So how can we hear these holy words that Paul speaks to us? How can we let go of worry? Paul suggests that prayer is the answer. Prayer shifts our focus from ourselves to God. Prayer acknowledges what we cannot control (almost everything!) and assures us that we are held in God's hand. Prayer justifies us, in the sense that it realigns us and puts us in right relationship with God. When we pray, we take the load of worry that weighs us down and hand it over to God. Maybe nothing in our situation or circumstance seems to change, but everything within us is different. The place once filled with worry now becomes a space for joy.

And what worries are to be the focus of our praying? Paul gives us yet another absolute—this one more comforting than challenging: we are to pray about everything!

Today, practice praying with every little worry that arises. Pay attention to what happens in your soul when you do that.

I've read somewhere that the command that appears most often in the Bible is "fear not." And God's command to fear not often comes with a reminder that God is with those receiving the command; acting on their behalf; protecting, providing, and guiding. Even after exile—the most lost and defeated place and time for God's chosen people—the command comes through the prophet Zephaniah: "Do not fear. . . . The LORD, your God, is in your midst."

But we find it hard not to be afraid. After all, fear is instinctive, a built-in physical response to threat. It prompts us to protect ourselves from danger. Chronic fear, however, can be disabling. Living in constant fear leaves us paralyzed between fight and flight and unable to respond at all. When we abandon ourselves to fear we become totally preoccupied with the future and its threat of terrible things to come. Then we miss the presence of the Holy in the here and now. Fear distracts us from seeing the God who is in our midst.

When God tells the people—then and now—not to be afraid, that command is coupled with the promise, spoken or implied, that God is in our midst. God does not hold us at arm's length or turn away from our failings or abandon us to our own worst selves. No, God is among us. To a broken people in ancient times that promise gave cause for rejoicing. It does for us too.

And here is a divine twist: It is not only God's people who rejoice. God also rejoices—over us. We experience renewal in God's love.

Imagine God rejoicing over you and renewing you. With this picture in mind, list those qualities of your life that make God glad. Then create a space of silence in your praying so you can listen for the love song God is singing to you.

The prophet says with confidence, "I will trust, and will not be afraid." Perfect love casts out fear (1 John 4:18) and so does faith it seems. Is this thought a comforting one, or does it mean that fear results from a lack of faith?

The prophet suggests that faith and fear are opposites; you can have one or the other but not both. Does being afraid demonstrate a lack of trust, a lack of faith? And if worry is the companion of fear, which I believe it is, is it a sin to worry? Does worry also signal a lack of faith?

While people often describe faith as something we have, almost a type of possession, that image suggests that it can easily slip through our fingers if we are careless, thoughtless, preoccupied, or sunk in the swampy places of life. We can lose our focus and our footing, and we can lose our faith.

Maybe faith is not a possession, a noun—but rather a verb. And instead of having faith or keeping the faith, maybe we choose to live out our faith as the way to banish fear. The second half of this verse echoes the song of thanksgiving from Exodus when Moses and the Israelites celebrated their deliverance from the Egyptians. Even in exile, the people choose faith over fear by recalling the saving activity of God in their past.

Choosing to be faithful seems to be an act that defies logic. It is the ability to see the Holy One in our midst when the world is blind to that presence. Faith is the willingness to give thanks even when things are at their worst and the courage to trust that God is in control and that God is love. Faith gives us the capacity to stand beside the sea, facing the unknown, facing the wilderness, and affirm with the ancient Israelites, "Surely God is my salvation; I will trust, and will not be afraid." We decide to believe this and trust God to make it so—even though we have considered all the facts!

Choose this day to act in faith. Believe that God is with you.

Igrew up on a farm, and my family depended on water to make our crops. Drought brought worry. But we could tap into the deep reservoirs underground, and those aquifers became wells of salvation for us. I still remember the cold, wet work of moving irrigation pipes in the night. But with the work came a joyful gratitude in knowing that much-needed water was soaking into the roots of our blueberries. Like our version of the miracle at Cana, the water would be transformed into sweet fruit, and the crop would be saved.

At the time, I felt that *our* effort primarily created this miracle. After all, we were the ones who did the work. But in reality, we could have accomplished nothing without access to the water. We could not save the crop all by ourselves.

Sometimes, good people, people of faith—people like us—approach their own salvation that way. We act as though the work is all up to us; that if we do enough good works, we will earn God's favor and grow and flourish. We are often so busy trying to save ourselves that we fail to notice what God has already done. We see the drought around us and get to work, and we lose sight of what is essential: God's gift of love and life stored up for us like water in deep wells.

God's wells are bottomless, holding a never-ending supply. This water of salvation is free and abundant; all we have to do is draw it up and drink it in. God has done the rest. The effort required on our part is to respond with joy and thanksgiving.

Reflect on the deep places of joy that God has created for you, and give thanks that you can draw from them in the dry places of your life.

In many churches tomorrow, participants will light a pink candle on the Advent wreath rather than the purple candle of penitence. This third Sunday of Advent is known as Gaudete Sunday, from the Latin word meaning "rejoice." But the scripture gives us a strange kind of rejoicing because this is also the Sunday that John the Baptist appears, preaching in the wilderness. Here he stands, right in the middle of December, as we are decking the halls and dashing through the snow, with his message of judgment and repentance.

John's preaching holds up a mirror before the crowds, reflecting to them their true selves, and it is not a pretty picture. They are a brood of vipers, children of chaos. And the rest of us who have gone out to be baptized have to look into that mirror as well. We have to confront who we have become, even as we are called to a more difficult confrontation—one with God, because that is what it means to bear fruits worthy of repentance. To be hell-bent on going our own way is to turn our backs to God, but to repent is to do an about-face that reorients us toward God.

Repentance is less about feeling sorry for our sins or worrying about our salvation and more about claiming anew our godly goal in life, which, according to the Westminster Catechism, is to glorify and enjoy God forever; in other words, to be in joy with God. If we do less than that, we end up cutting ourselves off from God. When we stop facing our own self-destruction and seek God's face instead, a holy joy must surely shine on, in, and through us, so that Christ's joy becomes complete—in us.

Rather than recounting your sins to God (who knows them anyway), focus on facing God and seeing yourself as God intends you to be.

THIRD SUNDAY OF ADVENT

The worries of this world are so weighty, the problems so intractable, we can feel overwhelmed by the enormity. It would be like trying to empty the ocean with a teaspoon. We cannot fix all that is wrong. What then should we do?

The holy answer is, in essence, don't worry. We don't have to save the world; God has already done that. We do not have to accomplish the impossible. We do not have to do everything, but we do have to do something. As the rabbi says, "You do not have to complete the work but neither are you free to desist from it" (*The Ethics of the Fathers*, Avot 2:21).

So John instructs us to do what we can. If you have something extra, share it with someone who has nothing. If you have food and people around you are hungry, feed them. If you are in a position of authority, avoid the abuse of power. Set right your relationships with others. Be satisfied with what you have and do not try to advance yourself at the expense of another. This approach is demanding but not impossible. And if we can't change the world in this way, we will perhaps change ourselves. Our preoccupied, distracted, crowded souls will be swept clean by holy wind and fire, leaving room for a fearless joy.

Soon we will hear the angel bring good news of great joy. That announcement will begin with instructions not to be afraid (Luke 2:10). When we know that God is in our midst, when we encounter Emmanuel, fear gives way to joy and worry gives way to peace. And "the peace of God, which surpasses all understanding, will guard [our] hearts and [our] minds in Christ Jesus (Phil. 4:7).

Make time in this too-busy season to perform one small task for someone, and do it with joy rather than from obligation.

Promise and Restoration

DECEMBER 14–20, 2015 • ELIZABETH CANHAM

MONDAY, DECEMBER 14 ~ *Read Micah 5:2-5a*

Promise. The prophets serve as the messengers of Yahweh, bringing hope in hard times and warning of consequences when the people stray in their faithfulness. The book of Micah opens in this manner: "The word of the LORD that came to Micah . . . . which he saw." The prophets speak from and for the Lord and not out of their unaided opinion. They listen for God's word, and often they see what God intends them to speak. They are people of faith who commit themselves to discerning the word of the Lord for their generation. The time of Micah's prophecies is uncertain but God's people need to hope and to trust in God's promise that a descendant of David will once again lead Israel.

Christians will immediately resonate with the words of promise in this section of Micah because they refer to Bethlehem as an insignificant, small town from which the future ruler of Israel will come to bring peace. Right away we recall the story of Jesus' birth and interpret this event as the fulfillment of Micah's prophecy; Jesus is the Good Shepherd who feeds and protects God's people. A people whose history included the struggles of wandering homeless through the desert, enduring war and loss of some tribes, and, possibly, the exile, would find fresh hope if they would but believe in God's faithfulness.

It is always a challenge to believe God's promises when circumstances are difficult and we do not yet see any fulfillment on the horizon. The prophets invite us to listen for God's word and see in daily experience the hand of God at work in the world.

God of peace, give me a listening heart and a willingness to see and become your word made visible in the world. Amen.

Episcopal priest and director of Hospites Mundi retreat and pilgrimage ministry; associate rector, Calvary Episcopal Church, Fletcher, North Carolina

*P*resence. Mary was probably still a teenager when she received the life-changing message of her pregnancy. Even after her willing acceptance of Gabriel's words, she has huge adjustments to make. She needs support as she comes to terms with how she now perceives herself, her relationships, and the inner wonder of the trust God is placing in her. She needs the presence of another woman, one whose wisdom she can trust. So she sets out on the long journey from Nazareth to the Judean hill country to visit her relative Elizabeth.

We can easily imagine the joyful reunion of the two women: Elizabeth now in old age, pregnant for the first time and Mary carrying a child before all the Jewish rites of marriage have been completed. For Elizabeth, the conception of a child meant an end to the shame she has endured for all the years she was "barren." These two women desire each other's support, but their celebration goes beyond their actual meeting to belief that God is bringing about in them the fulfillment of promise and hope. As Elizabeth feels the movement of her child she proclaims the now-familiar words of Mary's blessedness and the blessedness of the child in her womb—this child she honors as her Lord.

This scripture reveals the grace of the discerning presence of another on the journey of faith. A fellow traveler may enable us to remember the promises of God and to discover more deeply the awesome work of God in our lives. Mary shows great wisdom in choosing to visit Elizabeth, and Elizabeth's wisdom reinforces the amazing truth that Mary heard. The presence and support of another Christian friend may lift us out of fearful "not knowing" into deeper trust in God's purpose.

Living Christ, you indwell each of us; may we never miss the wonder of holy presence in ourselves and others. Amen.

Peace. This short passage from the prophecy of Micah ends with the statement "he shall be the one of peace." The obscurity of Bethlehem as one of the "little clans" is surpassed by the understanding that the origin of the ruler to come is from ancient days. This suggests a restoration of the house of David. Clearly God's people are suffering a time of great trial, which Micah compares to the labor pains of a woman. What they long for is not yet; some are still separated from the community, and the birth of a new age seems long overdue.

Waiting is a frequent theme in scripture—not only for people under stress but also for God who waits for the *kairos*, the right moment to act. It took years of struggle in the wilderness for a diverse group of Semitic tribes to be formed into a community with God's commandments as their foundation. But this was just a beginning, and we read of many occasions of the community turning away from Yahweh, becoming embattled, and longing for return. This is the context of Micah's words of promise that the leader to come will feed his flock, provide for their physical needs, and lead them into security.

Prophecies like this one led to messianic hope and later to the recognition of Jesus as the longed-for Messiah. In Micah the blessings given by the new ruler are material, but New Testament writers see them as spiritual. Peace is the gift of Jesus: "Peace I leave with you; my peace I give to you" (John 14:27). These words, spoken to anxious disciples anticipating losing their teacher, enabled them to live in a hostile world strengthened by his blessing. We too claim Jesus' promise, remembering when conflict threatens that "he is our peace" (Eph. 2:14). And so we live in hope.

O God, as we follow the risen Christ may we always find inner peace and be peacemakers in the earth. Amen.

*P*raise. Mary's song of praise reflects the words of Hannah spoken after the birth of Samuel. (See 1 Samuel 2:1-10.) Hannah had longed for a child and prayed earnestly that she might conceive, so earnestly that Eli the priest at Shiloh thought she might be drunk and scolded her! Nevertheless her prayer was answered, and she was no longer harassed by her rival Peninnah. She and Elkanah her husband celebrated Samuel's birth. Mary's story is different; her child is unexpected but her joy overflows into poetic form beginning, like Hannah, with blessing God whom she also names as Savior. Mary acknowledges her lowly origin, a simple peasant girl from the backwaters of Nazareth, and feels honored to bear the one named Jesus who will be called Son of the Most High and who will restore the Davidic reign in Israel.

Mary's song, the Magnificat, announces a reversal of fortune that Mary foresees as God's merciful action in the nation. Throughout the Hebrew Scriptures God refers to caring for the poor and disenfranchised, God's *anawim*, and often the prophets raised their voices to condemn the inequities of society. Now Mary announces that the powerful will be unseated, the poor lifted up, and the hungry filled because God has helped God's people Israel.

Our role comes in holding hope before others and discerning God's call to bring about the kind of realm God intends. We may feel little, insignificant, and limited, but Mary's song can become the message we also try to embody. Mary said yes to God's word through Gabriel, not knowing where willingness might lead her. The Christ born in Mary lives in us today and becomes visible through our words and actions as we challenge oppressive powers and welcome the poor.

Most Holy God, give us voices to praise you, trust in your promised realm of peace, and the courage to bring it about. Amen.

Preparation. The author of Hebrews writes primarily for Jewish readers to make clear that Christ is the fulfillment of the law and promises of God. He announces an end to the sacrificial practices of the Old Testament and, by repeated reference to scripture, seeks to prove that the new era of grace has arrived. In this passage he places in the mouth of Jesus words from Psalm 40:6-8, originally spoken as part of a psalm of thanksgiving for deliverance. Jesus says that God no longer desires sacrifices and offerings but has prepared for Jesus a human body. In Jesus, God no longer resides "up there" or "out there" but lives and walks among us, honoring humanity with divine presence. Christians came to understand that because Christ gave himself up to live and die on earth, he inaugurated a new relationship between God and the human family.

In our own lives we can often see, usually in retrospect, how God has been preparing us for the life and ministry that has unfolded in us. God has prepared specific bodies, yours and mine, and given specific gifts to be shared in the world. Sometimes we have experienced occasions when some scripture "came alive," and we saw it as part of our sensing of God's way. This passage attests to Jesus' understanding of the words of Psalm 40, probably known by heart, as an expression of his commitment to God's way: "I have come to do your will." We too can find the grace to do God's will by bearing witness to our faith by listening, by speaking, and by acting out the truth of God's will and way.

How does prayer enable you to listen for God's word? Who helps you discern your way of sharing the good news? As you look back on your life, what experiences do you think God has used to prepare you for your ministry?

Proclamation. The first verse of chapter 10 notes that the law, a formational construct for the people of God, offers only "a shadow of the good things to come." Those who lived under the law believed that atonement for sin came by means of animal sacrifice. But though burnt offerings were repeatedly offered, all the goats and bulls that died could not take away sins. Jesus comes as the "new," which displaces the old. He proclaims a message of hope and forgiveness through his self-offering. Through Jesus, God's light shone to reveal the new way of forgiveness and to take away the shadowy life of the sacrificial system.

At the heart of the gospel is Jesus' work as the One who fulfills God's will. His radical willingness to discern and obey God brings forgiveness, love, and compassion, which he makes visible through his life and in his death. Followers of Jesus are set apart (sanctified) as new people by virtue of their trust in his love. The old attempt at sanctification through repetitive sacrifices has been set aside "once for all" in Jesus' self-offering. In the once for all offering of himself, Jesus accomplishes what has never been done before and will never be done again.

While we gladly give lip service to the good news in Jesus, we can easily fall back into thinking of God as a distant being whom we have to appease. Grace is truly amazing! Faith in Christ frees us from the constraints of the law and brings us into a circle of belonging and reconciliation. Only when we forget who we are and whose we are do we wander into shadowy fears and doubt.

God of grace, we thank you for the new life that Jesus lived and proclaimed. May we be proclaimers of reconciliation and faith. Amen.

Fourth Sunday of Advent

Pilgrimage. As we approach the Christmas season, we are filled with hope and anticipation. Jesus' birth lies at the heart of our faith journey. And then we move into the coming year and recall his teaching and healing ministry. All too soon, opponents arise and begin to plot his death. We have a post-Resurrection view of Jesus, risen yet still present through the work of the Holy Spirit. But for early disciples it took time to let go of their dependence on the human Jesus. Their journey challenged their faith; they cried out to God for help and courage.

The scriptures are replete with stories about people on pilgrimage, those experiencing the ups and downs of life and always moving toward the realm of God. Christian believers continued to use the Psalter in their worship and to discover its relevance for their struggles and hope. In Psalm 80 the author reminds us that in the hard times we are to remember who God is as we cry out for help. Like Isaiah (6:1-8) he recalls the Temple and the awesome experience of God as supplicants wait amidst the smoke of incense where the Holy One is seated upon a throne. He also uses a far more intimate image of God as the Shepherd of Israel who leads the flock to safety and good pasture (Ps. 23.) The psalmist then requests God's restoration of the people so that they may be saved.

Wherever we are, in lostness and pain or faith-filled joy, we count on our awesome and holy Creator to lead us, like the Good Shepherd, in ways of truth and hope and to restore us to the fullness of our life in Christ.

Great Shepherd, lead us on our pilgrim journey; bring us home when we stray from your paths, and restore our faith. Amen.

Clothed in Love

DECEMBER 21–27, 2015 • NICOLA VIDAMOUR

MONDAY, DECEMBER 21 ~ *Read 1 Samuel 2:18-20, 26*

I wonder how Samuel reacted when his mother turned up each year with yet another new robe? We read that Hannah made this little outfit herself, and I feel sure that she did so with great love and care. I can picture her praying for her son and thanking God for him as she sewed. When her son wore this robe, he would know that he was not simply clothed in linen. He was wrapped in love and prayer.

This gift would also keep Samuel's mother close to him all year round. Hannah and Elkanah saw Samuel only once a year when they went up to offer the yearly sacrifice. Their present of the robe would serve as a constant reminder of their presence in his life.

We all have people in our lives whom we only see or hear from once a year, usually at Christmas. The gifts and the greetings we exchange at this time may be very similar to those that were offered last year. We may have begun to take them for granted. *Another Christmas—another pair of socks from Auntie Gladys!* we may think to ourselves. Do we take time to reflect on the love that these gifts symbolize and the ongoing presence they represent?

Like any child, Samuel would have needed new clothes each year. As he grew in size, he also grew in the prayerful love and gratitude to God with which his mother clothed him.

Ever-giving God, enlarge our hearts to receive the presence of love this Christmas. Amen.

How will you wrap your gifts with love and prayer this Christmas?

Methodist minister, London, England

How long does it take you to decide which clothes to put on in the morning? Have you already chosen the outfit you will wear on Christmas Day? Today's scripture passage reminds us that we are to put on more than what hangs in our closet. We are to clothe ourselves with "compassion, kindness, humility, meekness, and patience."

My wardrobe has a mirror fixed to the door so that after I dress I can see what I look like. The author of this letter shows us how we will look when we clothe ourselves with these gifts of God. We will see eyes full of forgiveness and hands stretched out to support rather than to write a letter of complaint!

When you view yourself in the mirror in the morning, don't just check that your collar is straight. Ask yourself if you look compassionate, kind, humble, meek, and patient. Every time you look in the mirror throughout the day, ask yourself again whether these gifts are present. When you undress in the evening, hold that mirror up again to look back on your day. Do you see those gifts reflected in your words and actions?

I own one item of jewelry that I wear nearly every day no matter what else I wear: a silver bracelet that consists of a chain of small hearts. I feel that I am not properly dressed without it. Colossians 3:14 tells us that love is the most important gift to clothe ourselves with. Love is the perfect accessory for every outfit since love "binds everything together in perfect harmony."

Forgiving God, may our words and actions today be a true reflection of your love. Amen.

What difference will it make to your day if you clothe yourself with love every morning?

Clothed in Love

Many of the Christmas cards I receive have images or words about peace. Peace is one gift of God that we celebrate particularly at this time of year. Angels proclaiming peace on earth announce the birth of the Prince of Peace to the shepherds. The rulers of the world continually struggle to achieve that vision. The good news is that even when wars rage around us, the peace of Christ can still rule in our hearts.

Other Christmas cards include Bible quotes and proclaim that "the Word became flesh and lived among us" (John 1:14). While the Bible passages about the birth of Christ are very familiar to us, we never tire of hearing or reading them. We recognize the treasure they contain and are glad that the word of God dwells in us richly.

Some Christmas cards contain lines from Christmas carols, and they encourage us to burst into song with gratitude in our hearts. Christmas would not be Christmas without those wonderful hymns that we sing as much as possible during this short season.

Other Christmas cards feature some of the many different names that Jesus has (Emmanuel, Savior, Messiah, Son of God) and remind us that Christmas itself is named after Christ. Everything we do at Christmas we do "in the name of the Lord Jesus."

Loving God, may your peace rule in our hearts and your word dwell richly in us as we sing songs of gratitude to you in the name of the Lord Jesus this Christmas and always. Amen.

How can you be an angel of peace this Christmas?

CHRISTMAS EVE

Luke tells us twice in this passage that the newborn baby Jesus was wrapped in bands of cloth. Swaddling remains a common practice in many cultures. When I lived in Russia, I would often see couples having their photographs taken on the steps of the birth house. The child was always wrapped from head to toe in white cloth with a pink or blue ribbon to denote its gender! Only the face was visible.

The swaddling clothes of Jesus remind us of his human nature. This newborn child needed to be kept warm. His soft skin needed protection from the roughness of the manger. Perhaps only his little face was visible to Mary and Joseph and the shepherds who came to visit—and yet in that face they saw the face of God.

Swaddling clothes remind me of Egyptian mummies. They make me think of death as well as birth. All four Gospel writers tell us that Jesus' body was wrapped in cloth for his burial. When we get to Easter we discover that Jesus has left his cloth wrappings behind in the empty tomb—a symbol of new life.

In the church where I serve we traditionally cover the bread and the wine with a white cloth until the point in the service when we come to the prayer of The Great Thanksgiving. When I remove that cloth on Christmas Eve it is as if we are uncovering the baby Jesus as he lies in the manger and recognizing that God comes to us as flesh and blood. As Charles Wesley writes in his Christmas carol "Hark! the Herald Angels Sing": "Veiled in flesh the Godhead see; hail th'incarnate Deity."

Word made flesh, may I treasure you and ponder you in my heart. Amen.

Save the planet! Wrap your gifts in cloth instead of paper this year!

CHRISTMAS DAY

The opening chapter of the letter to the Hebrews declares that the Son of God is superior to all the angels and any other messenger whom God has sent before. A modern-day paraphrase of this chapter might say that the batteries of the angels eventually run out but that Jesus runs on an everlasting battery! If you have children in your household who will receive a battery-operated gift today, I hope you have a good supply of batteries! Some toys can reach the end of their life before the day is over.

The author actually uses the example of clothing—which has been a running theme in our readings this week. "They will all wear out like clothing; like a cloak you will roll them up, and like clothing they will be changed. But you are the same, and your years will never end." These words, that echo Psalm 102:26-27, remind us that the author of this letter clothed himself in the Hebrew scriptures. They had become part of him, and he quotes relevant verses at will to support his message.

Today the Word of God becomes part of us. The Word becomes flesh and dwells among us (John 1:14). This Word is eternal. It never runs out of power or energy—and it empowers and energizes us. The Christmas story is so familiar to us—and yet, each year, its powerful message speaks to us again. We never tire of it, and it never wears out.

Eternal Word, I want you to dwell within me and become part of me. Amen.

What words of scripture do you want to wrap yourself in today?

Today is a good day to go out for a walk, especially after the amount of food you probably enjoyed yesterday! You may be wondering if you can still fit into your clothes after such a feast.

Today's psalm encourages us to join our praise with all the glorious gifts with which God has clothed creation. The skies are clothed with the sun, the moon, and the stars. The earth is clothed with water and fire, snow and frost, wind and hail. The world is clothed with mountains and trees, animals and insects, birds and people.

My friends sometimes laugh when they open my closet and see that nearly every piece of clothing is blue! Blue is my favorite color, and there are many different shades of blue. I rarely get bored with the variety of clothes that I can wear.

But God's palette extends far beyond my favorite color. I never cease to be amazed by the vast range of color and design with which God has clothed creation, to see the way in which the same place can look so different as the seasons and the weather change. My local park is beautiful all year round. In the winter it can be clothed in snow. In the spring it is clothed in daffodils. In the summer it is clothed with families having picnics. In the fall it is clothed in leaves.

You may go out for a walk today in a new item of clothing that you received as a gift yesterday. Take some time to look at the way in which creation is clothed today. It will differ from the apparel it wore yesterday—and it will be different again tomorrow! Join your voice of praise with all God's creation as we give thanks for the glory with which we are all clothed. Praise the Lord!

Let us praise the name of the Lord, for God commanded and we were created. (Based on Psalm 148:5)

What is creation wearing today?

When people are reported missing, police often circulate a description of what they look like and what they were wearing when last seen. I imagine that Mary and Joseph provided similar information about their son to everyone they met during their desperate three-day search for him. I picture Jesus at the time Mary and Joseph found him, sitting in the Temple with a prayer shawl draped over his shoulders.

The Gospel tells us that Mary and Joseph are astonished when they see him. Did they almost not recognize him? He fit their physical description, but he is clothed with a wisdom and understanding that surprises both his parents and the teachers in the Temple with whom he has been talking.

I recall movie scenes in which a young woman comes down the stairs dressed for a dance or for her wedding, and her father almost fails to recognize her. He suddenly realizes that his little girl is all grown up now.

I think this may be Mary and Joseph's experience. It suddenly dawns on them that their little boy has matured into a young man; he now has a deeper understanding of who he is than they do. "[Jesus] said to them, 'Why were you searching for me? Did you not know that I must be in my Father's house?' But they did not understand what he said to them."

We may experience times when we lose Jesus and don't know where to find him. Even the so-called wise ones look for him in the wrong place! Have we dressed Jesus in the wrong clothes? Are we prepared to let him mature into a man, or do we prefer that he remain a tiny baby?

Jesus, my teacher, help me to grow in wisdom and understanding. Amen.

Why are we searching for Jesus?

Bring Us Home

DECEMBER 28-31, 2015 • KENNETH M. LOCKE

MONDAY, DECEMBER 28 ~ *Read Jeremiah 31:7-9*

Christmas is finally over, and we may feel relieved. We are tired of delayed flights and missed connections. We are weary of staying with distant relatives. We have lost our taste for junk food. We are tired of the crush at the malls.

We are ready for a return to life the way it was, to what it should be. We want to be home, even if we haven't left!

Christmas powerfully brings home to us humanity's perennial condition. We are out of sorts, out of joint. Nothing is quite right. Things are not as they should be. And we desperately long to feel like we are home.

The post-Christmas days are a good time to reflect on what Christmas means for us. God is calling us to the way things should be. In Jesus Christ, God helps us put things right, come back to the lives we desire, the solid life we long for.

The invitation is for all people. Not just those of us "in the know" or who might be up for the spiritual journey, but for all people—even those who would otherwise faint along the way.

Christmas reminds us in a powerful way that we have wandered far from our spiritual home. If we had not, we would need no savior to guide us back. But thanks be to God, in Jesus we are offered a path back to the way things should be. In Jesus we are invited to step back and satisfy our longing for life as it should be: a life centered on God through loving others.

Lord God, we have wandered far away. In the life, love, and resurrection of Jesus please bring us home. Amen.

Pastor, Downtown Presbyterian Church, Nashville, Tennessee

I spend much of my ministry among the homeless and urban poor. Although they are all unique individuals, one quality they have in common is an unhealthy attitude toward what is "normal." In their world the violence of bone-crushing poverty and midnight attacks is normal. The indignity of locking up all one's possessions and sleeping in an assigned bunk or sleeping night after night in a car, is normal. Desperately seeking emotional connection or relief through sex and drugs is normal. But is that God's view of normal?

Our text today describes the "new normal" for the Israelites returning from exile in Babylon. First they are told that it is not something they can do for themselves. God has to ransom Jacob. Then they learn that there will be more than enough to eat and drink. Their physical needs will be met. No one will suffer from food insecurity or random violence.

Furthermore their minds will be at peace. Those returning from exile will not be troubled. They will be able to dance, make merry, and be joyful. They will be able to enjoy all that they have.

Finally, we find that there is even enough for the priests. The people will have enough that they can spare the precious fat of the animals for sacrifices. Or as we would say, the church's budget will be fully met and even exceeded.

It seems to me that what God wants us to have is both peace of mind and enough food and comfort to enjoy life.

Now that the excesses of Christmas are past we are in a good position to ask what should be normative for our lives. What implications does Jesus' birth have for our own view of normal?

O loving God, show us what you want our normal to be. In the miraculous birth; in the healing, self-giving love; in the triumphant, death-defeating resurrection of Jesus show us the normal for which we should strive. Amen.

I freely admit I am a "list" person. To-do lists, lists of positive affirmations, lists of thank-you notes to be written, lists of resolutions for the New Year: I keep them all. In keeping with my love for lists and the general theme of the import of Jesus' birth, our text today kindly lists out why Jesus' birth matters so much. In Jesus we are blessed with every spiritual blessing. Through Jesus we are adopted as God's children. Because of Jesus' blood we have forgiveness. Because of Jesus we have received from God the knowledge of the mystery of God's will. In Jesus we have obtained our divine inheritance!

It's quite a list and doubtless the author could have gone on longer. It's enough to make us proud, even a bit conceited. "Look at all the goodness that has accrued to me in the birth of Jesus. I must be pretty important to merit this many benefits. I bet I'm at the center of God's world!" Indeed, after our recent orgy of mostly receiving and a little giving it would seem pretty normal to attribute the gifts we have received in Jesus to our own goodness.

Fortunately for us, the text ends with a corrective. What God has done is "to the praise of his glory." That is, the benefits we receive through the birth of Jesus are ultimately not about us. They are about God! The gifts we receive remind us to praise and glorify God. They remind us our chief end is not to revel in our own self-worth but to know God and to serve God forever.

At Christmas it's easy to think that our salvation is at the center of the Incarnation. However, today's text reminds us that God is at the center of our salvation. Glory be to God!

Please God, forgive our Christmas arrogance. Remind us to put you at the center of all our living. Amen.

While every day is special in its own way, today is special because it marks the end of another year. Another year of love, toil, laughter, heartache, gain, and loss has come to an end. How should we celebrate this special day? Food and drink, song and revelry have their place but perhaps the best thing we can do is to stop and intentionally praise God.

For the last three days we have been considering the import and implications of Jesus' birth. Such study and contemplation have their place. They matter tremendously. But another aspect matters just as much: praising God. In the midst of our end-of-year activities and reports; in the midst of our planning for the future; in the midst of our search for how best to honor Jesus' sacrifice of becoming human, it is good to take a day and simply praise God.

So today we praise God. We praise God for our safety. We praise God for our progeny, both our children and the good we do that will live after us. We praise God for peace and for meeting our physical needs. We praise God for God's watchfulness over the universe, holding the laws of nature together. We praise God for divine ordinances and laws to guide our living so that we can enjoy our pleasures to the full.

This is how the psalmist praises God, and this list is a good place to begin. What other reasons do you have to praise God? From the glorious miracle of human birth to the mundane miracle of drawing breath, what are your reasons for praising God?

Every day is both special and ordinary. The last day of the year is as special and as ordinary as any other day. But this year let us make today special by setting it aside to praise God for God's goodness in the past and the goodness we know is yet to come.

Lord God, we praise you for. . . .

The Revised Common Lectionary* for 2015
Year B – Advent / Christmas Year C
(Disciplines Edition)

January 1–4
Isaiah 61:10–62:3
Psalm 148
Galatians 4:4-7
Luke 2:22-40

> **New Year's Day**
> Ecclesiastes 3:1-13
> Psalm 8
> Revelation 21:1-6a
> Matthew 25:31-46

January 6
EPIPHANY
(may be used for Sunday, Jan. 4)
Isaiah 60:1-6
Psalm 72:1-7, 10-14
Ephesians 3:1-12
Matthew 2:1-12

January 5–11
BAPTISM OF THE LORD
Genesis 1:1-5
Psalm 29
Acts 19:1-7
Mark 1:4-11

January 12–18
1 Samuel 3:1-20
Psalm 139:1-6, 13-18
1 Corinthians 6:12-20
John 1:43-51

January 19–25
Jonah 3:1-5, 10
Psalm 62:5-12
1 Corinthians 7:29-31
Mark 1:14-20

January 26–February 1
Deuteronomy 18:15-20
Psalm 111
1 Corinthians 8:1-13
Mark 1:21-28

February 2–8
Isaiah 40:21-31
Psalm 147:1-11, 20c
1 Corinthians 9:16-23
Mark 1:29-39

February 9–15
TRANSFIGURATION
2 Kings 2:1-12
Psalm 50:1-6
2 Corinthians 4:3-6
Mark 9:2-9

February 16–22
FIRST SUNDAY IN LENT
Genesis 9:8-17
Psalm 25:1-10
1 Peter 3:18-22
Mark 1:9-15

February 18
ASH WEDNESDAY
Joel 2:1-2, 12-17 (*or* Isaiah 58:1-12)
Psalm 51:1-17
2 Corinthians 5:20b–6:10
Matthew 6:1-6, 16-21

February 23–March 1
SECOND SUNDAY IN LENT
Genesis 17:1-7, 15-16
Psalm 22:23-31
Romans 4:13-25
Mark 8:31-38 *or* Mark 9:2-9

March 2–8
THIRD SUNDAY IN LENT
Exodus 20:1-17
Psalm 19
1 Corinthians 1:18-25
John 2:13-22

March 9–15
FOURTH SUNDAY IN LENT
Numbers 21:4-9
Psalm 107:1-3, 17-22
Ephesians 2:1-10
John 3:14-21

March 16–22
FIFTH SUNDAY IN LENT
Jeremiah 31:31-34
Psalm 51:1-12
(*or* Psalm 119:9-16)
Hebrews 5:5-10
John 12:20-33

March 23–29
PALM/PASSION SUNDAY
Liturgy of the Palms
Mark 11:1-11, 15-18
(*or* John 12:12-16)
Psalm 118:1-2, 19-29

Liturgy of the Passion
Isaiah 50:4-9a
Psalm 31:9-16
Philippians 2:5-11
Mark 14:1–15:47
 (*or* Mark 15:1-47)

March 30–April 5
HOLY WEEK

HOLY MONDAY
Isaiah 42:1-9
Psalm 36:5-11
Hebrews 9:11-15
John 12:1-11

HOLY TUESDAY
Isaiah 49:1-7
Psalm 71:1-14
1 Corinthians 1:18-31
John 12:20-36

HOLY WEDNESDAY
Isaiah 50:4-9a
Psalm 70
Hebrews 12:1-3
John 13:21-32

MAUNDY THURSDAY
Exodus 12:1-14
Psalm 116:1-4, 12-19
1 Corinthians 11:23-26
John 13:1-17, 31b-35

GOOD FRIDAY
Isaiah 52:13–53:12
Psalm 22
Hebrews 10:16-25
John 18:1–19:42

HOLY SATURDAY
Easter Vigil
Exodus 14:10-31
Isaiah 55:1-11
Psalm 114
Romans 6:3-11
Mark 16:1-8

EASTER SUNDAY
Acts 10:34-43
Psalm 118:1-2, 14-24
1 Corinthians 15:1-11
John 20:1-18
    (*or* Mark 16:1-8)

April 6–12
Acts 4:32-35
Psalm 133
1 John 1:1–2:2
John 20:19-31

April 13–19
Acts 3:12-19
Psalm 4
1 John 3:1-7
Luke 24:36b-48

April 20–26
Acts 4:5-12
Psalm 23
1 John 3:16-24
John 10:11-18

April 27–May 3
Acts 8:26-40
Psalm 22:25-31
1 John 4:7-21
John 15:1-8

May 4–10
Acts 10:44-48
Psalm 98
1 John 5:1-6
John 15:9-17

May 11–17
Acts 1:15-17, 21-26
Psalm 1
1 John 5:9-13
John 17:6-19

May 21
ASCENSION DAY
Acts 1:1-11
Psalm 47
Ephesians 1:15-23
Luke 24:44-53

May 18–24
PENTECOST
Acts 2:1-21
Psalm 104:24-34, 35b
Romans 8:22-27
John 15:26-27; 16:4b-15

May 25–31
TRINITY
Isaiah 6:1-8
Psalm 29
Romans 8:12-17
John 3:1-17

June 1–7
1 Samuel 8:4-20
Psalm 138
2 Corinthians 4:13–5:1
Mark 3:20-35

June 8–14
1 Samuel 15:34–16:13
Psalm 20
2 Corinthians 5:6-17
Mark 4:26-34

June 15–21
1 Samuel 17:1a, 4-11, 19-23, 32-49
Psalm 9:9-20
2 Corinthians 6:1-13
Mark 4:35-41

June 22–28
2 Samuel 1:1, 17-27
Psalm 130
2 Corinthians 8:7-15
Mark 5:21-43

June 29–July 5
2 Samuel 5:1-5, 9-10
Psalm 48
2 Corinthians 12:2-10
Mark 6:1-13

July 6–12
2 Samuel 6:1-5, 12b-19
Psalm 24
Ephesians 1:3-14
Mark 6:14-29

July 13–19
2 Samuel 7:1-14a
Psalm 89:20-37
Ephesians 2:11-22
Mark 6:30-34, 53-56

July 20–26
2 Samuel 11:1-15
Psalm 14
Ephesians 3:14-21
John 6:1-21

July 27–August 2
2 Samuel 11:26–12:13a
Psalm 51:1-12
Ephesians 4:1-16
John 6:24-35

August 3–9
2 Samuel 18:5-9, 15, 31-33
Psalm 34:1-8
Ephesians 4:25–5:2
John 6:35, 41-51

August 10–16
1 Kings 2:10-12; 3:3-14
Psalm 111
Ephesians 5:15-20
John 6:51-58

August 17–23
1 Kings 8:1, 6, 10-11, 22-30, 41-43
Psalm 84
Ephesians 6:10-20
John 6:56-69

August 24–30
Song of Solomon 2:8-13
Psalm 45:1-2, 6-9
James 1:17-27
Mark 7:1-8, 14-15, 21-23

August 31–September 6
Proverbs 22:1-2, 8-9, 22-23
Psalm 125
James 2:1-17
Mark 7:24-37

September 7–13
Proverbs 1:20-33
Psalm 19
James 3:1-12
Mark 8:27-38

September 14–20
Proverbs 31:10-31
Psalm 1
James 3:13–4:3, 7-8a
Mark 9:30-37

September 21–27
Esther 7:1-6, 9-10; 9:20-22
Psalm 124
James 5:13-20
Mark 9:38-50

September 28–October 4
Job 1:1; 2:1-10
Psalm 26
Hebrews 1:1-4; 2:5-12
Mark 10:2-16

October 5–11
Job 23:1-9, 16-17
Psalm 22:1-15
Hebrews 4:12-16
Mark 10:17-31

OCTOBER 12
THANKSGIVING DAY, CANADA
  Joel 2:21-27
  Psalm 126
  1 Timothy 2:1-7
  Matthew 6:25-33

October 12–18
Job 38:1-7, 34-41
Psalm 104:1-9, 24, 35c
Hebrews 5:1-10
Mark 10:35-45

October 19–25
Job 42:1-6, 10-17
Psalm 34:1-8, 19-22
Hebrews 7:23-28
Mark 10:46-52

October 26–November 1
Ruth 1:1-18
Psalm 146
Hebrews 9:11-14
Mark 12:28-34

November 1
ALL SAINTS DAY
Isaiah 25:6-9
Psalm 24
Revelation 21:1-6a
John 11:32-44

November 2–8
Ruth 3:1-5; 4:13-17
Psalm 127
Hebrews 9:24-28
Mark 12:38-44

November 9–15
1 Samuel 1:4-20
1 Samuel 2:1-10
Hebrews 10:11-25
Mark 13:1-8

November 16–22
THE REIGN OF CHRIST
2 Samuel 23:1-7
Psalm 132:1-18
Revelation 1:4b-8
John 18:33-37

November 26
THANKSGIVING DAY, USA
  Joel 2:21-27
  Psalm 126
  1 Timothy 2:1-7
  Matthew 6:25-33

November 23–29
FIRST SUNDAY OF ADVENT
Jeremiah 33:14-16
Psalm 25:1-10
1 Thessalonians 3:9-13
Luke 21:25-36

November 30–December 6
SECOND SUNDAY OF ADVENT
Malachi 3:1-4
Luke 1:68-79
Philippians 1:3-11
Luke 3:1-6

December 7–13
THIRD SUNDAY OF ADVENT
Zephaniah 3:14-20
Isaiah 12:2-6
Philippians 4:4-7
Luke 3:7-18

December 14–20
FOURTH SUNDAY OF ADVENT
Micah 5:2-5a
Luke 1:47-55
  (*or* Psalm 80:1-7)
Hebrews 10:5-10
Luke 1:39-55

December 21–27
FIRST SUNDAY AFTER
CHRISTMAS
    1 Samuel 2:18-20, 26
    Psalm 148
    Colossians 3:12-17
    Luke 2:41-52

December 24
CHRISTMAS EVE
Isaiah 9:2-7
Psalm 96
Titus 2:11-14
Luke 2:1-20

December 25
CHRISTMAS DAY
Isaiah 52:7-10
Psalm 98
Hebrews 1:1-12
John 1:1-14

December 28–31
    Jeremiah 31:7-14
    Psalm 147:12-20
    Ephesians 1:3-14
    John 1:1-18